Fundamentals of Programming Languages

Fundamentals of Programming Languages

Edited by
Chris Chancellor

Larsen & Keller
www.larsen-keller.com

Fundamentals of Programming Languages
Edited by Chris Chancellor
ISBN: 978-1-63549-680-2 (Hardback)

Larsen & Keller

Published by Larsen and Keller Education,
5 Penn Plaza,
19th Floor,
New York, NY 10001, USA

Cataloging-in-Publication Data

Fundamentals of programming languages / edited by Chris Chancellor.
    p. cm.
Includes bibliographical references and index.
ISBN 978-1-63549-680-2
    1. Programming languages (Electronic computers). 2. Languages, Artificial.
3. Electronic data processing. I. Chancellor, Chris.
QA76.7 .F86 2018
005.13--dc23

For more information regarding Larsen and Keller Education and its products, please visit the publisher's website www.larsen-keller.com

Table of Contents

Preface

The language of the computer which instructs it to perform various specific functions is known as programming language. It has some developing processes, which include syntax, dynamic semantics, static semantics, static typing, standard library, etc. This book is a valuable compilation of topics, ranging from the basic to the most complex theories and principles in the field of programming languages. The various sub-fields of the subject along with technological progress that have future implications are glanced at in it. For someone with an interest and eye for detail, this text covers the most significant topics in the field of programming languages. This textbook will serve as a reference to a broad spectrum of readers.

A short introduction to every chapter is written below to provide an overview of the content of the book:

Chapter 1 - The language used to develop programs, scripts or instructions which deliver the required output is known as programming languages. Speakeasy, Simula, Smalltalk, Prolog and ML are some of the programming languages. This chapter is an overview of the subject matter incorporating all the major aspects of programming language; **Chapter 2** - Computer programming includes the generation, development and analysis of algorithms. The other tasks of the subject are to test and maintain the source code. The types of programming languages discussed in the section are compiled language, scripting language and interpreted language. This chapter will provide an integrated understanding of computer programming and types of programming languages; **Chapter 3** - The set of rules that structures the symbols correctly to produce a programing language is called syntax. Computer language syntax can be divided into three levels, which are words, phrases and context. Data type, structured programming, control flow and programming style are significant and important topics related to programming languages. The following chapter unfolds its crucial aspects in a critical yet systematic manner; **Chapter 4** - Programming paradigms help in the categorization of programming languages based on their specifications. Object-oriented programming, aspect-oriented programming, automata-based programming, flow-based programming, non-structured programming and event-driven programming are some of the types of programming paradigm. The chapter on programming paradigm offers an insightful focus, keeping in mind the complex subject matter.

I extend my sincere thanks to the publisher for considering me worthy of this task. Finally, I thank my family for being a source of support and help.

Editor

An Overview of Programming Languages

The language used to develop programs, scripts or instructions which deliver the required output is known as programming languages. Speakeasy, Simula, Smalltalk, Prolog and ML are some of the programming languages. This chapter is an overview of the subject matter incorporating all the major aspects of programming language.

Programming Language

```c
1  /* This line basically imports the "stdio" header file, part of
2   * the standard library. It provides input and output functionality
3   * to the program.
4   */
5  #include <stdio.h>
6
7  /*
8   * Function (method) declaration. This outputs "Hello, world" to
9   * standard output when invoked.
10  */
11 void sayHello() {
12     // printf() in C outputs the specified text (with optional
13     // formatting options) when invoked.
14     printf("Hello, world!");
15 }
16
17 /*
18  * This is a "main function". The compiled program will run the code
19  * defined here.
20  */
21 void main() {
22     // Invoke the sayHello() function.
23     sayHello();
24 }
```

Source code of a simple computer program written in the C programming language,
which will output the "Hello, world!" message when compiled and run.

A programming language is a formal language that specifies a set of instructions that can be used to produce various kinds of output. Programming languages generally consist of instructions for a computer. Programming languages can be used to create programs that implement specific algorithms.

The earliest known programmable machine preceded the invention of the digital computer and is the automatic flute player described in the 9th century by the brothers Musa in Baghdad, "during the Islamic Golden Age". From the early 1800s, "programs" were used to direct the behavior of machines such as Jacquard looms and player pianos. Thousands of different programming languages have been created, mainly in the computer field, and many more still are being created every year. Many programming languages require computation to be specified in an imperative form (i.e., as a sequence of operations to perform) while other languages use other forms of program specification such as the declarative form (i.e. the desired result is specified, not how to achieve it).

The description of a programming language is usually split into the two components of syntax (form) and semantics (meaning). Some languages are defined by a specification document (for example, the C programming language is specified by an ISO Standard) while other languages (such as Perl) have a dominant implementation that is treated as a reference. Some languages have both, with the basic language defined by a standard and extensions taken from the dominant implementation being common.

Definitions

A programming language is a notation for writing programs, which are specifications of a computation or algorithm. Some, but not all, authors restrict the term "programming language" to those languages that can express *all* possible algorithms. Traits often considered important for what constitutes a programming language include:

Function and target

> A *computer programming language* is a language used to write computer programs, which involve a computer performing some kind of computation or algorithm and possibly control external devices such as printers, disk drives, robots, and so on. For example, PostScript programs are frequently created by another program to control a computer printer or display. More generally, a programming language may describe computation on some, possibly abstract, machine. It is generally accepted that a complete specification for a programming language includes a description, possibly idealized, of a machine or processor for that language. In most practical contexts, a programming language involves a computer; consequently, programming languages are usually defined and studied this way. Programming languages differ from natural languages in that natural languages are only used for interaction between people, while programming languages also allow humans to communicate instructions to machines.

Abstractions

> Programming languages usually contain abstractions for defining and manipulating data structures or controlling the flow of execution. The practical necessity that a programming language support adequate abstractions is expressed by the abstraction principle; this principle is sometimes formulated as a recommendation to the programmer to make proper use of such abstractions.

Expressive power

> The theory of computation classifies languages by the computations they are capable of expressing. All Turing complete languages can implement the same set of algorithms. ANSI/ISO SQL-92 and Charity are examples of languages that are not Turing complete, yet often called programming languages.

Markup languages like XML, HTML, or troff, which define structured data, are not usually considered programming languages. Programming languages may, however, share the syntax with markup languages if a computational semantics is defined. XSLT, for example, is a Turing complete XML dialect. Moreover, LaTeX, which is mostly used for structuring documents, also contains a Turing complete subset.

The term *computer language* is sometimes used interchangeably with programming language. However, the usage of both terms varies among authors, including the exact scope of each. One usage describes programming languages as a subset of computer languages. In this vein, languages used in computing that have a different goal than expressing computer programs are generically designated computer languages. For instance, markup languages are sometimes referred to as computer languages to emphasize that they are not meant to be used for programming.

Another usage regards programming languages as theoretical constructs for programming abstract machines, and computer languages as the subset thereof that runs on physical computers, which have finite hardware resources. John C. Reynolds emphasizes that formal specification languages are just as much programming languages as are the languages intended for execution. He also argues that textual and even graphical input formats that affect the behavior of a computer are programming languages, despite the fact they are commonly not Turing-complete, and remarks that ignorance of programming language concepts is the reason for many flaws in input formats.

History

Early Developments

The earliest computers were often programmed without the help of a programming language, by writing programs in absolute machine language. The programs, in decimal or binary form, were read in from punched cards or magnetic tape or toggled in on switches on the front panel of the computer. Absolute machine languages were later termed *first-generation programming languages* (1GL).

The next step was development of so-called *second-generation programming languages* (2GL) or assembly languages, which were still closely tied to the instruction set architecture of the specific computer. These served to make the program much more human-readable and relieved the programmer of tedious and error-prone address calculations.

The first *high-level programming languages*, or *third-generation programming languages* (3GL), were written in the 1950s. An early high-level programming language to be designed for a computer was Plankalkül, developed for the German Z3 by Konrad Zuse between 1943 and 1945. However, it was not implemented until 1998 and 2000.

John Mauchly's Short Code, proposed in 1949, was one of the first high-level languages ever developed for an electronic computer. Unlike machine code, Short Code statements represented mathematical expressions in understandable form. However, the program had to be translated into machine code every time it ran, making the process much slower than running the equivalent machine code.

At the University of Manchester, Alick Glennie developed Autocode in the early 1950s. A programming language, it used a compiler to automatically convert the language into machine code. The first code and compiler was developed in 1952 for the Mark 1 computer at the University of Manchester and is considered to be the first compiled high-level programming language.

The second autocode was developed for the Mark 1 by R. A. Brooker in 1954 and was called the "Mark 1 Autocode". Brooker also developed an autocode for the Ferranti Mercury in the 1950s in conjunction with the University of Manchester. The version for the EDSAC 2 was devised by D. F. Hartley of University of Cambridge Mathematical Laboratory in 1961. Known as EDSAC 2 Autocode, it was a straight development from Mercury Autocode adapted for local circumstances and was noted for its object code optimisation and source-language diagnostics which were advanced for the time. A contemporary but separate thread of development, Atlas Autocode was developed for the University of Manchester Atlas 1 machine.

In 1954, FORTRAN was invented at IBM by John Backus. It was the first widely used high-level general purpose programming language to have a functional implementation, as opposed to just a design on paper. It is still popular language for high-performance computing and is used for programs that benchmark and rank the world's fastest supercomputers.

Another early programming language was devised by Grace Hopper in the US, called FLOW-MATIC. It was developed for the UNIVAC I at Remington Rand during the period from 1955 until 1959. Hopper found that business data processing customers were uncomfortable with mathematical notation, and in early 1955, she and her team wrote a specification for an English programming language and implemented a prototype. The FLOW-MATIC compiler became publicly available in early 1958 and was substantially complete in 1959. Flow-Matic was a major influence in the design of COBOL, since only it and its direct descendant AIMACO were in actual use at the time.

Refinement

The increased use of high-level languages introduced a requirement for *low-level programming languages* or *system programming languages*. These languages, to varying degrees, provide facilities between assembly languages and high-level languages and can be used to perform tasks which require direct access to hardware facilities but still provide higher-level control structures and error-checking.

The period from the 1960s to the late 1970s brought the development of the major language paradigms now in use:

- APL introduced *array programming* and influenced functional programming.

- ALGOL refined both *structured procedural programming* and the discipline of language specification; the "Revised Report on the Algorithmic Language ALGOL 60" became a model for how later language specifications were written.

- Lisp, implemented in 1958, was the first dynamically typed *functional programming* language

- In the 1960s, Simula was the first language designed to support *object-oriented programming*; in the mid-1970s, Smalltalk followed with the first "purely" object-oriented language.

- C was developed between 1969 and 1973 as a system programming language for the Unix operating system and remains popular.

- Prolog, designed in 1972, was the first *logic programming* language.

- In 1978, ML built a polymorphic type system on top of Lisp, pioneering *statically typed functional programming* languages.

Each of these languages spawned descendants, and most modern programming languages count at least one of them in their ancestry.

The 1960s and 1970s also saw considerable debate over the merits of *structured programming*, and whether programming languages should be designed to support it. Edsger Dijkstra, in a famous 1968 letter published in the Communications of the ACM, argued that GOTO statements should be eliminated from all "higher level" programming languages.

Consolidation and Growth

A selection of textbooks that teach programming, in languages both popular and obscure.
These are only a few of the thousands of programming languages and dialects that have been designed in history.

The 1980s were years of relative consolidation. C++ combined object-oriented and systems programming. The United States government standardized Ada, a systems programming language derived from Pascal and intended for use by defense contractors. In Japan and elsewhere, vast sums were spent investigating so-called "fifth generation" languages that incorporated logic programming constructs. The functional languages community moved to standardize ML and Lisp. Rather than inventing new paradigms, all of these movements elaborated upon the ideas invented in the previous decades.

One important trend in language design for programming large-scale systems during the 1980s was an increased focus on the use of *modules* or large-scale organizational units of code. Modula-2, Ada, and ML all developed notable module systems in the 1980s, which were often wedded to generic programming constructs.

The rapid growth of the Internet in the mid-1990s created opportunities for new languages. Perl, originally a Unix scripting tool first released in 1987, became common in dynamic websites. Java came to be used for server-side programming, and bytecode virtual machines became popular again in commercial settings with their promise of "Write once, run anywhere" (UCSD Pascal had been popular for a time in the early 1980s). These developments were not fundamentally novel, rather they were refinements of many existing languages and paradigms (although their syntax was often based on the C family of programming languages).

Programming language evolution continues, in both industry and research. Current directions include security and reliability verification, new kinds of modularity (mixins, delegates, aspects), and database integration such as Microsoft's LINQ.

Fourth-generation programming languages (4GL) are a computer programming languages which aim to provide a higher level of abstraction of the internal computer hardware details than 3GLs. *Fifth generation programming languages* (5GL) are programming languages based on solving problems using constraints given to the program, rather than using an algorithm written by a programmer.

Elements

All programming languages have some primitive building blocks for the description of data and the processes or transformations applied to them (like the addition of two numbers or the selection of an item from a collection). These primitives are defined by syntactic and semantic rules which describe their structure and meaning respectively.

Syntax

A programming language's surface form is known as its syntax. Most programming languages are purely textual; they use sequences of text including words, numbers, and punctuation, much like written natural languages. On the other hand, there are some programming languages which are more graphical in nature, using visual relationships between symbols to specify a program.

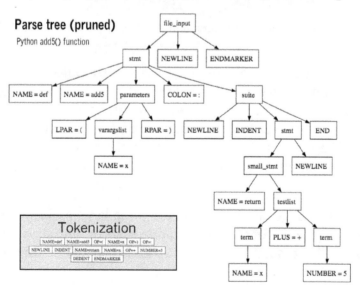

Parse tree of Python code with inset tokenization

The syntax of a language describes the possible combinations of symbols that form a syntactically correct program. The meaning given to a combination of symbols is handled by semantics (either formal or hard-coded in a reference implementation).

```
def add5(x):
    return x+5

def dotwrite(ast):
    nodename = getNodename()
    label=symbol.sym_name.get(int(ast[0]),ast[0])
    print ' %s [label="%s' % (nodename, label),
    if isinstance(ast[1], str):
        if ast[1].strip():
            print '= %s"];' % ast[1]
        else:
            print '"]'
    else:
        print '"];'
        children = []
        for n, child in enumerate(ast[1:]):
            children.append(dotwrite(child))
        print ' %s -> {' % nodename,
        for name in children:
            print '%s' % name,
```

Syntax highlighting is often used to aid programmers in recognizing elements of source code.
The language above is Python.

Programming language syntax is usually defined using a combination of regular expressions (for lexical structure) and Backus–Naur form (for grammatical structure). Below is a simple grammar, based on Lisp:

```
expression ::= atom | list

atom       ::= number | symbol

number     ::= [+-]?['0'-'9']+

symbol     ::= ['A'-'Z''a'-'z'].*

list       ::= '(' expression* ')'
```

This grammar specifies the following:

- an *expression* is either an *atom* or a *list*;

- an *atom* is either a *number* or a *symbol*;

- a *number* is an unbroken sequence of one or more decimal digits, optionally preceded by a plus or minus sign;

- a *symbol* is a letter followed by zero or more of any characters (excluding whitespace); and

- a *list* is a matched pair of parentheses, with zero or more *expressions* inside it.

The following are examples of well-formed token sequences in this grammar: 12345, () and (a b c232 (1)).

Not all syntactically correct programs are semantically correct. Many syntactically correct programs are nonetheless ill-formed, per the language's rules; and may (depending on the language specification and the soundness of the implementation) result in an error on translation or execution. In some cases, such programs may exhibit undefined behavior. Even when a program is well-defined within a language, it may still have a meaning that is not intended by the person who wrote it.

Using natural language as an example, it may not be possible to assign a meaning to a grammatically correct sentence or the sentence may be false:

- "Colorless green ideas sleep furiously." is grammatically well-formed but has no generally accepted meaning.

- "John is a married bachelor." is grammatically well-formed but expresses a meaning that cannot be true.

The following C language fragment is syntactically correct, but performs operations that are not semantically defined (the operation *p >> 4 has no meaning for a value having a complex type and p->im is not defined because the value of p is the null pointer):

```
complex *p = NULL;

complex abs_p = sqrt(*p >> 4 + p->im);
```

If the type declaration on the first line were omitted, the program would trigger an error on compilation, as the variable "p" would not be defined. But the program would still be syntactically correct since type declarations provide only semantic information.

The grammar needed to specify a programming language can be classified by its position in the Chomsky hierarchy. The syntax of most programming languages can be specified using a Type-2 grammar, i.e., they are context-free grammars. Some languages, including Perl and Lisp, contain constructs that allow execution during the parsing phase. Languages that have constructs that allow the programmer to alter the behavior of the parser make syntax analysis an undecidable problem, and generally blur the distinction between parsing and execution. In contrast to Lisp's macro system and Perl's BEGIN blocks, which may contain general computations, C macros are merely string replacements and do not require code execution.

Semantics

The term *semantics* refers to the meaning of languages, as opposed to their form (syntax).

Static Semantics

The static semantics defines restrictions on the structure of valid texts that are hard or impossible to express in standard syntactic formalisms. For compiled languages, static semantics essentially include those semantic rules that can be checked at compile time. Examples include checking that every identifier is declared before it is used (in languages that require such declarations) or that the labels on the arms of a case statement are distinct. Many important restrictions of this type, like checking that identifiers are used in the appropriate context (e.g. not adding an integer to a function name), or that subroutine calls have the appropriate number and type of arguments, can be enforced by defining them as rules in a logic called a type system. Other forms of static analyses like data flow analysis may also be part of static semantics. Newer programming languages like Java and C# have definite assignment analysis, a form of data flow analysis, as part of their static semantics.

Dynamic Semantics

Once data has been specified, the machine must be instructed to perform operations on the data. For example, the semantics may define the strategy by which expressions are evaluated to values, or the manner in which control structures conditionally execute statements. The *dynamic semantics* (also known as *execution semantics*) of a language defines how and when the various constructs of a language should produce a program behavior. There are many ways of defining execution semantics. Natural language is often used to specify the execution semantics of languages commonly used in practice. A significant amount of academic research went into formal semantics of programming languages, which allow execution semantics to be specified in a formal manner. Results from this field of research have seen limited application to programming language design and implementation outside academia.

Type System

A type system defines how a programming language classifies values and expressions into *types*, how it can manipulate those types and how they interact. The goal of a type system is to verify and usually enforce a certain level of correctness in programs written in that language by detecting certain incorrect operations. Any decidable type system involves a trade-off: while it rejects many incorrect programs, it can also prohibit some correct, albeit unusual programs. In order to bypass this downside, a number of languages have *type loopholes*, usually unchecked casts that may be used by the programmer to explicitly allow a normally disallowed operation between different types. In most typed languages, the type system is used only to type check programs, but a number of languages, usually functional ones, infer types, relieving the programmer from the need to write type annotations. The formal design and study of type systems is known as *type theory*.

Typed Versus Untyped Languages

A language is *typed* if the specification of every operation defines types of data to which the operation is applicable, with the implication that it is not applicable to other types. For example, the data represented by "this text between the quotes" is a string, and in many programming languages dividing a number by a string has no meaning and will be rejected by the compilers. The invalid operation may be detected when the program is compiled ("static" type checking) and will be rejected by the compiler with a compilation error message, or it may be detected when the program is run ("dynamic" type checking), resulting in a run-time exception. Many languages allow a function called an exception handler to be written to handle this exception and, for example, always return "-1" as the result.

A special case of typed languages are the *single-type* languages. These are often scripting or markup languages, such as REXX or SGML, and have only one data type—most commonly character strings which are used for both symbolic and numeric data.

In contrast, an *untyped language*, such as most assembly languages, allows any operation to be performed on any data, which are generally considered to be sequences of bits of various lengths. High-level languages which are untyped include BCPL, Tcl, and some varieties of Forth.

In practice, while few languages are considered typed from the point of view of type theory (verifying or rejecting *all* operations), most modern languages offer a degree of typing. Many production languages provide means to bypass or subvert the type system, trading type-safety for finer control over the program's execution.

Static Versus Dynamic Typing

In *static typing*, all expressions have their types determined prior to when the program is executed, typically at compile-time. For example, 1 and (2+2) are integer expressions; they cannot be passed to a function that expects a string, or stored in a variable that is defined to hold dates.

Statically typed languages can be either *manifestly typed* or *type-inferred*. In the first case, the programmer must explicitly write types at certain textual positions (for example, at variable declarations). In the second case, the compiler *infers* the types of expressions and declarations based on context. Most mainstream statically typed languages, such as C++, C# and Java, are manifestly typed. Complete type inference has traditionally been associated with less mainstream languages, such as Haskell and ML. However, many manifestly typed languages support partial type inference; for example, Java and C# both infer types in certain limited cases. Additionally, some programming languages allow for some types to be automatically converted to other types; for example, an int can be used where the program expects a float.

Dynamic typing, also called *latent typing*, determines the type-safety of operations at run time; in other words, types are associated with *run-time values* rather than *textual expressions*. As with type-inferred languages, dynamically typed languages do not require the programmer to write explicit type annotations on expressions. Among other things, this may permit a single variable to refer to values of different types at different points in the program execution. However, type errors cannot be automatically detected until a piece of code is actually executed, potentially making debugging more difficult. Lisp, Smalltalk, Perl, Python, JavaScript, and Ruby are all examples of dynamically typed languages.

Weak and Strong Typing

Weak typing allows a value of one type to be treated as another, for example treating a string as a number. This can occasionally be useful, but it can also allow some kinds of program faults to go undetected at compile time and even at run time.

Strong typing prevents the above. An attempt to perform an operation on the wrong type of value raises an error. Strongly typed languages are often termed *type-safe* or *safe*.

An alternative definition for "weakly typed" refers to languages, such as Perl and JavaScript, which permit a large number of implicit type conversions. In JavaScript, for example, the expression 2 * x implicitly converts x to a number, and this conversion succeeds even if x is null, undefined, an Array, or a string of letters. Such implicit conversions are often useful, but they can mask programming errors. *Strong* and *static* are now generally considered orthogonal concepts, but usage in the literature differs. Some use the term *strongly typed* to mean *strongly, statically typed*, or, even more confusingly, to mean simply *statically typed*. Thus C has been called both strongly typed and weakly, statically typed.

It may seem odd to some professional programmers that C could be "weakly, statically typed". However, notice that the use of the generic pointer, the void* pointer, does allow for casting of pointers to other pointers without needing to do an explicit cast. This is extremely similar to some-how casting an array of bytes to any kind of datatype in C without using an explicit cast, such as (int) or (char).

Standard Library and Run-time System

Most programming languages have an associated core library (sometimes known as the 'standard library', especially if it is included as part of the published language standard), which is conventionally made available by all implementations of the language. Core libraries typically include definitions for commonly used algorithms, data structures, and mechanisms for input and output.

The line between a language and its core library differs from language to language. In some cases, the language designers may treat the library as a separate entity from the language. However, a language's core library is often treated as part of the language by its users, and some language specifications even require that this library be made available in all implementations. Indeed, some languages are designed so that the meanings of certain syntactic constructs cannot even be described without referring to the core library. For example, in Java, a string literal is defined as an instance of the java.lang.String class; similarly, in Smalltalk, an anonymous function expression (a "block") constructs an instance of the library's BlockContext class. Conversely, Scheme contains multiple coherent subsets that suffice to construct the rest of the language as library macros, and so the language designers do not even bother to say which portions of the language must be implemented as language constructs, and which must be implemented as parts of a library.

Design and Implementation

Programming languages share properties with natural languages related to their purpose as vehicles for communication, having a syntactic form separate from its semantics, and showing *language families* of related languages branching one from another. But as artificial constructs, they also differ in fundamental ways from languages that have evolved through usage. A significant difference is that a programming language can be fully described and studied in its entirety, since it has a precise and finite definition. By contrast, natural languages have changing meanings given by their users in different communities. While constructed languages are also artificial languages designed from the ground up with a specific purpose, they lack the precise and complete semantic definition that a programming language has.

Many programming languages have been designed from scratch, altered to meet new needs, and combined with other languages. Many have eventually fallen into disuse. Although there have been attempts to design one "universal" programming language that serves all purposes, all of them have failed to be generally accepted as filling this role. The need for diverse programming languages arises from the diversity of contexts in which languages are used:

- Programs range from tiny scripts written by individual hobbyists to huge systems written by hundreds of programmers.

- Programmers range in expertise from novices who need simplicity above all else, to experts who may be comfortable with considerable complexity.

- Programs must balance speed, size, and simplicity on systems ranging from microcontrollers to supercomputers.

- Programs may be written once and not change for generations, or they may undergo continual modification.

- Programmers may simply differ in their tastes: they may be accustomed to discussing problems and expressing them in a particular language.

One common trend in the development of programming languages has been to add more ability to solve problems using a higher level of abstraction. The earliest programming languages were tied very closely to the underlying hardware of the computer. As new programming languages have developed, features have been added that let programmers express ideas that are more remote from simple translation into underlying hardware instructions. Because programmers are less tied to the complexity of the computer, their programs can do more computing with less effort from the programmer. This lets them write more functionality per time unit.

Natural language programming has been proposed as a way to eliminate the need for a specialized language for programming. However, this goal remains distant and its benefits are open to debate. Edsger W. Dijkstra took the position that the use of a formal language is essential to prevent the introduction of meaningless constructs, and dismissed natural language programming as "foolish". Alan Perlis was similarly dismissive of the idea. Hybrid approaches have been taken in Structured English and SQL.

A language's designers and users must construct a number of artifacts that govern and enable the practice of programming. The most important of these artifacts are the language *specification* and *implementation*.

Specification

The specification of a programming language is an artifact that the language users and the implementors can use to agree upon whether a piece of source code is a valid program in that language, and if so what its behavior shall be.

A programming language specification can take several forms, including the following:

- An explicit definition of the syntax, static semantics, and execution semantics of the language. While syntax is commonly specified using a formal grammar, semantic definitions may be written in natural language (e.g., as in the C language), or a formal semantics (e.g., as in Standard ML and Scheme specifications).

- A description of the behavior of a translator for the language (e.g., the C++ and Fortran specifications). The syntax and semantics of the language have to be inferred from this description, which may be written in natural or a formal language.

- A *reference* or *model* implementation, sometimes written in the language being specified (e.g., Prolog or ANSI REXX). The syntax and semantics of the language are explicit in the behavior of the reference implementation.

Implementation

An *implementation* of a programming language provides a way to write programs in that language and execute them on one or more configurations of hardware and software. There are, broadly, two approaches to programming language implementation: *compilation* and *interpretation*. It is generally possible to implement a language using either technique.

The output of a compiler may be executed by hardware or a program called an interpreter. In some implementations that make use of the interpreter approach there is no distinct boundary between compiling and interpreting. For instance, some implementations of BASIC compile and then execute the source a line at a time.

Programs that are executed directly on the hardware usually run several orders of magnitude faster than those that are interpreted in software.

One technique for improving the performance of interpreted programs is just-in-time compilation. Here the virtual machine, just before execution, translates the blocks of bytecode which are going to be used to machine code, for direct execution on the hardware.

Proprietary Languages

Although most of the most commonly used programming languages have fully open specifications and implementations, many programming languages exist only as proprietary programming languages with the implementation available only from a single vendor, which may claim that such a proprietary language is their intellectual property. Proprietary programming languages are commonly domain specific languages or internal scripting languages for a single product; some proprietary languages are used only internally within a vendor, while others are available to external users.

Some programming languages exist on the border between proprietary and open; for example, Oracle Corporation asserts proprietary rights to some aspects of the Java programming language, and Microsoft's C# programming language, which has open implementations of most parts of the system, also has Common Language Runtime (CLR) as a closed environment.

Many proprietary languages are widely used, in spite of their proprietary nature; examples include MATLAB and VBScript. Some languages may make the transition from closed to open; for example, Erlang was originally an Ericsson's internal programming language.

Usage

Thousands of different programming languages have been created, mainly in the computing field. Software is commonly built with 5 programming languages or more.

Programming languages differ from most other forms of human expression in that they require a greater degree of precision and completeness. When using a natural language to communicate with other people, human authors and speakers can be ambiguous and make small errors, and still expect their intent to be understood. However, figuratively speaking, computers "do exactly what they are told to do", and cannot "understand" what code the programmer intended to write. The combination of the language definition, a program, and the program's inputs must fully specify the external behavior that occurs when the program is executed, within the domain of control of that program. On the other hand, ideas about an algorithm can be communicated to humans without the precision required for execution by using pseudocode, which interleaves natural language with code written in a programming language.

A programming language provides a structured mechanism for defining pieces of data, and the operations or transformations that may be carried out automatically on that data. A programmer uses the abstractions present in the language to represent the concepts involved in a computation. These concepts are represented as a collection of the simplest elements available (called primitives). *Programming* is the process by which programmers combine these primitives to compose new programs, or adapt existing ones to new uses or a changing environment.

Programs for a computer might be executed in a batch process without human interaction, or a user might type commands in an interactive session of an interpreter. In this case the "commands" are simply programs, whose execution is chained together. When a language can run its commands through an interpreter (such as a Unix shell or other command-line interface), without compiling, it is called a scripting language.

Measuring Language Usage

It is difficult to determine which programming languages are most widely used, and what usage means varies by context. One language may occupy the greater number of programmer hours, a different one have more lines of code, and a third may consume the most CPU time. Some languages are very popular for particular kinds of applications. For example, COBOL is still strong in the corporate data center, often on large mainframes; Fortran in scientific and engineering applications; Ada in aerospace, transportation, military, real-time and embedded applications; and C in embedded applications and operating systems. Other languages are regularly used to write many different kinds of applications.

Various methods of measuring language popularity, each subject to a different bias over what is measured, have been proposed:

- counting the number of job advertisements that mention the language

- the number of books sold that teach or describe the language

- estimates of the number of existing lines of code written in the language – which may underestimate languages not often found in public searches

- counts of language references (i.e., to the name of the language) found using a web search engine.

Combining and averaging information from various internet sites, langpop.com claims that in 2013 the ten most popular programming languages are (in descending order by overall popularity): C, Java, PHP, JavaScript, C++, Python, Shell, Ruby, Objective-C and C#.

Taxonomies

There is no overarching classification scheme for programming languages. A given programming language does not usually have a single ancestor language. Languages commonly arise by combining the elements of several predecessor languages with new ideas in circulation at the time. Ideas that originate in one language will diffuse throughout a family of related languages, and then leap suddenly across familial gaps to appear in an entirely different family.

The task is further complicated by the fact that languages can be classified along multiple axes. For example, Java is both an object-oriented language (because it encourages object-oriented organization) and a concurrent language (because it contains built-in constructs for running multiple threads in parallel). Python is an object-oriented scripting language.

In broad strokes, programming languages divide into *programming paradigms* and a classification by *intended domain of use,* with general-purpose programming languages distinguished from domain-specific programming languages. Traditionally, programming languages have been regarded as describing computation in terms of imperative sentences, i.e. issuing commands. These are generally called imperative programming languages. A great deal of research in programming languages has been aimed at blurring the distinction between a program as a set of instructions and a program as an assertion about the desired answer, which is the main feature of declarative programming. More refined paradigms include procedural programming, object-oriented programming, functional programming, and logic programming; some languages are hybrids of paradigms or multi-paradigmatic. An assembly language is not so much a paradigm as a direct model of an underlying machine architecture. By purpose, programming languages might be considered general purpose, system programming languages, scripting languages, domain-specific languages, or concurrent/distributed languages (or a combination of these). Some general purpose languages were designed largely with educational goals.

A programming language may also be classified by factors unrelated to programming paradigm. For instance, most programming languages use English language keywords, while a minority do not. Other languages may be classified as being deliberately esoteric or not.

Low-level Programming Language

In computer science, a low-level programming language is a programming language that provides little or no abstraction from a computer's instruction set architecture—commands or functions in the language map closely to processor instructions. Generally this refers to either machine code or assembly language. The word "low" refers to the small or nonexistent amount of abstraction between the language and machine language; because of this, low-level languages are sometimes described as being "close to the hardware". Programs written in low-level languages tend to be relatively non-portable, mainly because of the close relationship between the language and the hardware architecture.

Low-level languages can convert to machine code without a compiler or interpreter— second-generation programming languages use a simpler processor called an assembler— and the resulting code runs directly on the processor. A program written in a low-level language can be made to run very quickly, with a small memory footprint. An equivalent program in a high-level language can be less efficient and use more memory. Low-level languages are simple, but considered difficult to use, due to numerous technical details that the programmer must remember. By comparison, a high-level programming language isolates execution semantics of a computer architecture from the specification of the program, which simplifies development.

Low-level programming languages are sometimes divided into two categories: *first generation* and *second generation*.

Machine Code

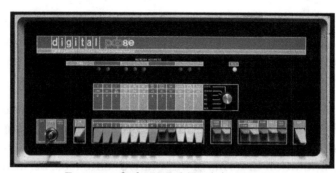

Front panel of a PDP-8/E minicomputer.
The row of switches at the bottom can be used to toggle in a machine language program.

Machine code is the only language a computer can process directly without a previous transformation. Currently, programmers almost never write programs directly in machine code, because it requires attention to numerous details that a high-level language handles automatically. Furthermore it requires memorizing or looking up numerical codes for every instruction, and is extremely difficult to modify.

True *machine code* is a stream of raw, usually binary, data. A programmer coding in "machine code" normally codes instructions and data in a more readable form such as decimal, octal, or hexadecimal which is translated to internal format by a program called a loader or toggled into the computer's memory from a front panel.

Although few programs are written in machine language, programmers often become adept at reading it through working with core dumps or debugging from the front panel.

Example: A function in hexadecimal representation of 32-bit x86 machine code to calculate the *n*th Fibonacci number:

```
8B542408  83FA0077  06B80000  0000C383

FA027706  B8010000  00C353BB  01000000

B9010000  008D0419  83FA0376  078BD989

C14AEBF1  5BC3
```

Assembly

Second-generation languages provide one abstraction level on top of the machine code. In the early days of coding on computers like the TX-0 and PDP-1, the first thing MIT hackers did was write assemblers. Assembly language has little semantics or formal specification, being only a mapping of human-readable symbols, including symbolic addresses, to opcodes, addresses, numeric constants, strings and so on. Typically, one machine instruction is represented as one line of assembly code. Assemblers produce object files that can link with other object files or be loaded on their own.

Most assemblers provide macros to generate common sequences of instructions.

Example: The same Fibonacci number calculator as above, but in x86 assembly language using MASM syntax:

```
fib:
    mov edx, [esp+8]

    cmp edx, 0

    ja @f

    mov eax, 0

    ret


@@:
cmp edx, 2

ja @f

mov eax, 1

ret


@@:
push ebx

mov ebx, 1

mov ecx, 1


@@:
        lea eax, [ebx+ecx]

        cmp edx, 3

        jbe @f

        mov ebx, ecx

        mov ecx, eax

        dec edx
```

```
jmp @b


@@:

pop ebx

ret
```

In this code example, hardware features of the x86 processor (its registers) are named and manipulated directly. The function loads its input from a precise location in the stack (8 bytes higher than the location stored in the ESP stack pointer) and performs its calculation by manipulating values in the EAX, EBX, ECX and EDX registers until it has finished and returns. Note that in this assembly language, there is no concept of returning a value. The result having been stored in the EAX register, the RET command simply moves code processing to the code location stored on the stack (usually the instruction immediately after the one that called this function) and it is up to the author of the calling code to know that this function stores its result in EAX and to retrieve it from there. x86 assembly language imposes no standard for returning values from a function (and so, in fact, has no concept of a function); it is up to the calling code to examine state after the procedure returns if it needs to extract a value.

Compare this with the same function in C:

```
unsigned int fib(unsigned int n) {

    if (n <= 0)

        return 0;

    else if (n <= 2)

        return 1;

    else {

        unsigned int a,b,c;

        a = 1;

        b = 1;

        while (1) {

            c = a + b;

            if (n <= 3) return c;

            a = b;

            b = c;

            n--;
```

```
            }

        }

}
```

This code is very similar in structure to the assembly language example but there are significant differences in terms of abstraction:

- While the input (parameter n) is loaded from the stack, its precise position on the stack is not specified. The C compiler calculates this based on the calling conventions of the target architecture.

- The assembly language version loads the input parameter from the stack into a register and in each iteration of the loop decrements the value in the register, never altering the value in the memory location on the stack. The C compiler could do the same or could update the value in the stack. Which one it chooses is an implementation decision completely hidden from the code author (and one with no side effects, thanks to C language standards).

- The local variables a, b and c are abstractions that do not specify any specific storage location on the hardware. The C compiler decides how to actually store them for the target architecture.

- The return function specifies the value to return, but does not dictate *how* it is returned. The C compiler for any specific architecture implements a standard mechanism for returning the value. Compilers for the x86 architecture typically (but not always) use the EAX register to return a value, as in the assembly language example (the author of the assembly language example has *chosen* to copy the C convention but assembly language does not require this).

These abstractions make the C code compilable without modification on any architecture for which a C compiler has been written. The x86 assembly language code is specific to the x86 architecture.

Low-level Programming in High-level Languages

In the late 1960s, high-level languages such as PL/S, BLISS, BCPL, extended ALGOL (for Burroughs large systems) and C included some degree of access to low-level programming functions. One method for this is Inline assembly, in which assembly code is embedded in a high-level language that supports this feature. Some of these languages also allow architecture-dependent compiler optimization directives to adjust the way a compiler uses the target processor architecture

Speakeasy (Computational Environment)

Speakeasy is a numerical computing interactive environment also featuring an interpreted programming language. It was initially developed for internal use at the Physics Division of Argonne National Laboratory by the theoretical physicist Stanley Cohen. He eventually founded Speakeasy Computing Corporation to make the program available commercially.

Speakeasy is a very long-lasting numerical package. In fact, the original version of the environment was built around a core dynamic data repository called "Named storage" developed in the early 1960s, while the most recent version has been released in 2006.

Speakeasy was aimed to make the computational work of the physicists at the Argonne National Laboratory easier. It was initially conceived to work on mainframes (the only kind of computers at that time), and was subsequently ported to new platforms (minicomputers, personal computers) as they became available. The porting of the same code on different platforms was made easier by using Mortran metalanguage macros to face systems dependencies and compilers deficiencies and differences. Speakeasy is currently available on several platforms : PCs running Windows, macOS, Linux, departmental computers and workstations running several flavors of Linux, AIX or Solaris.

Speakeasy was also among the first interactive numerical computing environments, having been implemented in such a way on a CDC 3600 system, and later on IBM TSO machines as one was in beta-testing at the Argonne National Laboratory at the time.

Almost since the beginning (as the dynamic linking functionality was made available in the operating systems) Speakeasy features the capability of expanding its operational vocabulary using separated modules, dynamically linked to the core processor as they are needed. For that reason such modules were called "linkules" (LINKable-modULES). They are functions with a generalized interface, which can be written in FORTRAN or in C. The independence of each of the new modules from the others and from the main processor is of great help in improving the system, especially it was in the old days.

This easy way of expanding the functionalities of the main processor was often exploited by the users to develop their own specialized packages. Besides the programs, functions and subroutines the user can write in the Speakeasy's own interpreted language, linkules add functionalities carried out with the typical performances of compiled programs.

Among the packages developed by the users, one of the most important is "Modeleasy", originally developed as "FEDeasy" in the early 1970s at the research department of the Federal Reserve Board of Governors in Washington D.C.. Modeleasy implements special objects and functions for large econometric models estimation and simulation. Its evolution led eventually to its distribution as an independent product.

Syntax

The symbol :_ (colon+underscore) is both the Speakeasy logo and the prompt of the interactive session.

The dollar sign is used for delimiting comments; the ampersand is used to continue a statement on the following physical line, in which case the prompt becomes :& (colon+ampersand); a semicolon can separate statements written on the same physical line.

```
$ suppose you have a very long statement,

$ you can write it on multiple physical lines using "&"

$ at the end of the line to be continued:
```

```
:_ the_return_value = this_is_a_function_with many_arguments(argument_1,
argument_2, &

:&                                       argument_3, argument_4, argument_5, ar-
gument_6)
```

```
$ on the other hand, you can collect several short statements

$ on a single physical line using ";"

:_ a=1; b=2; c=3; d=4
```

As its own name tells, Speakeasy was aimed to expose a syntax as friendly as possible to the user, and as close as possible to the spoken language. The best example of that is given by the set of commands for reading/writing data from/to the permanent storage. E.g. (the languages keywords are in upper case to clarify the point):

```
:_ GET my_data FROM LIBRARY my_project

:_ KEEP my_data AS a_new_name_for_mydata IN LIBRARY other_project
```

Variables (i.e. Speakeasy objects) are given a name up to 255 character long, when LONGNAME option is ON, up to 8 characters otherwise (for backward compatibility). They are dynamically typed, depending on the value assigned to them.

```
:_ a=1

:_ whatis a

A is a REAL SCALAR.

:_ a="now a character array"

:_ whatis a

A is a 21 element CHARACTER ARRAY.
```

Arguments of functions are usually not required to be surrounded by parenthesis or separated by commas, provided that the context remains clear and unambiguous. For example:

```
:_ sin(grid(-pi,pi,pi/32))     $ fully specified syntax
```

can be written :

```
:_ sin grid(-pi,pi,pi/32)      $ the argument of function sin is not sur-
rounded by parenthesis
```

or even

```
:_  sin grid(-pi pi pi/32)        $ the arguments of function grid can be
separated by spaces
```

Many other syntax simplifications are possible; for example, to define an object named 'a' valued to a ten-elements array of zeroes, one can write any of the following statements:

```
:_  a=array(10:0,0,0,0,0,0,0,0,0,0)
```

```
:_  a=0,0,0,0,0,0,0,0,0,0
```

```
:_  a=0 0 0 0 0 0 0 0 0 0
```

```
:_  a=ints(10)*0
```

```
:_  a=10:
```

Speakeasy is a vector-oriented language: giving a structured argument to a function of a scalar, the result is usually an object with the same structure of the argument, in which each element is the result of the function applied to the corresponding element of the argument. In the example given above, the result of function sin applied to the array (let us call it x) generated by the function grid is the array answer whose element answer(i) equals sin(x(i)) for each i from 1 to noels(x) (the number of elements of x). In other words, the statement

```
:_  a=sin(grid(-pi pi pi/32))
```

is equivalent to the following fragment of program:

```
x=grid(-pi pi pi/32) $ generates an array of real numbers from -pi to pi,
stepping by pi/32

for i = 1,noels(x)    $ loops on the elements of x

  a(i) = sin(x(i))    $ evaluates the i-th element of a

next i                $ increment the loop index
```

The *vector-oriented* statements avoid writing programs for such loops and are much faster than them.

Work Area and Objects

By the very first statement of the session, the user can define the size of the "named storage" (or "work area", or "allocator"), which is allocated once and for all at the beginning of the session. Within this fixed-size work area, the Speakeasy processor dynamically creates and destroys the work objects as needed. A user-tunable garbage collection mechanism is provided to maximize the size of the free block in the work area, packing the defined objects in the low end or in the high end of the allocator. At any time, the user can ask about used or remaining space in the work area.

```
:_  SIZE 100M $ very first statement: the work area will be 100MB
```

```
:_  SIZE      $ returns the size of the work area in the current session
```

```
:_ SPACELEFT $ returns the amount of data storage space currently unused

:_ SPACENOW  $ returns the amount of data storage space currently used

:_ SPACEPEAK $ returns the maximum amount of data storage space used in
the current session
```

(Raw) Object Orientation

Within reasonable conformity and compatibility constraints, the Speakeasy objects can be operated on using the same algebraic syntax.

From this point of view, and considering the dynamic and structured nature of the data held in the "named storage", it is possible to say that Speakeasy since the beginning implemented a very raw form of operator overloading, and a pragmatic approach to some features of what was later called "Object Oriented Programming", although it did not evolve further in that direction.

```
$ The following example shows how a Matrix-family object and an Ar-
ray-family object

$ with the same structure and values are operated on differently al-
though using the

$ same "*" and "/" operator: in the first case using the matrix algebra
and in the

$ second case operating on an element-by-element basis.
```

```
:_ a=matrix(2,2:1,2,3,4) ; a              :_ aa=array(2,2:1,2,3,4) ; aa

  A (A 2 by 2 Matrix)                         AA (A 2 by 2 Array)

  1   2                                       1   2

  3   4                                       3   4

:_ a*a                                     :_ aa*aa

  A*A (A 2 by 2 Matrix)                       AA*AA (A 2 by 2 Array)

  7    10                                     1    4

  15   22                                     9    16

:_ a/a                                     :_ aa/aa

  A/A (A 2 by 2 Matrix)                       AA/AA (A 2 by 2 Array)

  1   0                                       1   1

  0   1                                       1   1
```

The Object Families

Speakeasy provides a bunch of predefined "families" of data objects: scalars, arrays (up to 15 dimensions), matrices, sets, time series.

The elemental data can be of kind real (8-bytes), complex (2x8-bytes), character-literal or name-literal (matrices elements can be real or complex, time series values can only be real).

Missing Values

For time series processing, five types of missing values are provided. They are denoted by N.A. (not available), N.C. (not computable), N.D. (not defined), along with N.B. and N.E. the meaning of which is not predetermined and is left available for the linkules developer. They are internally represented by specific (and very small) numeric values, acting as codes.

All the time series operations take care of the presence of missing values, propagating them appropriately in the results.

Depending on a specific setting, missing values can be represented by the above notation, by a question mark symbol, or a blank (useful in tables). When used in input the question mark is interpreted as an N.A. missing value.

```
:_ b=timeseries(1,2,3,4 : 2010 1 4)
:_ b

  B (A Time Series with 4 Components)

  1  2  3  4
:_ b(2010 3) = ?
:_ showmval qmark
:_ b

  B (A Time Series with 4 Components)

  1  2  ?  4
:_ 1/b

  1/B (A Time Series with 4 Components)

  1    .5   ?    .25
:_ showmval explain
:_ b

  B (A Time Series with 4 Components)

  1    2    N.A.  4
:_ 1/b
```

```
1/B (A Time Series with 4 Components)

1      .5     N.C.    .25
```

In numerical objects other than time series, the concept of "missing values" is meaningless, and the numerical operations on them use the actual numeric values regardless they correspond to "missing values codes" or not (although "missing values codes" can be input and shown as such).

```
:_ 1+?

 1+? =   1.00

:_ 1/?

 1/? =   5.3033E36

:_ 1*?

 1*? = ?
```

Note that, in other contexts, a question mark may have a different meaning: for example, when used as the first (and possibly only) character of a command line, it means the request to show more pieces of a long error message (which ends with a "+" symbol).

```
:_ a=array(10000,10000:)

ARRAY(10000,10000:) In line "A=ARRAY(10000,10000:)"  Too much data.+

:_ ?

Allocator size must be at least    859387 kilobytes.+

:_ ?

Use FREE to remove no longer needed data

or

use CHECKPOINT to save allocator for later restart.+

:_ ?

Use NAMES to see presently defined names.

Use SIZE & RESTORE to restart with a larger allocator.

:_ ?

NO MORE INFORMATION AVAILABLE.
```

Logical Values

Some support is provided for logical values, relational operators (the Fortran syntax can be used) and logical expressions.

Logical values are stored actually as numeric values: with 0 meaning false and non-zero (1 on output) meaning true.

```
:_ a = 1 2 3 4 5

:_ b = 1 3 2 5 4

:_ a>b

  A>B (A 5 Component Array)

   0  0  1  0  1

:_ a<=b

  A<=B (A 5 Component Array)

   1  1  0  1  0

:_ a.eq.b

  A.EQ.B (A 5 Component Array)

   1  0  0  0  0

:_ logical(2) $ this changes the way logical values are shown

:_ a>b; a<=b; a.eq.b

  A>B (A 5 Component Array)

  F F T F T

  A<=B (A 5 Component Array)

  T T F T F

  A.EQ.B (A 5 Component Array)

  T F F F F
```

Programming

Special objects such as "PROGRAM", "SUBROUTINE" and "FUNCTION" objects (collectively referred to as *procedures*) can be defined for operations automation. Another way for running several instructions with a single command is to store them into a use-file and make the processor read them by mean of the USE command.

Use-files

"USEing" a use-file is the simplest way for performing several instruction with minimal typed input. (This operation roughly corresponds to what "source-ing" a file is in other scripting languages.)

A use-file is an alternate input source to the standard console and can contain all the commands a user can input by the keyboard (hence no multi-line flow control construct is allowed). The processor reads and executes use-files one line at a time.

Use-file execution can be concatenated but not nested, i.e. the control does not return to the caller at the completion of the called use-file.

Procedures

Full programming capability is achieved using "procedures". They are actually Speakeasy objects, which must be defined in the work area to be executed. An option is available in order to make the procedures being automatically retrieved and loaded from the external storage as they are needed.

Procedures can contain any of the execution flow control constructs available in the Speakeasy programming language.

Programs

A program can be run simply invoking its name or using it as the argument of the command EXECUTE. In the latter case, a further argument can identify a label from which the execution will begin. Speakeasy programs differs from the other procedures for being executed at the same scoping "level" they are referenced to, hence they have full visibility of all the objects defined at that level, and all the objects created during their execution will be left there for subsequent uses. For that reason no argument list is needed.

Subroutines and Functions

Subroutines and Functions are executed at a new scoping level, which is removed when they finish. The communication with the calling scoping level is carried out through the argument list (in both directions). This implements data hiding, i.e. objects created within a Subroutine or a Function are not visible to other Subroutine and Functions but through argument lists.

A global level is available for storing object which must be visible from within any procedure, e.g. the procedures themselves.

The Functions differ from the Subroutines because they also return a functional value; reference to them can be part of more complex statement and are replaced by the returned functional value when evaluating the statement.

In some extent, Speakeasy Subroutines and Functions are very similar to the Fortran procedures of the same name.

Flow Control

An IF-THEN-ELSE construct is available for conditional execution and two forms of FOR-NEXT construct are provided for looping.

```
IF (logical-expression) THEN

    true-block                   FOR  index = min,   FOR  value  IN  set-of-
                                 max [, step]        values
[ELSE
                                    loop-block          loop-block
    false-block]
                                 NEXT index          NEXT value
END IF
```

A "GO TO *label*" statement is provided for jumping, while a Fortran-like computed GO TO statement can be used fort multiple branching.

```
                                 $ In the following statement

                                 $ selector must be >= 1 and <= N



...                              GO TO label1, label2, ..., labelN : selector

IF (logical-expression)          ...
GO TO label
                                 label1:
...
                                 ...
label:
                                 label2:
...
                                 ...

                                 ...

                                 labelN:

                                 ...
```

An ON ERROR mechanism, with several options, provides a means for error handling.

Linkule Writing

Linkules are functions usually written in Fortran (or, unsupportedly, in C). With the aid of Mortran or C macros and an API library, they can interface the Speakeasy workarea for retrieving, defining, manipulating any Speakeasy object.

Most of the Speakeasy operational vocabulary is implemented via linkules. They can be statically linked to the core engine, or dynamically loaded as they are needed, provided they are properly compiled as shared objects (unix) or dll (windows).

Simula

Simula is the name of two simulation programming languages, Simula I and Simula 67, developed in the 1960s at the Norwegian Computing Center in Oslo, by Ole-Johan Dahl and Kristen Nygaard. Syntactically, it is a fairly faithful superset of ALGOL 60.

Simula 67 introduced objects, classes, inheritance and subclasses, virtual procedures, coroutines, and discrete event simulation, and features garbage collection. Also other forms of subtyping (besides inheriting subclasses) were introduced in Simula derivatives.

Simula is considered the first object-oriented programming language. As its name suggests, Simula was designed for doing simulations, and the needs of that domain provided the framework for many of the features of object-oriented languages today.

Simula has been used in a wide range of applications such as simulating VLSI designs, process modeling, protocols, algorithms, and other applications such as typesetting, computer graphics, and education. The influence of Simula is often understated, and Simula-type objects are reimplemented in C++, Object Pascal, Java, C# and several other languages. Computer scientists such as Bjarne Stroustrup, creator of C++, and James Gosling, creator of Java, have acknowledged Simula as a major influence.

History

The following account is based on Jan Rune Holmevik's historical essay.

Kristen Nygaard started writing computer simulation programs in 1957. Nygaard saw a need for a better way to describe the heterogeneity and the operation of a system. To go further with his ideas on a formal computer language for describing a system, Nygaard realized that he needed someone with more computer programming skills than he had. Ole-Johan Dahl joined him on his work January 1962. The decision of linking the language up to ALGOL 60 was made shortly after. By May 1962 the main concepts for a simulation language were set. "SIMULA I" was born, a special purpose programming language for simulating discrete event systems.

Kristen Nygaard was invited to UNIVAC late May 1962 in connection with the marketing of their new UNIVAC 1107 computer. At that visit Nygaard presented the ideas of Simula to Robert Bemer, the director of systems programming at Univac. Bemer was a sworn ALGOL fan and found the Simula project compelling. Bemer was also chairing a session at the second international conference on information processing hosted by IFIP. He invited Nygaard, who presented the paper "SIMULA -- An Extension of ALGOL to the Description of Discrete-Event Networks".

Norwegian Computing Center got a UNIVAC 1107 August 1963 at a considerable discount, on which Dahl implemented the SIMULA I under contract with UNIVAC. The implementation was based on the UNIVAC ALGOL 60 compiler. SIMULA I was fully operational on the UNIVAC 1107 by January 1965. In the following couple of years Dahl and Nygaard spent a lot of time teaching Simula. Simula spread to several countries around the world and SIMULA I was later implemented on Burroughs B5500 computers and the Russian URAL-16 computer.

In 1966 C. A. R. Hoare introduced the concept of record class construct, which Dahl and Nygaard extended with the concept of prefixing and other features to meet their requirements for a generalized process concept. Dahl and Nygaard presented their paper on Class and Subclass Declarations at the IFIP Working Conference on simulation languages in Oslo, May 1967. This paper became the first formal definition of Simula 67. In June 1967 a conference was held to standardize the language and initiate a number of implementations. Dahl proposed to unify the type and the class concept. This led to serious discussions, and the proposal was rejected by the board. SIMULA 67 was formally standardized on the first meeting of the SIMULA Standards Group (SSG) in February 1968.

Simula was influential in the development of Smalltalk and later object-oriented programming languages. It also helped inspire the actor model of concurrent computation although Simula only supports co-routines and not true concurrency.

In the late sixties and the early seventies there were four main implementations of Simula:

- UNIVAC 1100 by NCC

- System/360 and System/370 by NCC

- CDC 3000 by University of Oslo's Joint Computer Installation at Kjeller

- TOPS-10 by Swedish National Defence Research Institute (FOA)

These implementations were ported to a wide range of platforms. The TOPS-10 implemented the concept of public, protected, and private member variables and procedures, that later was integrated into Simula 87. Simula 87 is the latest standard and is ported to a wide range of platforms. There are mainly three implementations:

- Simula AS

- Lund Simula

- GNU Cim

In November 2001 Dahl and Nygaard were awarded the IEEE John von Neumann Medal by the Institute of Electrical and Electronic Engineers "For the introduction of the concepts underlying object-oriented programming through the design and implementation of SIMULA 67". In April 2002 they received the 2001 A. M. Turing Award by the Association for Computing Machinery (ACM), with the citation: "For ideas fundamental to the emergence of object oriented programming, through their design of the programming languages Simula I and Simula 67." Unfortunately neither Dahl nor Nygaard could make it to the ACM Turing Award Lecture, scheduled to be delivered at the November 2002 OOPSLA conference in Seattle, as they died in June and August of that year, respectively.

Simula Research Laboratory is a research institute named after the Simula language, and Nygaard held a part-time position there from the opening in 2001. The new Computer Science building at the University of Oslo is named Ole Johan Dahl's House, in Dahl's honour, and the main auditorium is named Simula.

Simula is still used for various types of university courses, for instance, Jarek Sklenar teaches Simula to students at University of Malta.

Sample Code

Minimal Program

The empty computer file is the minimal program in Simula, measured by the size of the source code. It consists of one thing only; a dummy statement.

However, the minimal program is more conveniently represented as an empty block:

```
Begin

End;
```

It begins executing and immediately terminates. The language does not have any return value from the program itself.

Classic Hello World

An example of a Hello world program in Simula:

```
Begin

    OutText ("Hello World!");

    Outimage;

End;
```

Simula is case-insensitive.

Classes, Subclasses and Virtual Procedures

A more realistic example with use of classes, subclasses and virtual procedures:

```
Begin

    Class Glyph;

        Virtual: Procedure print Is Procedure print;

    Begin

    End;


    Glyph Class Char (c);

        Character c;

    Begin

        Procedure print;
```

```
            OutChar(c);
    End;


Glyph Class Line (elements);
        Ref (Glyph) Array elements;
Begin
    Procedure print;
    Begin
        Integer i;
        For i:= 1 Step 1 Until UpperBound (elements, 1) Do
            elements (i).print;
        OutImage;
    End;
End;


Ref (Glyph) rg;
Ref (Glyph) Array rgs (1 : 4);


! Main program;
rgs (1):- New Char ('A');
rgs (2):- New Char ('b');
rgs (3):- New Char ('b');
rgs (4):- New Char ('a');
rg:- New Line (rgs);
rg.print;
End;
```

The above example has one super class (Glyph) with two subclasses (Char and Line). There is one virtual procedure with two implementations. The execution starts by executing the main program. Simula does not have the concept of abstract classes since classes with pure virtual procedures can be instantiated. This means that in the above example all classes can be instantiated. Calling a pure virtual procedure will however produce a run-time error.

Call by Name

Simula supports call by name so the Jensen's Device can easily be implemented. However, the default transmission mode for simple parameter is call by value, contrary to ALGOL which used call by name. The source code for the Jensen's Device must therefore specify call by name for the parameters when compiled by a Simula compiler.

Another much simpler example is the summation function $\sum$ which can be implemented as follows:

```
Real Procedure Sigma (k, m, n, u);

    Name k, u;

    Integer k, m, n; Real u;

Begin

    Real s;

    k:= m;

    While k <= n Do Begin s:= s + u; k:= k + 1; End;

    Sigma:= s;

End;
```

The above code uses call by name for the controlling variable (k) and the expression (u). This allows the controlling variable to be used in the expression.

Note that the Simula standard allows for certain restrictions on the controlling variable in a for loop. The above code therefore uses a while loop for maximum portability.

The following:

$$Z = \sum_{i=1}^{100} \frac{1}{(i+a)^2}$$

can then be implemented as follows:

```
Z:= Sigma (i, 1, 100, 1 / (i + a) ** 2);
```

Simulation

Simula includes a simulation package for doing discrete event simulations. This simulation package is based on Simula's object oriented features and its coroutine concept.

Sam, Sally, and Andy are shopping for clothes. They have to share one fitting room. Each one of them is browsing the store for about 12 minutes and then uses the fitting room exclusively for about three minutes, each following a normal distribution. A simulation of their fitting room experience is as follows:

```
Simulation Begin

    Class FittingRoom; Begin

        Ref (Head) door;

        Boolean inUse;

        Procedure request; Begin

            If inUse Then Begin

                Wait (door);

                door.First.Out;

            End;

            inUse:= True;

        End;

        Procedure leave; Begin

            inUse:= False;

            Activate door.First;

        End;

        door:- New Head;

    End;


    Procedure report (message); Text message; Begin

        OutFix (Time, 2, 0); OutText (": " & message); OutImage;

    End;


    Process Class Person (pname); Text pname; Begin

        While True Do Begin

            Hold (Normal (12, 4, u));
```

```
        report   (pname & " is requesting the fitting room");

        fittingroom1.request;

        report (pname & " has entered the fitting room");

        Hold (Normal (3, 1, u));

        fittingroom1.leave;

        report (pname & " has left the fitting room");

    End;

  End;


  Integer u;

  Ref (FittingRoom) fittingRoom1;


  fittingRoom1:- New FittingRoom;

  Activate New Person ("Sam");

  Activate New Person ("Sally");

  Activate New Person ("Andy");

  Hold (100);

End;
```

The main block is prefixed with Simulation for enabling simulation. The simulation package can be used on any block and simulations can even be nested when simulating someone doing simulations.

The fitting room object uses a queue (door) for getting access to the fitting room. When someone requests the fitting room and it's in use they must wait in this queue (Wait (door)). When someone leaves the fitting room the first one (if any) is released from the queue (Activate door.first) and accordingly removed from the door queue (door.First.Out).

Person is a subclass of Process and its activity is described using hold (time for browsing the store and time spent in the fitting room) and calls procedures in the fitting room object for requesting and leaving the fitting room.

The main program creates all the objects and activates all the person objects to put them into the event queue. The main program holds for 100 minutes of simulated time before the program terminates.

Smalltalk

Smalltalk is an object-oriented, dynamically typed, reflective programming language. Smalltalk was created as the language to underpin the "new world" of computing exemplified by "human–computer symbiosis." It was designed and created in part for educational use, more so for constructionist learning, at the Learning Research Group (LRG) of Xerox PARC by Alan Kay, Dan Ingalls, Adele Goldberg, Ted Kaehler, Scott Wallace, and others during the 1970s.

The language was first generally released as Smalltalk-80. Smalltalk-like languages are in continuing active development and have gathered loyal communities of users around them. ANSI Smalltalk was ratified in 1998 and represents the standard version of Smalltalk.

History

There are a large number of Smalltalk variants. The unqualified word *Smalltalk* is often used to indicate the Smalltalk-80 language, the first version to be made publicly available and created in 1980.

Smalltalk was the product of research led by Alan Kay at Xerox Palo Alto Research Center (PARC); Alan Kay designed most of the early Smalltalk versions, Adele Goldberg wrote most of the documentation, and Dan Ingalls implemented most of the early versions. The first version, known as Smalltalk-71, was created by Kay in a few mornings on a bet that a programming language based on the idea of message passing inspired by Simula could be implemented in "a page of code." A later variant actually used for research work is now known as Smalltalk-72 and influenced the development of the Actor model. Its syntax and execution model were very different from modern Smalltalk variants.

After significant revisions which froze some aspects of execution semantics to gain performance (by adopting a Simula-like class inheritance model of execution), Smalltalk-76 was created. This system had a development environment featuring most of the now familiar tools, including a class library code browser/editor. Smalltalk-80 added metaclasses, to help maintain the "everything is an object" (except private instance variables) paradigm by associating properties and behavior with individual classes, and even primitives such as integer and boolean values (for example, to support different ways of creating instances).

Smalltalk-80 was the first language variant made available outside of PARC, first as Smalltalk-80 Version 1, given to a small number of firms (Hewlett-Packard, Apple Computer, Tektronix, and DEC) and universities (UC Berkeley) for "peer review" and implementation on their platforms. Later (in 1983) a general availability implementation, known as Smalltalk-80 Version 2, was released as an image (platform-independent file with object definitions) and a virtual machine specification. ANSI Smalltalk has been the standard language reference since 1998.

Two of the currently popular Smalltalk implementation variants are descendants of those original Smalltalk-80 images. Squeak is an open source implementation derived from Smalltalk-80 Version 1 by way of Apple Smalltalk. VisualWorks is derived from Smalltalk-80 version 2 by way of Smalltalk-80 2.5 and ObjectWorks (both products of ParcPlace Systems, a Xerox PARC spin-off company formed to bring Smalltalk to the market). As an interesting link between generations, in 2001 Vassili Bykov implemented Hobbes, a virtual machine running Smalltalk-80 inside Visual-Works. (Dan Ingalls later ported Hobbes to Squeak.)

During the late 1980s to mid-1990s, Smalltalk environments—including support, training and add-ons—were sold by two competing organizations: ParcPlace Systems and Digitalk, both California based. ParcPlace Systems tended to focus on the Unix/Sun microsystems market, while Digitalk focused on Intel-based PCs running Microsoft Windows or IBM's OS/2. Both firms struggled to take Smalltalk mainstream due to Smalltalk's substantial memory needs, limited run-time performance, and initial lack of supported connectivity to SQL-based relational database servers. While the high price of ParcPlace Smalltalk limited its market penetration to mid-sized and large commercial organizations, the Digitalk products initially tried to reach a wider audience with a lower price. IBM initially supported the Digitalk product, but then entered the market with a Smalltalk product in 1995 called VisualAge/Smalltalk. Easel introduced Enfin at this time on Windows and OS/2. Enfin became far more popular in Europe, as IBM introduced it into IT shops before their development of IBM Smalltalk (later VisualAge). Enfin was later acquired by Cincom Systems, and is now sold under the name ObjectStudio, and is part of the Cincom Smalltalk product suite.

In 1995, ParcPlace and Digitalk merged into ParcPlace-Digitalk and then rebranded in 1997 as ObjectShare, located in Irvine, CA. ObjectShare (NASDAQ: OBJS) was traded publicly until 1999, when it was delisted and dissolved. The merged firm never managed to find an effective response to Java as to market positioning, and by 1997 its owners were looking to sell the business. In 1999, Seagull Software acquired the ObjectShare Java development lab (including the original Smalltalk/V and Visual Smalltalk development team), and still owns VisualSmalltalk, although worldwide distribution rights for the Smalltalk product remained with ObjectShare who then sold them to Cincom. VisualWorks was sold to Cincom and is now part of Cincom Smalltalk. Cincom has backed Smalltalk strongly, releasing multiple new versions of VisualWorks and ObjectStudio each year since 1999.

Cincom, Gemstone and Object Arts, plus other vendors continue to sell Smalltalk environments. IBM has 'end of life'd VisualAge Smalltalk having in the late 1990s decided to back Java and it is, as of 2006, supported by Instantiations, Inc. which has renamed the product VA Smalltalk and released several new versions. The open Squeak implementation has an active community of developers, including many of the original Smalltalk community, and has recently been used to provide the Etoys environment on the OLPC project, a toolkit for developing collaborative applications Croquet Project, and the Open Cobalt virtual world application. GNU Smalltalk is a free software implementation of a derivative of Smalltalk-80 from the GNU project. Pharo Smalltalk is a fork of Squeak oriented towards research and use in commercial environments.

A significant development, that has spread across all current Smalltalk environments, is the increasing usage of two web frameworks, Seaside and AIDA/Web, to simplify the building of complex web applications. Seaside has seen considerable market interest with Cincom, Gemstone and Instantiations incorporating and extending it.

Influences

Smalltalk was one of many object-oriented programming languages based on Simula. Smalltalk is also one of the most influential programming languages. Virtually all of the object-oriented languages that came after—Flavors, CLOS, Objective-C, Java, Python, Ruby, and many others—were influenced by Smalltalk. Smalltalk was also one of the most popular languages with the Agile Methods, Rapid Prototyping, and Software Patterns communities. The highly productive environment provided by Smalltalk platforms made them ideal for rapid, iterative development.

Smalltalk emerged from a larger program of ARPA funded research that in many ways defined the modern world of computing. In addition to Smalltalk, working prototypes of things such as hypertext, GUIs, multimedia, the mouse, telepresence, and the Internet were developed by ARPA researchers in the 1960s. Alan Kay (one of the inventors of Smalltalk) also described a tablet computer he called the Dynabook which resembles modern tablet computers like the iPad.

Smalltalk environments were often the first to develop what are now common object-oriented software design patterns. One of the most popular is the Model–view–controller pattern for User Interface design. The MVC pattern enables developers to have multiple consistent views of the same underlying data. It's ideal for software development environments, where there are various views (e.g., entity-relation, dataflow, object model, etc.) of the same underlying specification. Also, for simulations or games where the underlying model may be viewed from various angles and levels of abstraction.

In addition to the MVC pattern the Smalltalk language and environment were tremendously influential in the history of the Graphical User Interface (GUI) and the What You See Is What You Get (WYSIWYG) user interface, font editors, and desktop metaphors for UI design. The powerful built-in debugging and object inspection tools that came with Smalltalk environments set the standard for all the Integrated Development Environments, starting with Lisp Machine environments, that came after.

Object-oriented Programming

As in other object-oriented languages, the central concept in Smalltalk-80 (but not in Smalltalk-72) is that of an *object*. An object is always an *instance* of a *class*. Classes are "blueprints" that describe the properties and behavior of their instances. For example, a GUI's window class might declare that windows have properties such as the label, the position and whether the window is visible or not. The class might also declare that instances support operations such as opening, closing, moving and hiding. Each particular window object would have its own values of those properties, and each of them would be able to perform operations defined by its class.

A Smalltalk object can do exactly three things:

1. Hold state (references to other objects).

2. Receive a message from itself or another object.

3. In the course of processing a message, send messages to itself or another object.

The state an object holds is always private to that object. Other objects can query or change that state only by sending requests (messages) to the object to do so. Any message can be sent to any object: when a message is received, the receiver determines whether that message is appropriate. Alan Kay has commented that despite the attention given to objects, messaging is the most important concept in Smalltalk: "The big idea is 'messaging'—that is what the kernel of Smalltalk/Squeak is all about (and it's something that was never quite completed in our Xerox PARC phase)."

Smalltalk is a "pure" object-oriented programming language, meaning that, unlike Java and C++, there is no difference between values which are objects and values which are primitive types. In Smalltalk, primitive values such as integers, booleans and characters are also objects, in the sense that they are instances of corresponding classes, and operations on them are invoked by sending messages. A programmer can change or extend (through subclassing) the classes that implement primitive values, so that new behavior can be defined for their instances—for example, to implement new control structures—or even so that their existing behavior will be changed. This fact is summarized in the commonly heard phrase "In Smalltalk everything is an object", which may be more accurately expressed as "all values are objects", as variables are not.

Since all values are objects, classes themselves are also objects. Each class is an instance of the *metaclass* of that class. Metaclasses in turn are also objects, and are all instances of a class called Metaclass. Code blocks—Smalltalk's way of expressing anonymous functions—are also objects.

Reflection

Reflection is a term that computer scientists apply to software programs that have the capability to inspect their own structure, for example their parse tree or datatypes of input and output parameters. Reflection was first primarily a feature of interpreted languages such as Smalltalk and Lisp. The fact that statements are interpreted means that the programs have access to information created as they were parsed and can often even modify their own structure.

Reflection is also a feature of having a meta-model as Smalltalk does. The meta-model is the model that describes the language itself and developers can use the meta-model to do things like walk through, examine, and modify the parse tree of an object. Or find all the instances of a certain kind of structure (e.g., all the instances of the Method class in the meta-model).

Smalltalk-80 is a totally reflective system, implemented in Smalltalk-80 itself. Smalltalk-80 provides both structural and computational reflection. Smalltalk is a structurally reflective system whose structure is defined by Smalltalk-80 objects. The classes and methods that define the system are themselves objects and fully part of the system that they help define. The Smalltalk compiler compiles textual source code into method objects, typically instances of CompiledMethod. These get added to classes by storing them in a class's method dictionary. The part of the class hierarchy that defines classes can add new classes to the system. The system is extended by running Smalltalk-80 code that creates or defines classes and methods. In this way a Smalltalk-80 system is a "living" system, carrying around the ability to extend itself at run time.

Since the classes are themselves objects, they can be asked questions such as "what methods do you implement?" or "what fields/slots/instance variables do you define?". So objects can easily be inspected, copied, (de)serialized and so on with generic code that applies to any object in the system.

Smalltalk-80 also provides computational reflection, the ability to observe the computational state of the system. In languages derived from the original Smalltalk-80 the current activation of a method is accessible as an object named via a pseudo-variable (one of the six reserved words), thisContext. By sending messages to thisContext a method activation can ask questions like "who sent this message to me". These facilities make it possible to implement co-routines or Prolog-like back-tracking without modifying the virtual machine. The exception system is implemented using this facility. One of the more interesting uses of this is in the Seaside web framework which relieves the programmer of dealing with the complexity of a Web Browser's back button by storing continuations for each edited page and switching between them as the user navigates a web site. Programming the web server using Seaside can then be done using a more conventional programming style.

An example of how Smalltalk can use reflection is the mechanism for handling errors. When an object is sent a message that it does not implement, the virtual machine sends the object the doesNotUnderstand: message with a reification of the message as an argument. The message (another object, an instance of Message) contains the selector of the message and an Array of its arguments. In an interactive Smalltalk system the default implementation of doesNotUnderstand: is one that opens an error window (a Notifier) reporting the error to the user. Through this and the reflective facilities the user can examine the context in which the error occurred, redefine the offending code, and continue, all within the system, using Smalltalk-80's reflective facilities.

Syntax

Smalltalk-80 syntax is rather minimalist, based on only a handful of declarations and reserved words. In fact, only six "keywords" are reserved in Smalltalk: true, false, nil, self, super, and thisContext. These are actually called *pseudo-variables*, identifiers that follow the rules for variable identifiers but denote bindings that the programmer cannot change. The true, false, and nil pseudo-variables are singleton instances. self and super refer to the receiver of a message within a method activated in response to that message, but sends to super are looked up in the superclass of the method's defining class rather than the class of the receiver, which allows methods in subclasses to invoke methods of the same name in superclasses. thisContext refers to the current activation record. The only built-in language constructs are message sends, assignment, method return and literal syntax for some objects. From its origins as a language for children of all ages, standard Smalltalk syntax uses punctuation in a manner more like English than mainstream coding languages. The remainder of the language, including control structures for conditional evaluation and iteration, is implemented on top of the built-in constructs by the standard Smalltalk class library. (For performance reasons, implementations may recognize and treat as special some of those messages; however, this is only an optimization and is not hardwired into the language syntax.)

The adage that "Smalltalk syntax fits on a postcard" refers to a code snippet by Ralph Johnson, demonstrating all the basic standard syntactic elements of methods:

```
exampleWithNumber: x

    | y |

    true & false not & (nil isNil) ifFalse: [self halt].

    y := self size + super size.

    #($a #a "a" 1 1.0)

        do: [ :each |

            Transcript show: (each class name);

                    show: ' '].

    ^x < y
```

Literals

The following examples illustrate the most common objects which can be written as literal values in Smalltalk-80 methods.

Numbers. The following list illustrates some of the possibilities.

```
42
```

```
-42
```

```
123.45
```

```
1.2345e2
```

```
2r10010010
```

```
16rA000
```

The last two entries are a binary and a hexadecimal number, respectively. The number before the 'r' is the radix or base. The base does not have to be a power of two; for example 36rSMALLTALK is a valid number equal to 80738163270632 decimal.

Characters are written by preceding them with a dollar sign:

```
$A
```

Strings are sequences of characters enclosed in single quotes:

```
'Hello, world!'
```

To include a quote in a string, escape it using a second quote:

```
'I said, ''Hello, world!'' to them.'
```

Double quotes do not need escaping, since single quotes delimit a string:

```
'I said, "Hello, world!" to them.'
```

Two equal strings (strings are equal if they contain all the same characters) can be different objects residing in different places in memory. In addition to strings, Smalltalk has a class of character sequence objects called Symbol. Symbols are guaranteed to be unique—there can be no two equal symbols which are different objects. Because of that, symbols are very cheap to compare and are often used for language artifacts such as message selectors.

Symbols are written as # followed by a string literal. For example:

```
#'foo'
```

If the sequence does not include whitespace or punctuation characters, this can also be written as:

```
#foo
```

Arrays:

```
#(1 2 3 4)
```

defines an array of four integers.

Many implementations support the following literal syntax for ByteArrays:

```
#[1 2 3 4]
```

defines a ByteArray of four integers.

And last but not least, blocks (anonymous function literals)

```
[... Some smalltalk code...]
```

Blocks are explained in detail further in the text.

Many Smalltalk dialects implement additional syntaxes for other objects, but the ones above are the essentials supported by all.

Variable Declarations

The two kinds of variables commonly used in Smalltalk are instance variables and temporary variables. Other variables and related terminology depend on the particular implementation. For example, VisualWorks has class shared variables and namespace shared variables, while Squeak and many other implementations have class variables, pool variables and global variables.

Temporary variable declarations in Smalltalk are variables declared inside a method. They are declared at the top of the method as names separated by spaces and enclosed by vertical bars. For example:

```
| index |
```

declares a temporary variable named index. Multiple variables may be declared within one set of bars:

```
| index vowels |
```

declares two variables: index and vowels.

Assignment

A variable is assigned a value via the ':=' syntax. So:

```
vowels := 'aeiou'
```

Assigns the string 'aeiou' to the previously declared vowels variable. The string is an object (a sequence of characters between single quotes is the syntax for literal strings), created by the compiler at compile time.

In the original Parc Place image, the glyph of the underscore character (_) appeared as a left-facing arrow (like in the 1963 version of the ASCII code). Smalltalk originally accepted this left-arrow as the only assignment operator. Some modern code still contains what appear to be underscores acting as assignments, hearkening back to this original usage. Most modern Smalltalk implementations accept either the underscore or the colon-equals syntax.

Messages

The message is the most fundamental language construct in Smalltalk. Even control structures are implemented as message sends. Smalltalk adopts by default a synchronous, single dynamic message dispatch strategy (as contrasted to the asynchronous, multiple dispatch strategy adopted by some other object-oriented languages).

The following example sends the message 'factorial' to number 42:

```
42 factorial
```

In this situation 42 is called the message *receiver*, while 'factorial' is the message *selector*. The receiver responds to the message by returning a value (presumably in this case the factorial of 42). Among other things, the result of the message can be assigned to a variable:

```
aRatherBigNumber := 42 factorial
```

"factorial" above is what is called a *unary message* because only one object, the receiver, is involved. Messages can carry additional objects as *arguments*, as follows:

```
2 raisedTo: 4
```

In this expression two objects are involved: 2 as the receiver and 4 as the message argument. The message result, or in Smalltalk parlance, *the answer* is supposed to be 16. Such messages are called *keyword messages*. A message can have more arguments, using the following syntax:

```
'hello world' indexOf: $o startingAt: 6
```

which answers the index of character 'o' in the receiver string, starting the search from index 6. The selector of this message is "indexOf:startingAt:", consisting of two pieces, or *keywords*.

Such interleaving of keywords and arguments is meant to improve readability of code, since arguments are explained by their preceding keywords. For example, an expression to create a rectangle using a C++ or Java-like syntax might be written as:

```
new Rectangle(100, 200);
```

It's unclear which argument is which. By contrast, in Smalltalk, this code would be written as:

Rectangle width: 100 height: 200

The receiver in this case is "Rectangle", a class, and the answer will be a new instance of the class with the specified width and height.

Finally, most of the special (non-alphabetic) characters can be used as what are called *binary messages*. These allow mathematical and logical operators to be written in their traditional form:

```
3 + 4
```

which sends the message "+" to the receiver 3 with 4 passed as the argument (the answer of which will be 7). Similarly,

```
3 > 4
```

is the message ">" sent to 3 with argument 4 (the answer of which will be false).

Notice, that the Smalltalk-80 language itself does not imply the meaning of those operators. The outcome of the above is only defined by how the receiver of the message (in this case a Number instance) responds to messages "+" and ">".

A side effect of this mechanism is operator overloading. A message ">" can also be understood by other objects, allowing the use of expressions of the form "a > b" to compare them.

Expressions

An expression can include multiple message sends. In this case expressions are parsed according to a simple order of precedence. Unary messages have the highest precedence, followed by binary messages, followed by keyword messages. For example:

```
3 factorial + 4 factorial between: 10 and: 100
```

is evaluated as follows:

1. 3 receives the message "factorial" and answers 6

2. 4 receives the message "factorial" and answers 24

3. 6 receives the message "+" with 24 as the argument and answers 30

4. 30 receives the message "between:and:" with 10 and 100 as arguments and answers true

The answer of the last message sent is the result of the entire expression.

Parentheses can alter the order of evaluation when needed. For example,

```
(3 factorial + 4) factorial between: 10 and: 100
```

will change the meaning so that the expression first computes "3 factorial + 4" yielding 10. That 10 then receives the second "factorial" message, yielding 3628800. 3628800 then receives "between:and:", answering false.

Note that because the meaning of binary messages is not hardwired into Smalltalk-80 syntax, all of them are considered to have equal precedence and are evaluated simply from left to right. Because of this, the meaning of Smalltalk expressions using binary messages can be different from their "traditional" interpretation:

```
3 + 4 * 5
```

is evaluated as "(3 + 4) * 5", producing 35. To obtain the expected answer of 23, parentheses must be used to explicitly define the order of operations:

```
3 + (4 * 5)
```

Unary messages can be *chained* by writing them one after another:

```
3 factorial factorial log
```

which sends "factorial" to 3, then "factorial" to the result (6), then "log" to the result (720), producing the result 2.85733.

A series of expressions can be written as in the following (hypothetical) example, each separated by a period. This example first creates a new instance of class Window, stores it in a variable, and then sends two messages to it.

```
| window |

window := Window new.

window label: 'Hello'.

window open
```

If a series of messages are sent to the same receiver as in the example above, they can also be written as a *cascade* with individual messages separated by semicolons:

```
Window new

   label: 'Hello';

   open
```

This rewrite of the earlier example as a single expression avoids the need to store the new window in a temporary variable. According to the usual precedence rules, the unary message "new" is sent first, and then "label:" and "open" are sent to the answer of "new".

Code Blocks

A block of code (an anonymous function) can be expressed as a literal value (which is an object, since all values are objects.) This is achieved with square brackets:

```
[ :params | <message-expressions> ]
```

Where *:params* is the list of parameters the code can take. This means that the Smalltalk code:

```
[:x | x + 1]
```

can be understood as:

$$f : f(x) = x + 1 :$$

or expressed in lambda terms as:

$$\lambda x : x + 1$$

and

```
[:x | x + 1] value: 3
```

can be evaluated as

$$f(3) = 3 + 1$$

Or in lambda terms as:

$$(\lambda x : x + 1)3_\beta \rightarrow 4$$

The resulting block object can form a closure: it can access the variables of its enclosing lexical scopes at any time. Blocks are first-class objects.

Blocks can be executed by sending them the *value* message (compound variations exist in order to provide parameters to the block e.g. 'value:value:' and 'valueWithArguments:').

The literal representation of blocks was an innovation which on the one hand allowed certain code to be significantly more readable; it allowed algorithms involving iteration to be coded in a clear and concise way. Code that would typically be written with loops in some languages can be written concisely in Smalltalk using blocks, sometimes in a single line. But more importantly blocks allow control structure to be expressed using messages and polymorphism, since blocks defer computation and polymorphism can be used to select alternatives. So if-then-else in Smalltalk is written and implemented as

```
expr ifTrue: [statements to evaluate if expr] ifFalse: [statements to
evaluate if not expr]
```

True methods for evaluation

ifTrue: trueAlternativeBlock **ifFalse:** falseAlternativeBlock

        ^trueAlternativeBlock value

False methods for evaluation

ifTrue: trueAlternativeBlock **ifFalse:** falseAlternativeBlock

        ^falseAlternativeBlock value

```
positiveAmounts := allAmounts select: [:anAmount | anAmount isPositive]
```

Note that this is related to functional programming, wherein patterns of computation (here selection) are abstracted into higher-order functions. For example, the message *select:* on a Collection is equivalent to the higher-order function filter on an appropriate functor.

Control Structures

Control structures do not have special syntax in Smalltalk. They are instead implemented as messages sent to objects. For example, conditional execution is implemented by sending the message ifTrue: to a Boolean object, passing as an argument the block of code to be executed if and only if the Boolean receiver is true.

The following code demonstrates this:

```
result := a > b

    ifTrue:[ 'greater' ]

    ifFalse:[ 'less or equal' ]
```

Blocks are also used to implement user-defined control structures, enumerators, visitors, pluggable behavior and many other patterns. For example:

```
| aString vowels |

aString := 'This is a string'.

vowels := aString select: [:aCharacter | aCharacter isVowel].
```

In the last line, the string is sent the message select: with an argument that is a code block literal. The code block literal will be used as a predicate function that should answer true if and only if an element of the String should be included in the Collection of characters that satisfy the test represented by the code block that is the argument to the "select:" message.

A String object responds to the "select:" message by iterating through its members (by sending itself the message "do:"), evaluating the selection block ("aBlock") once with each character it contains as the argument. When evaluated (by being sent the message "value: each"), the selection block (referenced by the parameter "aBlock", and defined by the block literal "[:aCharacter | aCharacter isVowel]"), answers a boolean, which is then sent "ifTrue:". If the boolean is the object true, the character is added to a string to be returned. Because the "select:" method is defined in the abstract class Collection, it can also be used like this:

```
| rectangles aPoint collisions |

rectangles := OrderedCollection

  with: (Rectangle left: 0 right: 10 top: 100 bottom: 200)

  with: (Rectangle left: 10 right: 10 top: 110 bottom: 210).

aPoint := Point x: 20 y: 20.

collisions := rectangles select: [:aRect | aRect containsPoint: aPoint].
```

Classes

This is a stock class definition:

```
Object subclass: #MessagePublisher

    instanceVariableNames: ''
```

```
classVariableNames: ''

poolDictionaries: ''

category: 'Smalltalk Examples'
```

Often, most of this definition will be filled in by the environment. Notice that this is actually a message to the "Object"-class to create a subclass called "MessagePublisher". In other words: classes are first-class objects in Smalltalk which can receive messages just like any other object and can be created dynamically at execution time.

Methods

When an object receives a message, a method matching the message name is invoked. The following code defines a method publish, and so defines what will happen when this object receives the 'publish' message.

```
publish

    Transcript show: 'Hello World!'
```

The following method demonstrates receiving multiple arguments and returning a value:

```
quadMultiply: i1 and: i2

    "This method multiplies the given numbers by each other and the re-
sult by 4."

    | mul |

    mul := i1 * i2.

    ^mul * 4
```

The method's name is #quadMultiply:and:. The return value is specified with the ^ operator.

Note that objects are responsible for determining dynamically at runtime which method to execute in response to a message—while in many languages this may be (sometimes, or even always) determined statically at compile time.

Instantiating Classes

The following code:

```
MessagePublisher new
```

creates (and returns) a new instance of the MessagePublisher class. This is typically assigned to a variable:

```
publisher := MessagePublisher new
```

However, it is also possible to send a message to a temporary, anonymous object:

```
MessagePublisher new publish
```

Hello World Example

The Hello world program is used by virtually all texts to new programming languages as the first program learned to show the most basic syntax and environment of the language. For Smalltalk, the program is extremely simple to write. The following code, the message "show:" is sent to the object "Transcript" with the String literal 'Hello, world!' as its argument. Invocation of the "show:" method causes the characters of its argument (the String literal 'Hello, world!') to be displayed in the transcript ("terminal") window.

```
Transcript show: 'Hello, world!'.
```

Note that a Transcript window would need to be open in order to see the results of this example.

Image-based Persistence

Most popular programming systems separate static program code (in the form of class definitions, functions or procedures) from dynamic, or run time, program state (such as objects or other forms of program data). They load program code when a program starts, and any prior program state must be recreated explicitly from configuration files or other data sources. Any settings the program (and programmer) does not explicitly save must be set up again for each restart. A traditional program also loses much useful document information each time a program saves a file, quits, and reloads. This loses details such as undo history or cursor position. Image based systems don't force losing all that just because a computer is turned off, or an OS updates.

Many Smalltalk systems, however, do not differentiate between program data (objects) and code (classes). In fact, classes are objects themselves. Therefore, most Smalltalk systems store the entire program state (including both Class and non-Class objects) in an image file. The image can then be loaded by the Smalltalk virtual machine to restore a Smalltalk-like system to a prior state. This was inspired by FLEX, a language created by Alan Kay and described in his M.Sc. thesis.

Smalltalk images are similar to (restartable) core dumps and can provide the same functionality as core dumps, such as delayed or remote debugging with full access to the program state at the time of error. Other languages that model application code as a form of data, such as Lisp, often use image-based persistence as well. This method of persistence is powerful for rapid development because all the development information (e.g. parse trees of the program) is saved which facilitates debugging. However, it also has serious drawbacks as a true persistence mechanism. For one thing, developers may often want to hide implementation details and not make them available in a run time environment. For legal reasons as well as for maintenance reasons, allowing anyone to modify the program at run time inevitably introduces complexity and potential errors that would not be possible with a compiled system that does not expose source code in the run time environment. Also, while the persistence mechanism is easy to use it lacks the true persistence capabilities needed for most multi-user systems. The most obvious is the ability to do transactions with multiple users accessing the same database in parallel.

Level of Access

Everything in Smalltalk-80 is available for modification from within a running program. This means that, for example, the IDE can be changed in a running system without restarting it. In some implementations, the syntax of the language or the garbage collection implementation can also be changed on the fly. Even the statement true become: false is valid in Smalltalk, although executing it is not recommended. When used judiciously, this level of flexibility allows for one of the shortest required times for new code to enter a production system.

Just-in-time Compilation

Smalltalk programs are usually compiled to bytecode, which is then interpreted by a virtual machine or dynamically translated into machine-native code.

List of Implementations

- Amber Smalltalk Smalltalk running atop JavaScript

- Athena, Smalltalk scripting engine for Java ≥ 1.6

- Bistro

- Cincom has the following Smalltalk products: ObjectStudio, VisualWorks and WebVelocity.

  o Visual Smalltalk Enterprise, and family, including Smalltalk/V

- Cuis Smalltalk, open source, modern Smalltalk-80

- F-Script

- GemTalk Systems, GemStone/s

- GNU Smalltalk

  o Étoilé Pragmatic Smalltalk, Smalltalk for Étoilé, a GNUstep-based user environment

  o StepTalk, GNUstep scripting framework uses Smalltalk language on an Objective-C runtime

- Gravel Smalltalk, a Smalltalk implementation for the JVM

- Instantiations, VA Smalltalk being the follow-on to IBM VisualAge Smalltalk

  o VisualAge Smalltalk

- Little Smalltalk

- Object Arts, Dolphin Smalltalk

- Object Connect, Smalltalk MT Smalltalk for Windows

- Objective-Smalltalk, Smalltalk on Objective-C runtime with extensions for Software Architecture

  o LSW Vision-Smalltalk have partnered with Object Arts

- Panda Smalltalk, open source engine, written in C, has no dependencies except libc

- Pharo Smalltalk, Pharo Project's open-source multi-platform Smalltalk

- Pocket Smalltalk, runs on Palm Pilot

- Redline Smalltalk, runs on the Java virtual machine

- Refactory, produces #Smalltalk

- Smalltalk YX

- Smalltalk/X

- Squeak, open source Smalltalk

  - Cog, JIT VM written in Squeak Smalltalk

    - CogDroid, port of non-JIT variant of Cog VM to Android

  - eToys, eToys visual programming system for learning

  - iSqueak, Squeak interpreter port for iOS devices, iPhone/iPad

  - JSqueak, Squeak interpreter written in Java

    - Potato, Squeak interpreter written in Java, a direct derivative of JSqueak

  - RoarVM, RoarVM is a multi- and manycore interpreter for Squeak and Pharo

- Strongtalk, for Windows, offers optional strong typing

- Vista Smalltalk

- CalmoSoft Project for Vista Smalltalk

Prolog

Prolog is a general-purpose logic programming language associated with artificial intelligence and computational linguistics.

Prolog has its roots in first-order logic, a formal logic, and unlike many other programming languages, Prolog is declarative: the program logic is expressed in terms of relations, represented as facts and rules. A computation is initiated by running a *query* over these relations.

The language was first conceived by a group around Alain Colmerauer in Marseille, France, in the early 1970s and the first Prolog system was developed in 1972 by Colmerauer with Philippe Roussel.

Prolog was one of the first logic programming languages, and remains the most popular among such languages today, with several free and commercial implementations available. The language has been used for theorem proving, expert systems, type inference systems, and automated planning, as well as its original intended field of use, natural language processing. Modern Prolog environments support creating graphical user interfaces, as well as administrative and networked applications.

Prolog is well-suited for specific tasks that benefit from rule-based logical queries such as searching databases, voice control systems, and filling templates.

Syntax and Semantics

In Prolog, program logic is expressed in terms of relations, and a computation is initiated by running a *query* over these relations. Relations and queries are constructed using Prolog's single data type, the *term*. Relations are defined by *clauses*. Given a query, the Prolog engine attempts to find a resolution refutation of the negated query. If the negated query can be refuted, i.e., an instantiation for all free variables is found that makes the union of clauses and the singleton set consisting of the negated query false, it follows that the original query, with the found instantiation applied, is a logical consequence of the program. This makes Prolog (and other logic programming languages) particularly useful for database, symbolic mathematics, and language parsing applications. Because Prolog allows impure predicates, checking the truth value of certain special predicates may have some deliberate side effect, such as printing a value to the screen. Because of this, the programmer is permitted to use some amount of conventional imperative programming when the logical paradigm is inconvenient. It has a purely logical subset, called "pure Prolog", as well as a number of extralogical features.

Data Types

Prolog's single data type is the *term*. Terms are either *atoms, numbers, variables* or *compound terms.*

- An atom is a general-purpose name with no inherent meaning. Examples of atoms include x, red, 'Taco', and 'some atom'.

- Numbers can be floats or integers. ISO standard compatible Prolog systems can check the Prolog flag "bounded". Most of the major Prolog systems support arbitrary precision integer numbers.

- Variables are denoted by a string consisting of letters, numbers and underscore characters, and beginning with an upper-case letter or underscore. Variables closely resemble variables in logic in that they are placeholders for arbitrary terms.

- A compound term is composed of an atom called a "functor" and a number of "arguments", which are again terms. Compound terms are ordinarily written as a functor followed by a comma-separated list of argument terms, which is contained in parentheses. The number of arguments is called the term's arity. An atom can be regarded as a compound term with arity zero. Examples of compound terms are truck_year('Mazda', 1986) and 'Person_Friends'(zelda,[tom,jim]).

Special cases of compound terms:

- A *List* is an ordered collection of terms. It is denoted by square brackets with the terms separated by commas or in the case of the empty list, []. For example, [1,2,3] or [red,green,blue].

- *Strings*: A sequence of characters surrounded by quotes is equivalent to a list of (numeric) character codes, generally in the local character encoding, or Unicode if the system supports Unicode. For example, "to be, or not to be".

Rules and Facts

Prolog programs describe relations, defined by means of clauses. Pure Prolog is restricted to Horn clauses. There are two types of clauses: facts and rules. A rule is of the form

```
Head :- Body.
```

and is read as "Head is true if Body is true". A rule's body consists of calls to predicates, which are called the rule's goals. The built-in predicate ,/2 (meaning a 2-arity operator with name ,) denotes conjunction of goals, and ;/2 denotes disjunction. Conjunctions and disjunctions can only appear in the body, not in the head of a rule.

Clauses with empty bodies are called facts. An example of a fact is:

```
cat(tom).
```

which is equivalent to the rule:

```
cat(tom) :- true.
```

The built-in predicate true/0 is always true.

Given the above fact, one can ask:

is tom a cat?

```
 ?- cat(tom).

 Yes
```

what things are cats?

```
 ?- cat(X).

 X = tom
```

Clauses with bodies are called rules. An example of a rule is:

```
animal(X) :- cat(X).
```

If we add that rule and ask *what things are animals?*

```
 ?- animal(X).

 X = tom
```

Due to the relational nature of many built-in predicates, they can typically be used in several directions. For example, length/2 can be used to determine the length of a list (length(List, L), given a list List) as well as to generate a list skeleton of a given length (length(X, 5)), and also to generate both list skeletons and their lengths together (length(X, L)). Similarly, append/3 can be used both to append two lists (append(ListA, ListB, X) given lists ListA and ListB) as well as to split a given list into parts (append(X, Y, List), given a list List). For this reason, a comparatively small set of library predicates suffices for many Prolog programs.

As a general purpose language, Prolog also provides various built-in predicates to perform routine activities like input/output, using graphics and otherwise communicating with the operating system. These predicates are not given a relational meaning and are only useful for the side-effects they exhibit on the system. For example, the predicate write/1 displays a term on the screen.

Execution

Execution of a Prolog program is initiated by the user's posting of a single goal, called the query. Logically, the Prolog engine tries to find a resolution refutation of the negated query. The resolution method used by Prolog is called SLD resolution. If the negated query can be refuted, it follows that the query, with the appropriate variable bindings in place, is a logical consequence of the program. In that case, all generated variable bindings are reported to the user, and the query is said to have succeeded. Operationally, Prolog's execution strategy can be thought of as a generalization of function calls in other languages, one difference being that multiple clause heads can match a given call. In that case, the system creates a choice-point, unifies the goal with the clause head of the first alternative, and continues with the goals of that first alternative. If any goal fails in the course of executing the program, all variable bindings that were made since the most recent choice-point was created are undone, and execution continues with the next alternative of that choice-point. This execution strategy is called chronological backtracking. For example:

```
mother_child(trude, sally).

 father_child(tom, sally).

father_child(tom, erica).

father_child(mike, tom).


 sibling(X, Y)       :- parent_child(Z, X), parent_child(Z, Y).

 parent_child(X, Y) :- father_child(X, Y).

parent_child(X, Y) :- mother_child(X, Y).
```

This results in the following query being evaluated as true:

```
 ?- sibling(sally, erica).

 Yes
```

This is obtained as follows: Initially, the only matching clause-head for the query sibling(sally, erica) is the first one, so proving the query is equivalent to proving the body of that clause with the appropriate variable bindings in place, i.e., the conjunction (parent_child(Z,sally), parent_child(Z,erica)). The next goal to be proved is the leftmost one of this conjunction, i.e., parent_child(Z, sally). Two clause heads match this goal. The system creates a choice-point and tries the first alternative, whose body is father_child(Z, sally). This goal can be proved using the fact father_child(tom, sally), so the binding Z = tom is generated, and the next goal to be proved is the second part of the above conjunction: parent_child(tom, erica). Again, this can be proved by the corresponding fact. Since all goals could be proved, the query succeeds. Since the query contained no variables, no bindings are reported to the user. A query with variables, like:

```
?- father_child(Father, Child).
```

enumerates all valid answers on backtracking.

Notice that with the code as stated above, the query ?- sibling(sally, sally). also succeeds. One would insert additional goals to describe the relevant restrictions, if desired.

Loops and Recursion

Iterative algorithms can be implemented by means of recursive predicates.

Negation

The built-in Prolog predicate \+/1 provides negation as failure, which allows for non-monotonic reasoning. The goal \+ illegal(X) in the rule

```
legal(X) :- \+ illegal(X).
```

is evaluated as follows: Prolog attempts to prove illegal(X). If a proof for that goal can be found, the original goal (i.e., \+ illegal(X)) fails. If no proof can be found, the original goal succeeds. Therefore, the \+/1 prefix operator is called the "not provable" operator, since the query ?- \+ Goal. succeeds if Goal is not provable. This kind of negation is sound if its argument is "ground" (i.e. contains no variables). Soundness is lost if the argument contains variables and the proof procedure is complete. In particular, the query ?- legal(X). can now not be used to enumerate all things that are legal.

Programming in Prolog

In Prolog, loading code is referred to as *consulting*. Prolog can be used interactively by entering queries at the Prolog prompt ?-. If there is no solution, Prolog writes no. If a solution exists then it is printed. If there are multiple solutions to the query, then these can be requested by entering a semi-colon ;. There are guidelines on good programming practice to improve code efficiency, readability and maintainability.

Here follow some example programs written in Prolog.

Hello World

```
An example of a query:

?- write('Hello world!'), nl.

Hello world!

true.


?-
```

Compiler Optimization

Any computation can be expressed declaratively as a sequence of state transitions. As an example, an optimizing compiler with three optimization passes could be implemented as a relation between an initial program and its optimized form:

```
program_optimized(Prog0, Prog) :-

    optimization_pass_1(Prog0, Prog1),

    optimization_pass_2(Prog1, Prog2),

    optimization_pass_3(Prog2, Prog).
```

or equivalently using DCG notation:

```
program_optimized --> optimization_pass_1, optimization_pass_2, optimi-
zation_pass_3.
```

Quicksort

The quicksort sorting algorithm, relating a list to its sorted version:

```
partition([], _, [], []).

partition([X|Xs], Pivot, Smalls, Bigs) :-

    (   X @< Pivot ->

        Smalls = [X|Rest],

        partition(Xs, Pivot, Rest, Bigs)

    ;   Bigs = [X|Rest],

        partition(Xs, Pivot, Smalls, Rest)

    ).

quicksort([])      --> [].

quicksort([X|Xs]) -->

    { partition(Xs, X, Smaller, Bigger) },

    quicksort(Smaller), [X], quicksort(Bigger).
```

Design Patterns

A design pattern is a general reusable solution to a commonly occurring problem in software design. In Prolog, design patterns go under various names: skeletons and techniques, cliches, program schemata, and logic description schemata. An alternative to design patterns is higher order programming.

Higher-order Programming

A higher-order predicate is a predicate that takes one or more other predicates as arguments. Although support for higher-order programming takes Prolog outside the domain of first-order logic, which does not allow quantification over predicates, ISO Prolog now has some built-in higher-order predicates such as call/1, call/2, call/3, findall/3, setof/3, and bagof/3. Furthermore, since arbitrary Prolog goals can be constructed and evaluated at run-time, it is easy to write higher-order predicates like maplist/2, which applies an arbitrary predicate to each member of a given list, and sublist/3, which filters elements that satisfy a given predicate, also allowing for currying.

To convert solutions from temporal representation (answer substitutions on backtracking) to spatial representation (terms), Prolog has various all-solutions predicates that collect all answer substitutions of a given query in a list. This can be used for list comprehension. For example, perfect numbers equal the sum of their proper divisors:

```
perfect(N) :-
    between(1, inf, N), U is N // 2,
    findall(D, (between(1,U,D), N mod D =:= 0), Ds),
    sumlist(Ds, N).
```

This can be used to enumerate perfect numbers, and also to check whether a number is perfect.

As another example, the predicate maplist applies a predicate P to all corresponding positions in a pair of lists:

```
maplist(_, [], []).
maplist(P, [X|Xs], [Y|Ys]) :-
    call(P, X, Y),
    maplist(P, Xs, Ys).
```

When P is a predicate that for all X, P(X,Y) unifies Y with a single unique value, maplist(P, Xs, Ys) is equivalent to applying the map function in functional programming as Ys = map(Function, Xs).

Higher-order programming style in Prolog was pioneered in HiLog and λProlog.

Modules

For programming in the large, Prolog provides a module system. The module system is standardised by ISO. However, not all Prolog compilers support modules, and there are compatibility problems between the module systems of the major Prolog compilers. Consequently, modules written on one Prolog compiler will not necessarily work on others.

Parsing

There is a special notation called definite clause grammars (DCGs). A rule defined via -->/2 instead of :-/2 is expanded by the preprocessor (expand_term/2, a facility analogous to macros in other languages) according to a few straightforward rewriting rules, resulting in ordinary Prolog clauses. Most notably, the rewriting equips the predicate with two additional arguments, which can be used to implicitly thread state around, analogous to monads in other languages. DCGs are often used to write parsers or list generators, as they also provide a convenient interface to difference lists.

Meta-interpreters and Reflection

Prolog is a homoiconic language and provides many facilities for reflection. Its implicit execution strategy makes it possible to write a concise meta-circular evaluator (also called *meta-interpreter*) for pure Prolog code:

```
solve(true).

solve((Subgoal1,Subgoal2)) :-
    solve(Subgoal1),
    solve(Subgoal2).

solve(Head) :-
    clause(Head, Body),
    solve(Body).
```

where true represents an empty conjunction, and clause(Head, Body) unifies with clauses in the database of the form Head :- Body.

Since Prolog programs are themselves sequences of Prolog terms (:-/2 is an infix operator) that are easily read and inspected using built-in mechanisms (like read/1), it is possible to write customized interpreters that augment Prolog with domain-specific features. For example, Sterling and Shapiro present a meta-interpreter that performs reasoning with uncertainty, reproduced here with slight modifications:

```
solve(true, 1) :- !.

solve((Subgoal1,Subgoal2), Certainty) :-
    !,
    solve(Subgoal1, Certainty1),
    solve(Subgoal2, Certainty2),
    Certainty is min(Certainty1, Certainty2).

solve(Goal, 1) :-
    builtin(Goal), !,
    Goal.
```

```
solve(Head, Certainty) :-
    clause_cf(Head, Body, Certainty1),
    solve(Body, Certainty2),
    Certainty is Certainty1 * Certainty2.
```

This interpreter uses a table of built-in Prolog predicates of the form

```
builtin(A is B).
```

```
builtin(read(X)).
```

```
% etc.
```

and clauses represented as clause_cf(Head, Body, Certainty). Given those, it can be called as solve(Goal, Certainty) to execute Goal and obtain a measure of certainty about the result.

Turing Completeness

Pure Prolog is based on a subset of first-order predicate logic, Horn clauses, which is Turing-complete. Turing completeness of Prolog can be shown by using it to simulate a Turing machine:

```
turing(Tape0, Tape) :-
    perform(q0, [], Ls, Tape0, Rs),
    reverse(Ls, Ls1),
    append(Ls1, Rs, Tape).


perform(qf, Ls, Ls, Rs, Rs) :- !.
perform(Q0, Ls0, Ls, Rs0, Rs) :-
    symbol(Rs0, Sym, RsRest),
    once(rule(Q0, Sym, Q1, NewSym, Action)),
    action(Action, Ls0, Ls1, [NewSym|RsRest], Rs1),
    perform(Q1, Ls1, Ls, Rs1, Rs).


  symbol([], b, []).
symbol([Sym|Rs], Sym, Rs).


action(left, Ls0, Ls, Rs0, Rs) :- left(Ls0, Ls, Rs0, Rs).
```

```
action(stay, Ls, Ls, Rs, Rs).

action(right, Ls0, [Sym|Ls0], [Sym|Rs], Rs).


left([], [], Rs0, [b|Rs0]).

left([L|Ls], Ls, Rs, [L|Rs]).
```

A simple example Turing machine is specified by the facts:

```
rule(q0, 1, q0, 1, right).

rule(q0, b, qf, 1, stay).
```

This machine performs incrementation by one of a number in unary encoding: It loops over any number of "1" cells and appends an additional "1" at the end. Example query and result:

```
?- turing([1,1,1], Ts).

Ts = [1, 1, 1, 1] ;
```

This illustrates how any computation can be expressed declaratively as a sequence of state transitions, implemented in Prolog as a relation between successive states of interest.

Implementation

ISO Prolog

The ISO Prolog standard consists of two parts. ISO/IEC 13211-1, published in 1995, aims to standardize the existing practices of the many implementations of the core elements of Prolog. It has clarified aspects of the language that were previously ambiguous and leads to portable programs. There are two corrigenda: Cor.1:2007 and Cor.2:2012. ISO/IEC 13211-2, published in 2000, adds support for modules to the standard. The standard is maintained by the ISO/IEC JTC1/SC22/WG17 working group. ANSI X3J17 is the US Technical Advisory Group for the standard.

Compilation

For efficiency, Prolog code is typically compiled to abstract machine code, often influenced by the register-based Warren Abstract Machine (WAM) instruction set. Some implementations employ abstract interpretation to derive type and mode information of predicates at compile time, or compile to real machine code for high performance. Devising efficient implementation methods for Prolog code is a field of active research in the logic programming community, and various other execution methods are employed in some implementations. These include clause binarization and stack-based virtual machines.

Tail Recursion

Prolog systems typically implement a well-known optimization method called tail call optimization (TCO) for deterministic predicates exhibiting tail recursion or, more generally, tail calls: A clause's stack frame is discarded before performing a call in a tail position. Therefore, deterministic tail-recursive predicates are executed with constant stack space, like loops in other languages.

Term Indexing

Finding clauses that are unifiable with a term in a query is linear in the number of clauses. Term indexing uses a data structure that enables sub-linear-time lookups. Indexing only affects program performance, it does not affect semantics. Most Prologs only use indexing on the first term, as indexing on all terms is expensive, but techniques based on *field-encoded words* or *superimposed codewords* provide fast indexing across the full query and head.

Hashing

Some Prolog systems, such as LPA Prolog and SWI-Prolog, now implement hashing to help handle large datasets more efficiently. This tends to yield very large performance gains when working with large corpora such as WordNet.

Tabling

Some Prolog systems, (BProlog, XSB, SWI-Prolog, Yap, B-Prolog and Ciao), implement a memoization method called *tabling*, which frees the user from manually storing intermediate results.

Subgoals encountered in a query evaluation are maintained in a table, along with answers to these subgoals. If a subgoal is re-encountered, the evaluation reuses information from the table rather than re-performing resolution against program clauses.

Tabling is a space-time tradeoff; execution time can be reduced by using more memory to store intermediate results.

Implementation in Hardware

During the Fifth Generation Computer Systems project, there were attempts to implement Prolog in hardware with the aim of achieving faster execution with dedicated architectures. Furthermore, Prolog has a number of properties that may allow speed-up through parallel execution. A more recent approach has been to compile restricted Prolog programs to a field programmable gate array. However, rapid progress in general-purpose hardware has consistently overtaken more specialised architectures.

Limitations

Although Prolog is widely used in research and education, Prolog and other logic programming languages have not had a significant impact on the computer industry in general. Most applications are small by industrial standards, with few exceeding 100,000 lines of code. Programming in the large is considered to be complicated because not all Prolog compilers support modules, and there are compatibility problems between the module systems of the major Prolog compilers. Portability of Prolog code across implementations has also been a problem, but developments since 2007 have meant: "the portability within the family of Edinburgh/Quintus derived Prolog implementations is good enough to allow for maintaining portable real-world applications."

Software developed in Prolog has been criticised for having a high performance penalty compared to conventional programming languages. In particular, Prolog's non-deterministic evaluation strategy can be problematic when programming deterministic computations, or when even using "don't care non-determinism" (where a single choice is made instead of backtracking over all possibilities). Cuts and other language constructs may have to be used to achieve desirable performance, destroying one of Prolog's main attractions, the ability to run programs "backwards and forwards".

Prolog is not purely declarative: because of constructs like the cut operator, a procedural reading of a Prolog program is needed to understand it. The order of clauses in a Prolog program is significant, as the execution strategy of the language depends on it. Other logic programming languages, such as Datalog, are truly declarative but restrict the language. As a result, many practical Prolog programs are written to conform to Prolog's depth-first search order, rather than as purely declarative logic programs.

Extensions

Various implementations have been developed from Prolog to extend logic programming capabilities in numerous directions. These include types, modes, constraint logic programming (CLP), object-oriented logic programming (OOLP), concurrency, linear logic (LLP), functional and higher-order logic programming capabilities, plus interoperability with knowledge bases:

Types

Prolog is an untyped language. Attempts to introduce types date back to the 1980s, and as of 2008 there are still attempts to extend Prolog with types. Type information is useful not only for type safety but also for reasoning about Prolog programs.

Modes

The syntax of Prolog does not specify which arguments of a predicate are inputs and which are outputs. However, this information is significant and it is recommended that it be included in the comments. Modes provide valuable information when reasoning about Prolog programs and can also be used to accelerate execution.

Constraints

Constraint logic programming extends Prolog to include concepts from constraint satisfaction. A constraint logic program allows constraints in the body of clauses, such as: A(X,Y) :- X+Y>0. It is suited to large-scale combinatorial optimisation problems. and is thus useful for applications in industrial settings, such as automated time-tabling and production scheduling. Most Prolog systems ship with at least one constraint solver for finite domains, and often also with solvers for other domains like rational numbers.

Object-orientation

Flora-2 is an object-oriented knowledge representation and reasoning system based on F-logic and incorporates HiLog, Transaction logic, and defeasible reasoning.

Logtalk is an object-oriented logic programming language that can use most Prolog implementations as a back-end compiler. As a multi-paradigm language, it includes support for both prototypes and classes.

Oblog is a small, portable, object-oriented extension to Prolog by Margaret McDougall of EdCAAD, University of Edinburgh.

Objlog was a frame-based language combining objects and Prolog II from CNRS, Marseille, France.

Prolog++ was developed by Logic Programming Associates and first released in 1989 for MS-DOS PCs. Support for other platforms was added, and a second version was released in 1995. A book about Prolog++ by Chris Moss was published by Addison-Wesley in 1994.

Graphics

Prolog systems that provide a graphics library are SWI-prolog, Visual-prolog, LPA Prolog for Windows and B-Prolog.

Concurrency

Prolog-MPI is an open-source SWI-Prolog extension for distributed computing over the Message Passing Interface. Also there are various concurrent Prolog programming languages.

Web programming

Some Prolog implementations, notably SWI-Prolog and Ciao, support server-side web programming with support for web protocols, HTML and XML. There are also extensions to support semantic web formats such as RDF and OWL. Prolog has also been suggested as a client-side language.

Adobe Flash

Cedar is a free and basic Prolog interpreter. From version 4 and above Cedar has a FCA (Flash Cedar App) support. This provides a new platform to programming in Prolog through ActionScript.

Other

- F-logic extends Prolog with frames/objects for knowledge representation.

- Transaction logic extends Prolog with a logical theory of state-changing update operators. It has both a model-theoretic and procedural semantics.

- OW Prolog has been created in order to answer Prolog's lack of graphics and interface.

Interfaces to Other Languages

Frameworks exist which can bridge between Prolog and other languages:

- The LPA Intelligence Server allows the embedding of LPA Prolog within C, C#, C++, Java, VB, Delphi, .Net, Lua, Python and other languages. It exploits the dedicated string data-type which LPA Prolog provides

- The Logic Server API allows both the extension and embedding of Prolog in C, C++, Java, VB, Delphi, .NET and any language/environment which can call a .dll or .so. It is implemented for Amzi! Prolog Amzi! Prolog + Logic Server but the API specification can be made available for any implementation.

- JPL is a bi-directional Java Prolog bridge which ships with SWI-Prolog by default, allowing Java and Prolog to call each other (recursively). It is known to have good concurrency support and is under active development.

- InterProlog, a programming library bridge between Java and Prolog, implementing bi-directional predicate/method calling between both languages. Java objects can be mapped into Prolog terms and vice versa. Allows the development of GUIs and other functionality in Java while leaving logic processing in the Prolog layer. Supports XSB, with support for SWI-Prolog and YAP planned for 2013.

- Prova provides native syntax integration with Java, agent messaging and reaction rules. Prova positions itself as a rule-based scripting (RBS) system for middleware. The language breaks new ground in combining imperative and declarative programming.

- PROL An embeddable Prolog engine for Java. It includes a small IDE and a few libraries.

- GNU Prolog for Java is an implementation of ISO Prolog as a Java library (gnu.prolog)

- Ciao provides interfaces to C, C++, Java, and relational databases.

- C#-Prolog is a Prolog interpreter written in (managed) C#. Can easily be integrated in C# programs. Characteristics: reliable and fairly fast interpreter, command line interface, Windows-interface, builtin DCG, XML-predicates, SQL-predicates, extendible. The complete source code is available, including a parser generator that can be used for adding special purpose extensions.

- Jekejeke Prolog API provides tightly coupled concurrent call-in and call-out facilities between Prolog and Java or Android, with the marked possibility to create individual knowledge base objects. It can be used to embed the ISO Prolog interpreter in standalones, applets, servlets, APKs, etc..

- A Warren Abstract Machine for PHP A Prolog compiler and interpreter in PHP 5.3. A library that can be used standalone or within Symfony2.1 framework

History

The name *Prolog* was chosen by Philippe Roussel as an abbreviation for *programmation en logique* (French for *programming in logic*). It was created around 1972 by Alain Colmerauer with Philippe Roussel, based on Robert Kowalski's procedural interpretation of Horn clauses. It was motivated in part by the desire to reconcile the use of logic as a declarative knowledge representation language with the procedural representation of knowledge that was popular in North America in the late 1960s and early 1970s. According to Robert Kowalski, the first Prolog system was developed in 1972 by Colmerauer and Phillipe Roussel. The first implementations of Prolog were interpreters. However, David H. D. Warren created the Warren Abstract Machine, an early and influential Prolog compiler which came to define the "Edinburgh Prolog" dialect which served as the basis for the syntax of most modern implementations.

European AI researchers favored Prolog while Americans favored Lisp, reportedly causing many nationalistic debates on the merits of the languages. Much of the modern development of Prolog came from the impetus of the Fifth Generation Computer Systems project (FGCS), which developed a variant of Prolog named *Kernel Language* for its first operating system.

Pure Prolog was originally restricted to the use of a resolution theorem prover with Horn clauses of the form:

```
H :- B₁, ..., Bₙ.
```

The application of the theorem-prover treats such clauses as procedures:

```
to show/solve H, show/solve B₁ and ... and Bₙ.
```

Pure Prolog was soon extended, however, to include negation as failure, in which negative conditions of the form $not(B_i)$ are shown by trying and failing to solve the corresponding positive conditions B_i.

Subsequent extensions of Prolog by the original team introduced constraint logic programming abilities into the implementations.

Use in Industry

Prolog has been used in Watson. Watson uses IBM's DeepQA software and the Apache UIMA (Unstructured Information Management Architecture) framework. The system was written in various languages, including Java, C++, and Prolog, and runs on the SUSE Linux Enterprise Server 11 operating system using Apache Hadoop framework to provide distributed computing. Prolog is used for pattern matching over natural language parse trees. The developers have stated: "We required a language in which we could conveniently express pattern matching rules over the parse trees and other annotations (such as named entity recognition results), and a technology that could execute these rules very efficiently. We found that Prolog was the ideal choice for the language due to its simplicity and expressiveness."

ML (Programming Language)

ML is a general-purpose functional programming language developed by Robin Milner and others in the early 1970s at the University of Edinburgh, whose syntax is inspired by ISWIM. It has roots in the Lisp language, and has been characterized as "LISP with types". Historically, ML stands for *MetaLanguage*: it was conceived to develop proof tactics in the LCF theorem prover (whose language, *pplambda*, a combination of the first-order predicate calculus and the simply-typed polymorphic lambda calculus, had ML as its metalanguage). It is known for its use of the Hindley–Milner type system, whose type inference algorithm can automatically assign the types of most expressions without requiring explicit type annotations. Additionally, the use of this algorithm ensures type safety – there is a formal proof that a well-typed ML program does not cause runtime type errors.

Overview

Features of ML include a call-by-value evaluation strategy, first-class functions, automatic memory management through garbage collection, parametric polymorphism, static typing, type inference, algebraic data types, pattern matching, and exception handling. ML uses static scoping rules.

ML can be referred to as an *impure* functional language, because although it encourages functional programming, it does allow side-effects (like languages such as Lisp, but unlike a purely functional language such as Haskell). Like most programming languages, ML uses eager evaluation, meaning that all subexpressions are always evaluated, though lazy evaluation can be achieved through the use of closures. Thus one can create and use infinite streams as in Haskell, but their expression is indirect.

Today there are several languages in the ML family; the two major dialects are Standard ML (SML) and Caml, but others exist, including F# – a language that Microsoft supports for their .NET platform. Ideas from ML have influenced numerous other languages, like Haskell, Cyclone, Nemerle, ATS, and Elm.

ML's strengths are mostly applied in language design and manipulation (compilers, analyzers, theorem provers), but it is a general-purpose language also used in bioinformatics, financial systems, and applications including a genealogical database, a peer-to-peer client/server program, etc.

Examples

The following examples use the syntax of Standard ML. The other most widely used ML dialect, OCaml, differs in various insubstantial ways.

Factorial

The factorial function expressed as pure ML:

```
fun fac (0 : int) : int = 1

  | fac (n : int) : int = n * fac (n - 1)
```

This describes the factorial as a recursive function, with a single terminating base case. It is similar to the descriptions of factorials found in mathematics textbooks. Much of ML code is similar to mathematics in facility and syntax.

Part of the definition shown is optional, and describes the *types* of this function. The notation E : t can be read as *expression E has type t*. For instance, the argument n is assigned type *integer* (int), and fac (n : int), the result of applying fac to the integer n, also has type integer. The function fac as a whole then has type *function from integer to integer* (int -> int), that is, fac accepts an integer as an argument and returns an integer result. Thanks to type inference, the type annotations can be omitted and will be derived by the compiler. Rewritten without the type annotations, the example looks like:

```
fun fac 0 = 1

  | fac n = n * fac (n - 1)
```

The function also relies on pattern matching, an important part of ML programming. Note that parameters of a function are not necessarily in parentheses but separated by spaces. When the function's argument is 0 (zero) it will return the integer 1 (one). For all other cases the second line is tried. This is the recursion, and executes the function again until the base case is reached.

This implementation of the factorial function is not guaranteed to terminate, since a negative argument causes an infinite descending chain of recursive calls. A more robust implementation would check for a nonnegative argument before recursing, as follows:

```
fun fact n = let

  fun fac 0 = 1

    | fac n = n * fac (n - 1)

  in

    if (n < 0) then raise Fail "negative argument"

    else fac n

  end
```

The problematic case (when n is negative) demonstrates a use of ML's exception system.

The function can be improved further by writing its inner loop in a tail-recursive style, such that the call stack need not grow in proportion to the number of function calls. This is achieved by adding an extra, "accumulator", parameter to the inner function. At last, we arrive at

```
fun factorial n = let

  fun fac (0, acc) = acc

    | fac (n, acc) = fac (n - 1, n * acc)

  in

    if (n < 0) then raise Fail "negative argument"

    else fac (n, 1)

  end
```

List Reverse

The following function "reverses" the elements in a list. More precisely, it returns a new list whose elements are in reverse order compared to the given list.

```
fun reverse [] = []

  | reverse (x::xs) = (reverse xs) @ [x]
```

This implementation of reverse, while correct and clear, is inefficient, requiring quadratic time for execution. The function can be rewritten to execute in linear time in the following more efficient, though less easy-to-read, style:

```
fun reverse xs = let

  fun rev [] acc = acc

    | rev (hd::tl) acc = rev tl (hd::acc)

in

  rev xs []

end
```

Notably, this function is an example of parametric polymorphism. That is, it can consume lists whose elements have any type, and return lists of the same type.

System Programming

System programming (or systems programming) is the activity of programming computer system software. The primary distinguishing characteristic of systems programming when compared to application programming is that application programming aims to produce software which provides services to the user directly (e.g. word processor), whereas systems programming aims to produce software and software platforms which provide services to other software, are performance constrained, or both (e.g. operating systems, computational science applications, game engines and AAA video games, industrial automation, and software as a service applications).

System programming requires a great degree of hardware awareness. Its goal is to achieve efficient use of available resources, either because the software itself is performance critical (AAA video games) or because even small efficiency improvements directly transform into significant monetary savings for the service provider (cloud based word processors).

Overview

The following attributes characterize systems programming:

- The programmer can make assumptions about the hardware and other properties of the system that the program runs on, and will often exploit those properties, for example by using an algorithm that is known to be efficient when used with specific hardware.

- Usually a low-level programming language or programming language dialect is used so that:

    o Programs can operate in resource-constrained environments

    o Programs written to be efficient with little runtime overhead, they may have a small runtime library, or none at all

- o   Programs may use direct and "raw" control over memory access and control flow

- o   The programmer may write parts of the program directly in assembly language

- Often systems programs cannot be run in a debugger. Running the program in a simulated environment can sometimes be used to reduce this problem.

Systems programming is sufficiently different from application programming that programmers tend to specialize in one or the other.

In system programming, often limited programming facilities are available. The use of automatic garbage collection is not common and debugging is sometimes hard to do. The runtime library, if available at all, is usually far less powerful, and does less error checking. Because of those limitations, monitoring and logging are often used; operating systems may have extremely elaborate logging subsystems.

Implementing certain parts in operating systems and networking requires systems programming, for example implementing paging (virtual memory) or a device driver for an operating system.

History

Originally systems programmers invariably wrote in assembly language. Experiments with hardware support in high level languages in the late 1960s led to such languages as PL/S, BLISS, BCPL, and extended ALGOL for Burroughs large systems. Forth also has applications as a systems language. In the 1980s, C became ubiquitous, aided by the growth of Unix. More recently C++ has seen some use, for instance a subset of it is used in the I/O Kit drivers of Mac OS X.

Alternate Usage

For historical reasons, some organizations use the term *systems programmer* to describe a job function which would be more accurately termed systems administrator. This is particularly true in organizations whose computer resources have historically been dominated by mainframes, although the term is even used to describe job functions which do not involve mainframes. This usage arose because administration of IBM mainframes often involved the writing of custom assembler code (IBM's Basic Assembly Language (BAL)), which integrated with the operating system such as OS/MVS, DOS/VSE or VM/CMS. Indeed, some IBM software products had substantial code contributions from customer programming staff. This type of programming is progressively less common, but the term *systems programmer* is still the de facto job title for staff directly administering IBM mainframes.

System Programming Language

A system programming language usually refers to a programming language used for system programming; such languages are designed for writing system software, which usually requires different development approaches when compared with application software.

System software is computer software designed to operate and control the computer hardware, and to provide a platform for running application software. System software includes software categories such as operating systems, utility software, device drivers, compilers, and linkers.

Features

In contrast with application languages, system programming languages typically offer more-direct access to the physical hardware of the machine: an archetypical system programming language in this sense was BCPL. System programming languages often lack built-in input/output (I/O) facilities because a system-software project usually develops its own I/O mechanisms or builds on top of basic monitor I/O or screen management facilities. The distinction between languages used for system programming and application programming became blurred over time with the widespread popularity of PL/I, C and Pascal.

History

The earliest system software was written in assembly language primarily because there was no alternative, but also for reasons including efficiency of object code, compilation time, and ease of debugging. Application languages such as FORTRAN were used for system programming, although they usually still required some routines to be written in assembly language.

Mid-level Languages

Mid-level languages "have much of the syntax and facilities of a higher level language, but also provide direct access in the language (as well as providing assembly language) to machine features." The earliest of these was ESPOL on Burroughs mainframes in about 1960, followed by Niklaus Wirth's PL360 (initially written on a Burroughs system as a cross compiler), which had the general syntax of ALGOL 60 but whose statements directly manipulated CPU registers and memory. Other languages in this category include MOL-360 and PL/S.

As an example, a typical PL360 statement is R9 := R8 and R7 shll 8 or R6, signifying that registers 8 and 7 should be and'ed together, the result shifted left 8 bits, the result of that or'ed with the contents of register 6, and the result placed into register 9.

Higher-level Languages

While PL360 is at the semantic level of assembly language, another kind of system programming language operates at a higher semantic level, but has specific extensions designed to make the language suitable for system programming. An early example of this kind of language is LRLTRAN, which extended Fortran with features for character and bit manipulation, pointers, and directly addressed jump tables.

Subsequently, languages such as C were developed, where the combination of features was sufficient to write system software, and a compiler could be developed that generated efficient object programs on modest hardware. Such a language generally omits features that cannot be implemented efficiently, and adds a small number of machine-dependent features needed to access specific hardware capabilities; inline assembly code, such as C's asm statement, is often used for this purpose. Although many such languages were developed, C and C++ are the ones that have survived.

System Programming Language (SPL) is also the name of a specific language on the HP 3000 computer series, used for its operating system HP Multi-Programming Executive, and other parts of its system software.

History of Programming Languages

Early History

During a nine-month period in 1842–1843, Ada Lovelace translated the memoir of Italian mathematician Luigi Menabrea about Charles Babbage's newest proposed machine, the analytical engine. With the article she appended a set of notes which specified in complete detail a method for calculating Bernoulli numbers with the engine, recognized by some historians as the world's first computer program.

Herman Hollerith realized that he could encode information on punch cards when he observed that train conductors encode the appearance of the ticket holders on the train tickets using the position of punched holes on the tickets. Hollerith then encoded the 1890 American census data on punch cards.

The first computer codes were specialized for their applications. In the first decades of the 20th century, numerical calculations were based on decimal numbers. Eventually it was realized that logic could be represented with numbers, not only with words. For example, Alonzo Church was able to express the lambda calculus in a formulatic way. The Turing machine was an abstraction of the operation of a tape-marking machine, for example, in use at the telephone companies. Turing machines set the basis for storage of programs as data in the von Neumann architecture of computers by representing a machine through a finite number. However, unlike the lambda calculus, Turing's code does not serve well as a basis for higher-level languages—its principal use is in rigorous analyses of algorithmic complexity.

Like many "firsts" in history, the first modern programming language is hard to identify. From the start, the restrictions of the hardware defined the language. Punch cards allowed 80 columns, but some of the columns had to be used for a sorting number on each card. FORTRAN included some keywords which were the same as English words, such as "IF", "GOTO" (go to) and "CONTINUE". The use of a magnetic drum for memory meant that computer programs also had to be interleaved with the rotations of the drum. Thus the programs were more hardware-dependent.

To some people, what was the first modern programming language depends on how much power and human-readability is required before the status of "programming language" is granted. Jacquard Looms and Charles Babbage's Difference Engine both had simple, extremely limited languages for describing the actions that these machines should perform. One can even regard the punch holes on a player piano scroll as a limited domain-specific language, albeit not designed for human consumption.

First Programming Languages

In the 1940s, the first recognizably modern electrically powered computers were created. The limited speed and memory capacity forced programmers to write hand tuned assembly language programs. It was eventually realized that programming in assembly language required a great deal of intellectual effort and was error-prone.

The first programming languages designed to communicate instructions to a computer were written in the 1950s. An early high-level programming language to be designed for a computer was Plankalkül, developed by the Germans for Z1 by Konrad Zuse between 1943 and 1945. However, it was not implemented until 1998 and 2000.

John Mauchly's Short Code, proposed in 1949, was one of the first high-level languages ever developed for an electronic computer. Unlike machine code, Short Code statements represented mathematical expressions in understandable form. However, the program had to be translated into machine code every time it ran, making the process much slower than running the equivalent machine code.

At the University of Manchester, Alick Glennie developed Autocode in the early 1950s. A programming language, it used a compiler to automatically convert the language into machine code. The first code and compiler was developed in 1952 for the Mark 1 computer at the University of Manchester and is considered to be the first compiled high-level programming language.

The second autocode was developed for the Mark 1 by R. A. Brooker in 1954 and was called the "Mark 1 Autocode". Brooker also developed an autocode for the Ferranti Mercury in the 1950s in conjunction with the University of Manchester. The version for the EDSAC 2 was devised by D. F. Hartley of University of Cambridge Mathematical Laboratory in 1961. Known as EDSAC 2 Autocode, it was a straight development from Mercury Autocode adapted for local circumstances, and was noted for its object code optimisation and source-language diagnostics which were advanced for the time. A contemporary but separate thread of development, Atlas Autocode was developed for the University of Manchester Atlas 1 machine.

In 1954, language FORTRAN was invented at IBM by John Backus; it was the first widely used high level general purpose programming language to have a functional implementation, as opposed to just a design on paper. It is still a popular language for high-performance computing and is used for programs that benchmark and rank the world's fastest supercomputers.

Another early programming language was devised by Grace Hopper in the US, called FLOW-MATIC. It was developed for the UNIVAC I at Remington Rand during the period from 1955 until 1959. Hopper found that business data processing customers were uncomfortable with mathematical notation, and in early 1955, she and her team wrote a specification for an English programming language and implemented a prototype. The FLOW-MATIC compiler became publicly available in early 1958 and was substantially complete in 1959. Flow-Matic was a major influence in the design of COBOL, since only it and its direct descendent AIMACO were in actual use at the time.

Other languages still in use today include LISP (1958), invented by John McCarthy and COBOL (1959), created by the Short Range Committee. Another milestone in the late 1950s was the publication, by a committee of American and European computer scientists, of "a new language for algorithms"; the ALGOL 60 Report (the "ALGOrithmic Language"). This report consolidated many ideas circulating at the time and featured three key language innovations:

- nested block structure: code sequences and associated declarations could be grouped into blocks without having to be turned into separate, explicitly named procedures;

- lexical scoping: a block could have its own private variables, procedures and functions, invisible to code outside that block, that is, information hiding.

Another innovation, related to this, was in how the language was described:

- a mathematically exact notation, Backus–Naur form (BNF), was used to describe the language's syntax. Nearly all subsequent programming languages have used a variant of BNF to describe the context-free portion of their syntax.

Algol 60 was particularly influential in the design of later languages, some of which soon became more popular. The Burroughs large systems were designed to be programmed in an extended subset of Algol.

Algol's key ideas were continued, producing ALGOL 68:

- syntax and semantics became even more orthogonal, with anonymous routines, a recursive typing system with higher-order functions, etc.;

- not only the context-free part, but the full language syntax and semantics were defined formally, in terms of Van Wijngaarden grammar, a formalism designed specifically for this purpose.

Algol 68's many little-used language features (for example, concurrent and parallel blocks) and its complex system of syntactic shortcuts and automatic type coercions made it unpopular with implementers and gained it a reputation of being *difficult*. Niklaus Wirth actually walked out of the design committee to create the simpler Pascal language.

Fortran

Some notable languages that were developed in this period include:

- 1951 – Regional Assembly Language
- 1952 – Autocode
- 1954 – IPL (forerunner to LISP)
- 1955 – FLOW-MATIC (led to COBOL)
- 1957 – FORTRAN (First compiler)

- 1959 – RPG
- 1962 – APL
- 1962 – Simula
- 1962 – SNOBOL
- 1963 – CPL (forerunner to C)

- 1957 – COMTRAN (precursor to COBOL)
- 1958 – LISP
- 1958 – ALGOL 58
- 1959 – FACT (forerunner to COBOL)
- 1959 – COBOL
- 1964 – Speakeasy (computational environment)
- 1964 – BASIC
- 1964 – PL/I
- 1966 – JOSS
- 1967 – BCPL (forerunner to C)

Establishing Fundamental Paradigms

Smalltalk

Scheme

The period from the late 1960s to the late 1970s brought a major flowering of programming languages. Most of the major language paradigms now in use were invented in this period:

- Speakeasy (computational environment), developed in 1964 at Argonne National Laboratory (ANL) by Stanley Cohen, is an OOPS (object-oriented programming, much like the later MATLAB, IDL (programming language) and Mathematica) numerical package. Speakeasy has a clear Fortran foundation syntax. It first addressed efficient physics computation internally at ANL, was modified for research use (as "Modeleasy") for the Federal Reserve Board in the early 1970s and then was made available commercially; Speakeasy and Modeleasy are still in use currently.

- Simula, invented in the late 1960s by Nygaard and Dahl as a superset of Algol 60, was the first language designed to support object-oriented programming.

- C, an early systems programming language, was developed by Dennis Ritchie and Ken Thompson at Bell Labs between 1969 and 1973.

- Smalltalk (mid-1970s) provided a complete ground-up design of an object-oriented language.

- Prolog, designed in 1972 by Colmerauer, Roussel, and Kowalski, was the first logic programming language.

- ML built a polymorphic type system (invented by Robin Milner in 1973) on top of Lisp, pioneering statically typed functional programming languages.

Each of these languages spawned an entire family of descendants, and most modern languages count at least one of them in their ancestry.

The 1960s and 1970s also saw considerable debate over the merits of "structured programming", which essentially meant programming without the use of "goto". A significant fraction of programmers believed that, even in languages that provide "goto", it is bad programming style to use it except in rare circumstances. This debate was closely related to language design: some languages did not include a "goto" at all, which forced structured programming on the programmer.

To provide even faster compile times, some languages were structured for "one-pass compilers" which expect subordinate routines to be defined first, as with Pascal, where the main routine, or driver function, is the final section of the program listing.

Some notable languages that were developed in this period include:

- 1968 – Logo
- 1969 – B (forerunner to C)
- 1970 – Pascal
- 1970 – Forth
- 1972 – C

- 1972 – Smalltalk
- 1972 – Prolog
- 1973 – ML
- 1975 – Scheme
- 1978 – SQL (a query language, later extended)

1980s: Consolidation, Modules, Performance

MATLAB   Erlang   Tcl

The 1980s were years of relative consolidation in imperative languages. Rather than inventing new paradigms, all of these movements elaborated upon the ideas invented in the previous decade. C++ combined object-oriented and systems programming. The United States government standardized Ada, a systems programming language intended for use by defense contractors. In Japan and elsewhere, vast sums were spent investigating so-called fifth-generation programming languages that incorporated logic programming constructs. The functional languages community moved to standardize ML and Lisp. Research in Miranda, a functional language with lazy evaluation, began to take hold in this decade.

One important new trend in language design was an increased focus on programming for large-scale systems through the use of *modules,* or large-scale organizational units of code. Modula, Ada, and ML all developed notable module systems in the 1980s. Module systems were often wedded to generic programming constructs---generics being, in essence, parametrized modules.

Although major new paradigms for imperative programming languages did not appear, many researchers expanded on the ideas of prior languages and adapted them to new contexts. For example, the languages of the Argus and Emerald systems adapted object-oriented programming to distributed systems.

The 1980s also brought advances in programming language implementation. The RISC movement in computer architecture postulated that hardware should be designed for compilers rather than for human assembly programmers. Aided by processor speed improvements that enabled increasingly aggressive compilation techniques, the RISC movement sparked greater interest in compilation technology for high-level languages.

Language technology continued along these lines well into the 1990s.

Some notable languages that were developed in this period include:

1990s: the Internet Age

| Haskell | Lua | Rebol | D Programming Language |

The rapid growth of the Internet in the mid-1990s was the next major historic event in programming languages. By opening up a radically new platform for computer systems, the Internet created an opportunity for new languages to be adopted. In particular, the JavaScript programming language rose to popularity because of its early integration with the Netscape Navigator web browser. Various other scripting languages achieved widespread use in developing customized applications for web servers such as PHP. The 1990s saw no fundamental novelty in imperative languages, but much recombination and maturation of old ideas. This era began the spread of functional languages. A big driving philosophy was programmer productivity. Many "rapid application development" (RAD) languages emerged, which usually came with an IDE, garbage collection, and were descendants of older languages. All such languages were object-oriented. These included Object Pascal, Visual Basic, and Java. Java in particular received much attention.

More radical and innovative than the RAD languages were the new scripting languages. These did not directly descend from other languages and featured new syntaxes and more liberal incorporation of features. Many consider these scripting languages to be more productive than even the RAD languages, but often because of choices that make small programs simpler but large programs more difficult to write and maintain. Nevertheless, scripting languages came to be the most prominent ones used in connection with the Web.

Some notable languages that were developed in this period include:

Current Trends

Programming language evolution continues, in both industry and research. Some of the recent trends have included:

- Increasing support for functional programming in mainstream languages used commercially, including pure functional programming for making code easier to reason about and easier to parallelise (at both micro- and macro- levels)

- Constructs to support concurrent and distributed programming.

- Mechanisms for adding security and reliability verification to the language: extended static checking, dependent typing, information flow control, static thread safety.

- Alternative mechanisms for composability and modularity: mixins, traits, delegates, aspects.

- Component-oriented software development.

- Metaprogramming, reflection or access to the abstract syntax tree

  - AOP or Aspect Oriented Programming allowing developers to insert code in another module or class at "join points"

  - Domain specific languages and code generation

    - XML for graphical interface (XUL, XAML)

- Increased interest in distribution and mobility.

- Integration with databases, including XML and relational databases.

- Open source as a developmental philosophy for languages, including the GNU Compiler Collection and languages such as Python, Ruby, and Scala.

- Massively parallel languages for coding 2000 processor GPU graphics processing units and supercomputer arrays including OpenCL

- Early research into (as-yet-unimplementable) quantum computing programming languages

Groovy

Rust

Some notable languages developed during this period include:

- 2000 – ActionScript
- 2001 – C#
- 2003 – Apache Groovy
- 2003 – Scala
- 2005 – F#
- 2006 – Windows PowerShell
- 2007 – Clojure

- 2009 – Go
- 2010 – Rust
- 2011 – Dart
- 2011 – Kotlin
- 2012 – Julia
- 2014 – Swift
- 2017 – Ion (programming language)

References

- Kowalski, R. A. (1988). "The early years of logic programming" (PDF). Communications of the ACM. 31: 38. doi:10.1145/35043.35046

- Goldberg, Adele; David Robson (1989). Smalltalk-80 The Language. Addison Wesley. pp. 31, 75–89. ISBN 0-201-13688-0

- Kay, Alan; Stefan Ram (2003-07-23). "E-Mail of 2003-07-23". Dr. Alan Kay on the Meaning of "Object-Oriented Programming". Retrieved 2009-01-03

- Krasner, Glen; Stephen Pope (August–September 1988). "A Cookbook for Using the Model-View-Controller User Interface Paradigm in Smalltalk -80". Journal of Object-Oriented Programming

- Taki, K.; Nakajima, K.; Nakashima, H.; Ikeda, M. (1987). "Performance and architectural evaluation of the PSI machine". ACM SIGPLAN Notices. 22 (10): 128. doi:10.1145/36205.36195

- Clocksin, William F.; Mellish, Christopher S . (2003). Programming in Prolog. Berlin ; New York: Springer-Verlag. ISBN 978-3-540-00678-7

- Cannon, Howard. "Flavors A non-hierarchical approach to object-oriented programming" (PDF). softwarepreservation.org. Retrieved 17 December 2013

- Stickel, M. E. (1988). "A prolog technology theorem prover: Implementation by an extended prolog compiler". Journal of Automated Reasoning. 4 (4): 353–380. doi:10.1007/BF00297245

- Swift, T.; Warren, D. S. (2011). "XSB: Extending Prolog with Tabled Logic Programming". Theory and Practice of Logic Programming. 12: 157. doi:10.1017/S1471068411000500

- Bratko, Ivan (2001). Prolog programming for artificial intelligence. Harlow, England ; New York: Addison Wesley. ISBN 0-201-40375-7

- Foote, Brian; Ralph Johnson (1–6 October 1989). "Reflective Facilities in Smalltalk-80". OOPSLA '89. Retrieved 16 December 2013

- Colomb, Robert M. (1991). "Enhancing unification in PROLOG through clause indexing". The Journal of Logic Programming. 10: 23. doi:10.1016/0743-1066(91)90004-9

- Swift, T. (1999). "Tabling for non-monotonic programming". Annals of Mathematics and Artificial Intelligence. 25 (3/4): 201–200. doi:10.1023/A:1018990308362

- Covington, Michael A. (1994). Natural language processing for Prolog programmers. Englewood Cliffs, N.J.: Prentice Hall. ISBN 978-0-13-629213-5

- Naish, Lee (1996). Higher-order logic programming in Prolog (Report). Department of Computer Science, University of Melbourne. Retrieved 2010-11-02

- Jaffar, J. (1994). "Constraint logic programming: a survey". The Journal of Logic Programming. 19-20: 503–581. doi:10.1016/0743-1066(94)90033-7

- Van Roy, P.; Despain, A. M. (1992). "High-performance logic programming with the Aquarius Prolog compiler". Computer. 25: 54. doi:10.1109/2.108055

- Shapiro, Ehud Y.; Sterling, Leon (1994). The Art of Prolog: Advanced Programming Techniques. Cambridge, Mass: MIT Press. ISBN 0-262-19338-8

- Wulf, W.A.; Russell, D.B.; Haberman, A.N. (December 1971). "BLISS: A Language for Systems Programming". CACM. 14 (12): 780–790. Retrieved January 11, 2014

- Robin Milner. A theory of type polymorphism in programming. Journal of Computer and System Sciences, 17(3):348–375, 1978

- Colmerauer, A.; Roussel, P. (1993). "The birth of Prolog" (PDF). ACM SIGPLAN Notices. 28 (3): 37. doi:10.1145/155360.155362

Computer Programming and Types of Programming Languages

Computer programming includes the generation, development and analysis of algorithms. The other tasks of the subject are to test and maintain the source code. The types of programming languages discussed in the section are compiled language, scripting language and interpreted language. This chapter will provide an integrated understanding of computer programming and types of programming languages.

Computer Programming

Computer programming (often shortened to programming) is a process that leads from an original formulation of a computing problem to executable computer programs. Programming involves activities such as analysis, developing understanding, generating algorithms, verification of requirements of algorithms including their correctness and resources consumption, and implementation (commonly referred to as coding) of algorithms in a target programming language. Source code is written in one or more programming languages. The purpose of programming is to find a sequence of instructions that will automate performing a specific task or solving a given problem. The process of programming thus often requires expertise in many different subjects, including knowledge of the application domain, specialized algorithms, and formal logic.

Related tasks include testing, debugging, and maintaining the source code, implementation of the build system, and management of derived artifacts such as machine code of computer programs. These might be considered part of the programming process, but often the term *software development* is used for this larger process with the term *programming*, *implementation*, or *coding* reserved for the actual writing of source code. Software engineering combines engineering techniques with software development practices.

Overview

Within software engineering, programming (the *implementation*) is regarded as one phase in a software development process.

There is an ongoing debate on the extent to which the writing of programs is an art form, a craft, or an engineering discipline. In general, good programming is considered to be the measured application of all three, with the goal of producing an efficient and evolvable software solution (the criteria for "efficient" and "evolvable" vary considerably). The discipline differs from many other technical professions in that programmers, in general, do not need to be licensed or pass any standardized (or governmentally regulated) certification tests in order to call themselves "program-mers" or even "software engineers" - but note that use of the term "engineer" *is* tighty regulated in many parts of the world.

Because the discipline covers many areas, which may or may not include critical applications, it is debatable whether licensing is required for the profession as a whole. In most cases, the discipline is self-governed by the entities which require the programming, and sometimes very strict environments are defined (e.g. United States Air Force use of AdaCore and security clearance). Another ongoing debate is the extent to which the programming language used in writing computer programs affects the form that the final program takes. This debate is analogous to that surrounding the Sapir–Whorf hypothesis in linguistics and cognitive science, which postulates that a particular spoken language's nature influences the habitual thought of its speakers. Different language patterns yield different patterns of thought. This idea challenges the possibility of representing the world perfectly with language because it acknowledges that the mechanisms of any language condition the thoughts of its speaker community.

History

Ada Lovelace, whose notes added to the end of Luigi Menabrea's paper included the first algorithm designed for processing by an Analytical Engine. She is often recognized as history's first computer programmer.

Programmable devices have existed at least as far back as 1206 AD, when the automata of Al-Jazari were programmable, via pegs and cams, to play various rhythms and drum patterns; and the 1801 Jacquard loom could produce entirely different weaves using different used by changing the "program" - a series of pasteboard cards with holes punched in them.

However, the first computer program is generally dated to 1843, when mathematician Ada Lovelace published an algorithm to calculate a sequence of Bernoulli numbers, intended to be carried out by Charles Babbage's Analytical Engine.

In the 1880s Herman Hollerith invented the concept of storing *data* in machine-readable form. Later a control panel (plugboard) added to his 1906 Type I Tabulator allowed it to be programmed for different jobs, and by the late 1940s, unit record equipment such as the IBM 602 and IBM 604, were programmed by control panels in a similar way; as were the first electronic computers. However, with the concept of the stored-program computers introduced in 1949, both programs and data were stored and manipulated in the same way in computer memory.

Data and instructions were once stored on external punched cards,
which were kept in order and arranged in program decks.

Machine code was the language of early programs, written in the instruction set of the particular machine, often in binary notation. Assembly languages were soon developed that let the programmer specify instruction in a text format, (e.g., ADD X, TOTAL), with abbreviations for each operation code and meaningful names for specifying addresses. However, because an assembly language is little more than a different notation for a machine language, any two machines with different instruction sets also have different assembly languages.

Wired control panel for an IBM 402 Accounting Machine

High-level languages allow the programmer to write programs in terms that are more abstract, and less bound to the underlying hardware. They harness the power of computers to make programming easier by allowing programmers to specify calculations by entering a formula directly (e.g., $Y = X*2 + 5*X + 9$). FORTRAN, the first widely used high-level language to have a functional implementation, came out in 1957 and many other languages were soon developed - in particular, COBOL aimed at commercial data processing, and Lisp for computer research.

Programs were mostly still entered using punched cards or paper tape. By the late 1960s, data storage devices and computer terminals became inexpensive enough that programs could be created by typing directly into the computers. Text editors were developed that allowed changes and corrections to be made much more easily than with punched cards.

Modern Programming

Quality Requirements

Whatever the approach to development may be, the final program must satisfy some fundamental properties. The following properties are among the most important:

- Reliability: how often the results of a program are correct. This depends on conceptual correctness of algorithms, and minimization of programming mistakes, such as mistakes in resource management (e.g., buffer overflows and race conditions) and logic errors (such as division by zero or off-by-one errors).

- Robustness: how well a program anticipates problems due to errors (not bugs). This includes situations such as incorrect, inappropriate or corrupt data, unavailability of needed resources such as memory, operating system services and network connections, user error, and unexpected power outages.

- Usability: the ergonomics of a program: the ease with which a person can use the program for its intended purpose or in some cases even unanticipated purposes. Such issues can make or break its success even regardless of other issues. This involves a wide range of textual, graphical and sometimes hardware elements that improve the clarity, intuitiveness, cohesiveness and completeness of a program's user interface.

- Portability: the range of computer hardware and operating system platforms on which the source code of a program can be compiled/interpreted and run. This depends on differences in the programming facilities provided by the different platforms, including hardware and operating system resources, expected behavior of the hardware and operating system, and availability of platform specific compilers (and sometimes libraries) for the language of the source code.

- Maintainability: the ease with which a program can be modified by its present or future developers in order to make improvements or customizations, fix bugs and security holes, or adapt it to new environments. Good practices during initial development make the difference in this regard. This quality may not be directly apparent to the end user but it can significantly affect the fate of a program over the long term.

- Efficiency/performance: Measure of system resources a program consumes (processor time, memory space, slow devices such as disks, network bandwidth and to some extent even user interaction): the less, the better. This also includes careful management of resources, for example cleaning up temporary files and eliminating memory leaks.

Readability of Source Code

In computer programming, readability refers to the ease with which a human reader can comprehend the purpose, control flow, and operation of source code. It affects the aspects of quality above, including portability, usability and most importantly maintainability.

Readability is important because programmers spend the majority of their time reading, trying to understand and modifying existing source code, rather than writing new source code. Unreadable code often leads to bugs, inefficiencies, and duplicated code. A study found that a few simple readability transformations made code shorter and drastically reduced the time to understand it.

Following a consistent programming style often helps readability. However, readability is more than just programming style. Many factors, having little or nothing to do with the ability of the computer to efficiently compile and execute the code, contribute to readability. Some of these factors include:

- Different indent styles (whitespace)

- Comments

- Decomposition

- Naming conventions for objects (such as variables, classes, procedures, etc.)

The presentation aspects of this (such as indents, line breaks, color highlighting, and so on) are often handled by the source code editor, but the content aspects reflect the programmer's talent and skills.

Various visual programming languages have also been developed with the intent to resolve readability concerns by adopting non-traditional approaches to code structure and display. Integrated development environments (IDEs) aim to integrate all such help. Techniques like Code refactoring can enhance readability.

Algorithmic Complexity

The academic field and the engineering practice of computer programming are both largely concerned with discovering and implementing the most efficient algorithms for a given class of problem. For this purpose, algorithms are classified into *orders* using so-called Big O notation, which expresses resource use, such as execution time or memory consumption, in terms of the size of an input. Expert programmers are familiar with a variety of well-established algorithms and their respective complexities and use this knowledge to choose algorithms that are best suited to the circumstances.

Methodologies

The first step in most formal software development processes is requirements analysis, followed by testing to determine value modeling, implementation, and failure elimination (debugging). There exist a lot of differing approaches for each of those tasks. One approach popular for requirements analysis is Use Case analysis. Many programmers use forms of Agile software development where the various stages of formal software development are more integrated together into short cycles that take a few weeks rather than years. There are many approaches to the Software development process.

Popular modeling techniques include Object-Oriented Analysis and Design (OOAD) and Model-Driven Architecture (MDA). The Unified Modeling Language (UML) is a notation used for both the OOAD and MDA.

A similar technique used for database design is Entity-Relationship Modeling (ER Modeling).

Implementation techniques include imperative languages (object-oriented or procedural), functional languages, and logic languages.

Measuring Language Usage

It is very difficult to determine what are the most popular of modern programming languages. Methods of measuring programming language popularity include: counting the number of job advertisements that mention the language, the number of books sold and courses teaching the language (this overestimates the importance of newer languages), and estimates of the number of existing lines of code written in the language (this underestimates the number of users of business languages such as COBOL).

Some languages are very popular for particular kinds of applications, while some languages are regularly used to write many different kinds of applications. For example, COBOL is still strong in corporate data centers often on large mainframe computers, Fortran in engineering applications, scripting languages in Web development, and C in embedded software. Many applications use a mix of several languages in their construction and use. New languages are generally designed around the syntax of a prior language with new functionality added, (for example C++ adds object-orientation to C, and Java adds memory management and bytecode to C++, but as a result, loses efficiency and the ability for low-level manipulation).

Debugging

The bug from 1947 which is at the origin of a popular (but incorrect)
etymology for the common term for a software defect.

Debugging is a very important task in the software development process since having defects in a program can have significant consequences for its users. Some languages are more prone to some kinds of faults because their specification does not require compilers to perform as much checking as other languages. Use of a static code analysis tool can help detect some possible problems.

Debugging is often done with IDEs like Eclipse, Visual Studio, Kdevelop, NetBeans and Code::-Blocks. Standalone debuggers like GDB are also used, and these often provide less of a visual environment, usually using a command line. Some text editors such as Emacs allow GDB to be invoked through them, to provide a visual environment.

Programming Languages

Different programming languages support different styles of programming (called *programming paradigms*). The choice of language used is subject to many considerations, such as company policy, suitability to task, availability of third-party packages, or individual preference. Ideally, the programming language best suited for the task at hand will be selected. Trade-offs from this ideal involve finding enough programmers who know the language to build a team, the availability of compilers for that language, and the efficiency with which programs written in a given language execute. Languages form an approximate spectrum from "low-level" to "high-level"; "low-level" languages are typically more machine-oriented and faster to execute, whereas "high-level" languages are more abstract and easier to use but execute less quickly. It is usually easier to code in "high-level" languages than in "low-level" ones.

Allen Downey, in his book *How To Think Like A Computer Scientist*, writes:

The details look different in different languages, but a few basic instructions appear in just about every language:

- Input: Gather data from the keyboard, a file, or some other device.

- Output: Display data on the screen or send data to a file or other device.

- Arithmetic: Perform basic arithmetical operations like addition and multiplication.

- Conditional Execution: Check for certain conditions and execute the appropriate sequence of statements.

- Repetition: Perform some action repeatedly, usually with some variation.

Many computer languages provide a mechanism to call functions provided by shared libraries. Provided the functions in a library follow the appropriate run-time conventions (e.g., method of passing arguments), then these functions may be written in any other language.

Programmers

Computer programmers are those who write computer software. Their jobs usually involve:

- Coding
- Debugging
- Documentation
- Integration
- Maintenance
- Requirements analysis
- Software architecture
- Software testing
- Specification

Compiled Language

A compiled language is a programming language whose implementations are typically compilers (translators that generate machine code from source code), and not interpreters (step-by-step executors of source code, where no pre-runtime translation takes place).

The term is somewhat vague. In principle, any language can be implemented with a compiler or with an interpreter. A combination of both solutions is also common: a compiler can translate the source code into some intermediate form (often called p-code or bytecode), which is then passed to an interpreter which executes it.

Advantages and Disadvantages

Programs compiled into native code at compile time tend to be faster than those translated at run time, due to the overhead of the translation process. Newer technologies such as just-in-time compilation, and general improvements in the translation process are starting to narrow this gap, though. Mixed solutions using bytecode tend toward intermediate efficiency.

Low-level programming languages are typically compiled, especially when efficiency is the main concern, rather than cross-platform support. For such languages, there are more one-to-one correspondences between the programmed code and the hardware operations performed by machine code, making it easier for programmers to control use of central processing unit (CPU) and memory in fine detail.

With some effort, it is always possible to write compilers even for traditionally interpreted languages. For example, Common lisp can be compiled to Java bytecode (then interpreted by the Java virtual machine), C code (then compiled to native machine code), or directly to native code. Programming languages that support multiple compiling targets give more control to developers to choose either execution speed or cross-platform compatibility.

Languages

Some languages that are commonly considered to be compiled:

- Ada
- ALGOL
  - ALGOL 60
  - ALGOL 68
  - SMALL
- BASIC
  - Visual Basic
  - PureBasic
- C

- C++
- Objective-C
  - Swift
- D
- C# (to bytecode)
- Java (to bytecode)

- CLEO
- COBOL
- Cobra
- Crystal
- eC
- Eiffel
  - Sather
  - Ubercode
- Erlang (to bytecode)
- F# (to bytecode)
- Factor (later versions)
- Forth
- Fortran
- Go
- Haskell
- Haxe (to bytecode or C++)
- JOVIAL
- Julia
- LabVIEW, G
- Lisp
  - Common Lisp
- Lush

- Mercury
- ML
  - Standard ML
    - Alice
  - OCaml
- Nim (to C, C++, or Objective-C)
- Open-URQ
- Pascal
  - Object Pascal
    - Delphi
  - Modula-2
  - Modula-3
  - Oberon
- PL/I
- RPG
- Rust
- Scala (to bytecode)
- Seed7
- SPITBOL
- Visual Foxpro
- Visual Prolog

Tools

- ANTLR
- CodeWorker
- Lex
- Flex
- GNU bison
- Yacc

Interpreted Language

An interpreted language is a programming language for which most of its implementations execute instructions directly, without previously compiling a program into machine-language instructions. The interpreter executes the program directly, translating each statement into a sequence of one or more subroutines already compiled into machine code.

The terms *interpreted language* and *compiled language* are not well defined because, in theory, any programming language can be either interpreted or compiled. In modern programming language implementation it is increasingly popular for a platform to provide both options.

Interpreted languages can also be contrasted with machine languages. Functionally, both execution and interpretation mean the same thing — fetching the next instruction/statement from the program and executing it. Although interpreted byte code is additionally identical to machine code in form and has an assembler representation, the term "interpreted" is practically reserved for "software processed" languages (by virtual machine or emulator) on top of the native (i.e. hardware) processor.

In principle, programs in many languages may be compiled or interpreted, emulated or executed natively, so this designation is applied solely based on common implementation practice, rather than representing an essential property of a language.

Many languages have been implemented using both compilers and interpreters, including BASIC, C, Lisp, Pascal, and Python. Java and C# are compiled into bytecode, the virtual machine-friendly interpreted language. Lisp implementations can freely mix interpreted and compiled code.

Historical Background

In the early days of computing, language design was heavily influenced by the decision to use compiling or interpreting as a mode of execution. For example, Smalltalk (1980), which was designed to be interpreted at run-time, allows generic objects to dynamically interact with each other.

Initially, interpreted languages were compiled line-by-line; that is, each line was compiled as it was about to be executed, and if a loop or subroutine caused certain lines to be executed multiple times, they would be recompiled every time. This has become much less common. Most so-called interpreted languages use an intermediate representation, which combines compiling and interpreting.

Examples include:

- JavaScript

- Python

- Ruby (similarly, it uses an abstract syntax tree as intermediate representation)

- Forth

The intermediate representation can be compiled once and for all (as in Java), each time before execution (as in Perl or Ruby), or each time a change in the source is detected before execution (as in Python).

Advantages

Interpreting a language gives implementations some additional flexibility over compiled implementations. Features that are often easier to implement in interpreters than in compilers include:

- platform independence (Java's byte code, for example)

- reflection and reflective use of the evaluator (e.g. a first-order eval function)

- dynamic typing

- smaller executable program size (since implementations have flexibility to choose the instruction code)

- dynamic scoping

Furthermore, source code can be read and copied, giving users more freedom.

Disadvantages

Disadvantages of interpreted languages are:

- Without static type-checking, which is usually performed by a compiler, programs can be less reliable, because type checking eliminates a class of programming errors.

- Interpreters can be susceptible to Code injection attacks.

- Slower execution compared to direct native machine code execution on the host CPU. A technique used to improve performance is just-in-time compilation which converts frequently executed sequences of interpreted instruction to host machine code. JIT is most often combined with compilation to byte-code as in Java.

- Source code can be read and copied (e.g. JavaScript in web pages), or more easily reverse engineered through reflection in applications where intellectual property has a commercial advantage. In some cases obfuscation can be used to encrypt source code or obscure its purpose.

List of Frequently Used Interpreted Languages

- APL A vector oriented language using an unusual character set

  o   J An APL variant in which tacit definition provides some of the benefits of compiling

- BASIC (although the original version, Dartmouth BASIC, was compiled, as are many modern BASICs)

  o   thinBasic

- Equation manipulation and solving systems

  o   GNU Octave

  o   Interactive Data Language (IDL)

- o   TK Solver
- o   Mathematica
- o   MATLAB
- Euphoria Interpreted or compiled.
- Game Maker Language
- Forth
- Lava
- Lisp
  - o   Logo
  - o   Scheme
- Madness Script
- MUMPS
- Perl
- PHP
- PostScript
- REXX
- Seed7
- Smalltalk
  - o   Bistro
  - o   Dolphin Smalltalk
  - o   F-Script
  - o   Little Smalltalk
  - o   Squeak
  - o   VisualAge
  - o   VisualWorks
- Spreadsheets
  - o   Excel
- S

- R

- Tcl

  - XOTcl

- VBScript

- PowerShell

- XMLmosaic An xml contained C# like programming language interpreted by a console application written in Visual Basic .NET

Languages Usually Compiled to a Bytecode

Many languages are first compiled to bytecode. Sometimes, bytecode can also be compiled to a native binary using an AOT compiler or executed natively, by hardware processor.

- Java (is compiled into Java bytecode to be interpreted by JVM)

  - Clojure

  - Groovy

  - ColdFusion

  - Scala

- Lua

- .NET Framework languages (translated to bytecode, called CIL).

  - C++/CLI

  - C#

  - Visual Basic .NET

  - F#

- Pike

- Python

- Squeak Smalltalk

- Ruby

- Visual FoxPro

- Lisp

- AppleScript

Scripting Language

A scripting or script language is a programming language that supports scripts: programs written for a special run-time environment that automate the execution of tasks that could alternatively be executed one-by-one by a human operator. Scripting languages are often interpreted (rather than compiled). Primitives are usually the elementary tasks or API calls, and the language allows them to be combined into more complex programs. Environments that can be automated through scripting include software applications, web pages within a web browser, the shells of operating systems (OS), embedded systems, as well as numerous games. A scripting language can be viewed as a domain-specific language for a particular environment; in the case of scripting an application, this is also known as an extension language. Scripting languages are also sometimes referred to as very high-level programming languages, as they operate at a high level of abstraction, or as control languages, particularly for job control languages on mainframes.

The term "scripting language" is also used loosely to refer to dynamic high-level general-purpose languages, such as Perl, Tcl, and Python, with the term "script" often used for small programs (up to a few thousand lines of code) in such languages, or in domain-specific languages such as the text-processing languages sed and AWK. Some of these languages were originally developed for use within a particular environment, and later developed into portable domain-specific or general-purpose languages. Conversely, many general-purpose languages have dialects that are used as scripting languages.

The spectrum of scripting languages ranges from very small and highly domain-specific languages to general-purpose programming languages used for scripting. Standard examples of scripting languages for specific environments include: Bash, for the Unix or Unix-like operating systems; ECMAScript (JavaScript), for web browsers; and Visual Basic for Applications, for Microsoft Office applications. Lua is a language designed and widely used as an extension language. Python is a general-purpose language that is also commonly used as an extension language, while ECMAScript is still primarily a scripting language for web browsers, but is also used as a general-purpose language. The Emacs Lisp dialect of Lisp (for the Emacs editor) and the Visual Basic for Applications dialect of Visual Basic are examples of scripting language dialects of general-purpose languages. Some game systems, notably the Second Life virtual world and the Trainz franchise of Railroad simulators have been extensively extended in functionality by scripting extensions. In other games like Wesnoth, the variety of actual games played by players are scripts written by other users.

Characteristics

Typically scripting languages are intended to be very fast to learn and write in, either as short source code files or interactively in a read–eval–print loop (REPL, language shell). This generally implies relatively simple syntax and semantics; typically a "script" (code written in the scripting language) is executed from start to finish, as a "script", with no explicit entry point.

For example, it is uncommon to characterise Java as a scripting language because of its lengthy syntax and rules about which classes exist in which files, and it is not directly possible to execute Java interactively, because source files can only contain definitions that must be invoked externally by a host application or application launcher.

```
public class HelloWorld {

  public void printHelloWorld() {

    System.out.println("Hello World");

  }

}
```

This piece of code intended to print "Hello World" does nothing as main() is not declared in HelloWorld class.

In contrast, Python allows definition of some functions in a single file, or to avoid functions altogether and use imperative programming style, or even use it interactively.

```
print ("Hello World")
```

This one line of python code prints "Hello World"; no *declarative* statement like *main()* is required here.

A scripting language is usually interpreted from source code or bytecode. By contrast, the software environment the scripts are written for is typically written in a compiled language and distributed in machine code form.

Scripting languages may be designed for use by end users of a program—end-user development—or may be only for internal use by developers, so they can write portions of the program in the scripting language. Scripting languages typically use abstraction, a form of information hiding, to spare users the details of internal variable types, data storage, and memory management.

Scripts are often created or modified by the person executing them, but they are also often distributed, such as when large portions of games are written in a scripting language.

History

Early mainframe computers (in the 1950s) were non-interactive, instead using batch processing. IBM's Job Control Language (JCL) is the archetype of languages used to control batch processing.

The first interactive shells were developed in the 1960s to enable remote operation of the first time-sharing systems, and these used shell scripts, which controlled running computer programs within a computer program, the shell. Calvin Mooers in his TRAC language is generally credited with inventing *command substitution*, the ability to embed commands in scripts that when interpreted insert a character string into the script. Multics calls these *active functions*. Louis Pouzin wrote an early processor for command scripts called RUNCOM for CTSS around 1964. Stuart Madnick at MIT wrote a scripting language for IBM's CP/CMS in 1966. He originally called this processor COMMAND, later named EXEC. Multics included an offshoot of CTSS RUNCOM, also called RUNCOM. EXEC was eventually replaced by EXEC 2 and REXX.

Languages such as Tcl and Lua were specifically designed as general-purpose scripting languages that could be embedded in any application. Other languages such as Visual Basic for Applications (VBA) provided strong integration with the automation facilities of an underlying system. Embedding of such general-purpose scripting languages instead of developing a new language for each application also had obvious benefits, relieving the application developer of the need to code a language translator from scratch and allowing the user to apply skills learned elsewhere.

Some software incorporates several different scripting languages. Modern web browsers typically provide a language for writing extensions to the browser itself, and several standard embedded languages for controlling the browser, including JavaScript (a dialect of ECMAScript) or XUL.

Types

Glue Languages

Scripting is often contrasted with system programming, as in Ousterhout's dichotomy or "programming in the large and programming in the small". In this view, scripting is particularly glue code, connecting software components, and a language specialized for this purpose is a *glue language*. Pipelines and shell scripting are archetypal examples of glue languages, and Perl was initially developed to fill this same role. Web development can be considered a use of glue languages, interfacing between a database and web server. But if a substantial amount of logic is written in script, it is better characterized as simply another software component, not "glue".

Glue languages are especially useful for writing and maintaining:

- custom commands for a command shell;

- smaller programs than those that are better implemented in a compiled language;

- "wrapper" programs for executables, like a batch file that moves or manipulates files and does other things with the operating system before or after running an application like a word processor, spreadsheet, data base, assembler, compiler, etc.;

- scripts that may change;

- rapid prototypes of a solution eventually implemented in another, usually compiled, language.

Glue language examples:

- AppleScript
- ColdFusion
- DCL
- Embeddable Common Lisp
- ecl
- Erlang
- JCL
- CoffeeScript
- JScript and JavaScript
- Lua

- m4
- Modern Pascal
- Perl
- PHP
- Pure
- Python
- Rebol
- Red
- Rexx
- Ruby

- Scheme
- Tcl
- Unix Shell scripts (ksh, csh, bash, sh and others)
- VBScript
- Work Flow Language
- Windows PowerShell
- XSLT

Macro languages exposed to operating system or application components can serve as glue languages. These include Visual Basic for Applications, WordBasic, LotusScript, CorelScript, Hummingbird Basic, QuickScript, SaxBasic, and WinWrap Basic. Other tools like AWK can also be considered glue languages, as can any language implemented by an Windows Script Host engine (VBScript, JScript and VBA by default in Windows and third-party engines including implementations of Rexx, Perl, Tcl, Python, XSLT, Ruby, Modern Pascal, Delphi, & C). A majority of applications can access and use operating system components via the object models or its own functions.

Other devices like programmable calculators may also have glue languages; the operating systems of PDAs such as Windows CE may have available native or third-party macro tools that glue applications together, in addition to implementations of common glue languages—including Windows NT, MS-DOS and some Unix shells, Rexx, Modern Pascal, PHP, and Perl. Depending upon the OS version, WSH and the default script engines (VBScript and JScript) are available.

Programmable calculators can be programmed in glue languages in three ways. For example, the Texas Instruments TI-92, by factory default can be programmed with a command script language. Inclusion of the scripting and glue language Lua in the TI-NSpire series of calculators could be seen as a successor to this. The primary on-board high-level programming languages of most graphing calculators (most often Basic variants, sometimes Lisp derivatives, and more uncommonly, C derivatives) in many cases can glue together calculator functions—such as graphs, lists, matrices, etc. Third-party implementations of more comprehensive Basic version that may be closer to variants listed as glue languages are available and attempts to implement Perl, Rexx, or various operating system shells on the TI and HP graphing calculators are also mentioned. PC-based C cross-compilers for some of the TI and HP machines used in conjunction with tools that convert between C and Perl, Rexx, AWK, as well as shell scripts to Perl, Modern Pascal, VBScript to and from Perl make it possible to write a program in a glue language for eventual implementation (as a compiled program) on the calculator.

Job Control Languages and Shells

A major class of scripting languages has grown out of the automation of job control, which relates to starting and controlling the behavior of system programs. (In this sense, one might think of shells as being descendants of IBM's JCL, or Job Control Language, which was used for exactly this purpose.) Many of these languages' interpreters double as command-line interpreters such as the Unix shell or the MS-DOS COMMAND.COM. Others, such as AppleScript offer the use of English-like commands to build scripts.

GUI Scripting

With the advent of graphical user interfaces, a specialized kind of scripting language emerged for controlling a computer. These languages interact with the same graphic windows, menus, buttons, and so on that a human user would. They do this by simulating the actions of a user. These languages are typically used to automate user actions. Such languages are also called "macros" when control is through simulated key presses or mouse clicks, as well as tapping or pressing on a touch-activated screen.

These languages could in principle be used to control any GUI application; but, in practice their use is limited because their use needs support from the application and from the operating system.

There are a few exceptions to this limitation. Some GUI scripting languages are based on recognizing graphical objects from their display screen pixels. These GUI scripting languages do not depend on support from the operating system or application.

Application-specific Languages

Application specific languages can be split in many different categories, i.e. standalone based app languages (executable) or internal application specific languages (postscript, xml, gscript as some of the widely distributed scripts, respectively implemented by Adobe, MS and Google) among others include an idiomatic scripting language tailored to the needs of the application user. Likewise, many computer game systems use a custom scripting language to express the programmed actions of non-player characters and the game environment. Languages of this sort are designed for a single application; and, while they may superficially resemble a specific general-purpose language (e.g. QuakeC, modeled after C), they have custom features that distinguish them. Emacs Lisp, while a fully formed and capable dialect of Lisp, contains many special features that make it most useful for extending the editing functions of Emacs. An application-specific scripting language can be viewed as a domain-specific programming language specialized to a single application.

Extension/embeddable Languages

A number of languages have been designed for the purpose of replacing application-specific scripting languages by being embeddable in application programs. The application programmer (working in C or another systems language) includes "hooks" where the scripting language can control the application. These languages may be technically equivalent to an application-specific extension language but when an application embeds a "common" language, the user gets the advantage of being able to transfer skills from application to application. A more generic alternative is simply to provide a library (often a C library) that a general-purpose language can use to control the application, without modifying the language for the specific domain.

JavaScript began as and primarily still is a language for scripting inside web browsers; however, the standardization of the language as ECMAScript has made it popular as a general-purpose embeddable language. In particular, the Mozilla implementation SpiderMonkey is embedded in several environments such as the Yahoo! Widget Engine. Other applications embedding ECMAScript implementations include the Adobe products Adobe Flash (ActionScript) and Adobe Acrobat (for scripting PDF files).

Tcl was created as an extension language but has come to be used more frequently as a general-purpose language in roles similar to Python, Perl, and Ruby. On the other hand, Rexx was originally created as a job control language, but is widely used as an extension language as well as a general-purpose language. Perl is a general-purpose language, but had the Oraperl (1990) dialect, consisting of a Perl 4 binary with Oracle Call Interface compiled in. This has however since been replaced by a library (Perl Module), DBD::Oracle.

Other complex and task-oriented applications may incorporate and expose an embedded programming language to allow their users more control and give them more functionality than can be available through a user interface, no matter how sophisticated. For example, Autodesk Maya 3D authoring tools embed the MEL scripting language, or Blender which uses Python to fill this role.

Some other types of applications that need faster feature addition or tweak-and-run cycles (e.g. game engines) also use an embedded language. During the development, this allows them to prototype features faster and tweak more freely, without the need for the user to have intimate knowledge of the inner workings of the application or to rebuild it after each tweak (which can take a significant amount of time). The scripting languages used for this purpose range from the more common and more famous Lua and Python to lesser-known ones such as AngelScript and Squirrel.

Ch is another C compatible scripting option for the industry to embed into C/C++ application programs.

Generic Programming

Generic programming is a style of computer programming in which algorithms are written in terms of types *to-be-specified-later* that are then *instantiated* when needed for specific types provided as parameters. This approach, pioneered by ML in 1973, permits writing common functions or types that differ only in the set of types on which they operate when used, thus reducing duplication. Such software entities are known as *generics* in Ada, C#, Delphi, Eiffel, F#, Java, Objective-C, Rust, Swift, and Visual Basic .NET. They are known as *parametric polymorphism* in ML, Scala, Haskell (the Haskell community also uses the term "generic" for a related but somewhat different concept) and Julia; *templates* in C++ and D; and *parameterized types* in the influential 1994 book *Design Patterns*. The authors of *Design Patterns* note that this technique, especially when combined with delegation, is very powerful, however,

Dynamic, highly parameterized software is harder to understand than more static software.

— Gang of Four, Design Patterns

The term generic programming was originally coined by David Musser and Alexander Stepanov in a more specific sense than the above, to describe a programming paradigm whereby fundamental requirements on types are abstracted from across concrete examples of algorithms and data structures and formalised as concepts, with generic functions implemented in terms of these concepts, typically using language genericity mechanisms as described above.

Stepanov–Musser and Other Generic Programming Paradigms

Generic programming is defined in Musser & Stepanov (1989) as follows,

Generic programming centers around the idea of abstracting from concrete, efficient algorithms to obtain generic algorithms that can be combined with different data representations to produce a wide variety of useful software.

— Musser, David R.; Stepanov, Alexander A., Generic Programming

Generic programming paradigm is an approach to software decomposition whereby fundamental requirements on types are abstracted from across concrete examples of algorithms and data structures and formalised as concepts, analogously to the abstraction of algebraic theories in abstract algebra. Early examples of this programming approach were implemented in Scheme and Ada, although the best known example is the Standard Template Library (STL), which developed a theory of iterators that is used to decouple sequence data structures and the algorithms operating on them.

For example, given N sequence data structures, e.g. singly linked list, vector etc., and M algorithms to operate on them, e.g. find, sort etc., a direct approach would implement each algorithm specifically for each data structure, giving $N \times M$ combinations to implement. However, in the generic programming approach, each data structure returns a model of an iterator concept (a simple value type that can be dereferenced to retrieve the current value, or changed to point to another value in the sequence) and each algorithm is instead written generically with arguments of such iterators, e.g. a pair of iterators pointing to the beginning and end of the subsequence to process. Thus, only $N + M$ data structure-algorithm combinations need be implemented. Several iterator concepts are specified in the STL, each a refinement of more restrictive concepts e.g. forward iterators only provide movement to the next value in a sequence (e.g. suitable for a singly linked list or a stream of input data), whereas a random-access iterator also provides direct constant-time access to any element of the sequence (e.g. suitable for a vector). An important point is that a data structure will return a model of the most general concept that can be implemented efficiently—computational complexity requirements are explicitly part of the concept definition. This limits the data structures a given algorithm can be applied to and such complexity requirements are a major determinant of data structure choice. Generic programming similarly has been applied in other domains, e.g. graph algorithms.

Note that although this approach often utilizes language features of compile-time genericity/templates, it is in fact independent of particular language-technical details. Generic programming pioneer Alexander Stepanov wrote,

Generic programming is about abstracting and classifying algorithms and data structures. It gets its inspiration from Knuth and not from type theory. Its goal is the incremental construction of systematic catalogs of useful, efficient and abstract algorithms and data structures. Such an undertaking is still a dream.

—Alexander Stepanov, Short History of STL

I believe that iterator theories are as central to Computer Science as theories of rings or Banach spaces are central to Mathematics.

—Alexander Stepanov, An Interview with A. Stepanov

Bjarne Stroustrup noted,

Following Stepanov, we can define generic programming without mentioning language features: Lift algorithms and data structures from concrete examples to their most general and abstract form.

—Bjarne Stroustrup, Evolving a language in and for the real world: C++ 1991-2006

Other programming paradigms that have been described as generic programming include *Datatype generic programming* as described in "Generic Programming — an Introduction". The *Scrap your boilerplate* approach is a lightweight generic programming approach for Haskell.

We distinguish the high-level programming paradigms of *generic programming*, above, from the lower-level programming language *genericity mechanisms* used to implement them.

Programming Language Support For Genericity

Genericity facilities have existed in high-level languages since at least the 1970s in languages such as ML, CLU and Ada, and were subsequently adopted by many object-based and object-oriented languages, including BETA, C++, D, Eiffel, Java, and DEC's now defunct Trellis-Owl language.

Genericity is implemented and supported differently in various programming languages; the term "generic" has also been used differently in various programming contexts. For example, in Forth the compiler can execute code while compiling and one can create new *compiler keywords* and new implementations for those words on the fly. It has few *words* that expose the compiler behaviour and therefore naturally offers *genericity* capacities that, however, are not referred to as such in most Forth texts. Similarly, dynamically typed languages, especially interpreted ones, usually offer *genericity* by default as both passing values to functions and value assignment are type-indifferent and such behavior is often utilized for abstraction or code terseness, however this is not typically labeled *genericity* as it's a direct consequence of dynamic typing system employed by the language. The term has been used in functional programming, specifically in Haskell-like languages, which use a structural type system where types are always parametric and the actual code on those types is generic. These usages still serve a similar purpose of code-saving and the rendering of an abstraction.

Arrays and structs can be viewed as predefined generic types. Every usage of an array or struct type instantiates a new concrete type, or reuses a previous instantiated type. Array element types and struct element types are parameterized types, which are used to instantiate the corresponding generic type. All this is usually built-in in the compiler and the syntax differs from other generic constructs. Some extensible programming languages try to unify built-in and user defined generic types.

A broad survey of genericity mechanisms in programming languages follows.

In Object-oriented Languages

When creating container classes in statically typed languages, it is inconvenient to write specific implementations for each datatype contained, especially if the code for each datatype is virtually identical. For example, in C++, this duplication of code can be circumvented by defining a class template:

```
template<typename T>

class List

{

    /* class contents */
```

```
};
```

```
List<Animal> list_of_animals;
```

```
List<Car> list_of_cars;
```

Above, T is a placeholder for whatever type is specified when the list is created. These "containers-of-type-T", commonly called templates, allow a class to be reused with different datatypes as long as certain contracts such as subtypes and signature are kept. This genericity mechanism should not be confused with *inclusion polymorphism*, which is the algorithmic usage of exchangeable sub-classes: for instance, a list of objects of type Moving_Object containing objects of type Animal and Car. Templates can also be used for type-independent functions as in the Swap example below:

```
template<typename T>

void Swap(T & a, T & b)  //"&" passes parameters by reference

{

    T temp = b;

    b = a;

    a = temp;

}
```

```
string hello = "world!", world = "Hello, ";

Swap( world, hello );

cout << hello << world << endl; //Output is "Hello, World!"
```

The C++ template construct used above is widely cited as the genericity construct that popularized the notion among programmers and language designers and supports many generic programming idioms. The D programming language also offers fully generic-capable templates based on the C++ precedent but with a simplified syntax. The Java programming language has provided genericity facilities syntactically based on C++'s since the introduction of J2SE 5.0.

C# 2.0, Oxygene 1.5 (also known as Chrome) and Visual Basic .NET 2005 have constructs that take advantage of the support for generics present in the Microsoft .NET Framework since version 2.0.

Generics in Ada

Ada has had generics since it was first designed in 1977–1980. The standard library uses generics to provide many services. Ada 2005 adds a comprehensive generic container library to the standard library, which was inspired by C++'s standard template library.

A *generic unit* is a package or a subprogram that takes one or more *generic formal parameters*.

A *generic formal parameter* is a value, a variable, a constant, a type, a subprogram, or even an instance of another, designated, generic unit. For generic formal types, the syntax distinguishes between discrete, floating-point, fixed-point, access (pointer) types, etc. Some formal parameters can have default values.

To *instantiate* a generic unit, the programmer passes *actual* parameters for each formal. The generic instance then behaves just like any other unit. It is possible to instantiate generic units at run-time, for example inside a loop.

Example

The specification of a generic package:

```
generic

    Max_Size : Natural; -- a generic formal value

    type Element_Type is private; -- a generic formal type; accepts any
nonlimited type

package Stacks is

    type Size_Type is range 0 .. Max_Size;

    type Stack is limited private;

    procedure Create (S : out Stack;

                    Initial_Size : in Size_Type := Max_Size);

    procedure Push (Into : in out Stack; Element : in Element_Type);

    procedure Pop (From : in out Stack; Element : out Element_Type);

    Overflow : exception;

    Underflow : exception;

private

    subtype Index_Type is Size_Type range 1 .. Max_Size;

    type Vector is array (Index_Type range <>) of Element_Type;

    type Stack (Allocated_Size : Size_Type := 0) is record

        Top : Index_Type;

        Storage : Vector (1 .. Allocated_Size);

    end record;

end Stacks;
```

Instantiating the generic package:

```
type Bookmark_Type is new Natural;

-- records a location in the text document we are editing

package Bookmark_Stacks is new Stacks (Max_Size => 20,

                                        Element_Type => Bookmark_Type);

-- Allows the user to jump between recorded locations in a document
```

Using an instance of a generic package:

```
type Document_Type is record

    Contents : Ada.Strings.Unbounded.Unbounded_String;

    Bookmarks : Bookmark_Stacks.Stack;

end record;


procedure Edit (Document_Name : in String) is

    Document : Document_Type;

begin

    -- Initialise the stack of bookmarks:

    Bookmark_Stacks.Create (S => Document.Bookmarks, Initial_Size => 10);

    -- Now, open the file Document_Name and read it in...

end Edit;
```

Advantages and Limitations

The language syntax allows precise specification of constraints on generic formal parameters. For example, it is possible to specify that a generic formal type will only accept a modular type as the actual. It is also possible to express constraints *between* generic formal parameters; for example:

```
generic

    type Index_Type is (<>); -- must be a discrete type

    type Element_Type is private; -- can be any nonlimited type

    type Array_Type is array (Index_Type range <>) of Element_Type;
```

In this example, Array_Type is constrained by both Index_Type and Element_Type. When instantiating the unit, the programmer must pass an actual array type that satisfies these constraints.

The disadvantage of this fine-grained control is a complicated syntax, but, because all generic formal parameters are completely defined in the specification, the compiler can instantiate generics without looking at the body of the generic.

Unlike C++, Ada does not allow specialised generic instances, and requires that all generics be instantiated explicitly. These rules have several consequences:

- the compiler can implement *shared generics*: the object code for a generic unit can be shared between all instances. As further consequences:

  o there is no possibility of code bloat (code bloat is common in C++ and requires special care, as explained below).

  o it is possible to instantiate generics at run-time, as well as at compile time, since no new object code is required for a new instance.

  o actual objects corresponding to a generic formal object are always considered to be nonstatic inside the generic

- all instances of a generic being exactly the same, it is easier to review and understand programs written by others; there are no "special cases" to take into account.

- all instantiations being explicit, there are no hidden instantiations that might make it difficult to understand the program.

- Ada does not permit "template metaprogramming", because it does not allow specialisations.

Templates in C++

C++ uses templates to enable generic programming techniques. The C++ Standard Library includes the Standard Template Library or STL that provides a framework of templates for common data structures and algorithms. Templates in C++ may also be used for template metaprogramming, which is a way of pre-evaluating some of the code at compile-time rather than run-time. Using template specialization, C++ Templates are considered Turing complete.

Technical Overview

There are two kinds of templates: function templates and class templates. A *function template* is a pattern for creating ordinary functions based upon the parameterizing types supplied when instantiated. For example, the C++ Standard Template Library contains the function template max(x, y) that creates functions that return either *x* or *y*, whichever is larger. max() could be defined like this:

```
template <typename T>

T max(T x, T y)

{
```

```
    return x < y ? y : x;

}
```

Specializations of this function template, instantiations with specific types, can be called just like an ordinary function:

```
cout << max(3, 7);    // outputs 7
```

The compiler examines the arguments used to call max and determines that this is a call to max-(int, int). It then instantiates a version of the function where the parameterizing type T is int, making the equivalent of the following function:

```
int max(int x, int y)

{

    return x < y ? y : x;

}
```

This works whether the arguments x and y are integers, strings, or any other type for which the expression x < y is sensible, or more specifically, for any type for which operator< is defined. Common inheritance is not needed for the set of types that can be used, and so it is very similar to duck typing. A program defining a custom data type can use operator overloading to define the meaning of < for that type, thus allowing its use with the max() function template. While this may seem a minor benefit in this isolated example, in the context of a comprehensive library like the STL it allows the programmer to get extensive functionality for a new data type, just by defining a few operators for it. Merely defining < allows a type to be used with the standard sort(), stable_sort(), and binary_search() algorithms or to be put inside data structures such as sets, heaps, and associative arrays.

C++ templates are completely type safe at compile time. As a demonstration, the standard type complex does not define the < operator, because there is no strict order on complex numbers. Therefore, max(x, y) will fail with a compile error, if x and y are complex values. Likewise, other templates that rely on < cannot be applied to complex data unless a comparison (in the form of a functor or function) is provided. E.g.: A complex cannot be used as key for a map unless a comparison is provided. Unfortunately, compilers historically generate somewhat esoteric, long, and unhelpful error messages for this sort of error. Ensuring that a certain object adheres to a method protocol can alleviate this issue. Languages which use compare instead of < can also use complex values as keys.

The second kind of template, a *class template,* extends the same concept to classes. A class template specialization is a class. Class templates are often used to make generic containers. For example, the STL has a linked list container. To make a linked list of integers, one writes list<int>. A list of strings is denoted list<string>. A list has a set of standard functions associated with it, that work for any compatible parameterizing types.

Template Specialization

A powerful feature of C++'s templates is *template specialization*. This allows alternative implementations to be provided based on certain characteristics of the parameterized type that is being instantiated. Template specialization has two purposes: to allow certain forms of optimization, and to reduce code bloat.

For example, consider a sort() template function. One of the primary activities that such a function does is to swap or exchange the values in two of the container's positions. If the values are large (in terms of the number of bytes it takes to store each of them), then it is often quicker to first build a separate list of pointers to the objects, sort those pointers, and then build the final sorted sequence. If the values are quite small however it is usually fastest to just swap the values in-place as needed. Furthermore, if the parameterized type is already of some pointer-type, then there is no need to build a separate pointer array. Template specialization allows the template creator to write different implementations and to specify the characteristics that the parameterized type(s) must have for each implementation to be used.

Unlike function templates, class templates can be partially specialized. That means that an alternate version of the class template code can be provided when some of the template parameters are known, while leaving other template parameters generic. This can be used, for example, to create a default implementation (the *primary specialization*) that assumes that copying a parameterizing type is expensive and then create partial specializations for types that are cheap to copy, thus increasing overall efficiency. Clients of such a class template just use specializations of it without needing to know whether the compiler used the primary specialization or some partial specialization in each case. Class templates can also be *fully specialized*, which means that an alternate implementation can be provided when all of the parameterizing types are known.

Advantages and Disadvantages

Some uses of templates, such as the max() function, were previously filled by function-like preprocessor macros (a legacy of the C programming language). For example, here is a possible max() macro:

```
#define max(a,b)  ((a) < (b) ? (b) : (a))
```

Macros are expanded by preprocessor, before compilation proper; templates are expanded at compile time. Macros are always expanded inline; templates can also be expanded as inline functions when the compiler deems it appropriate. Thus both function-like macros and function templates have no run-time overhead.

However, templates are generally considered an improvement over macros for these purposes. Templates are type-safe. Templates avoid some of the common errors found in code that makes heavy use of function-like macros, such as evaluating parameters with side effects twice. Perhaps most importantly, templates were designed to be applicable to much larger problems than macros.

There are three primary drawbacks to the use of templates: compiler support, poor error messages, and code bloat. Many compilers historically have poor support for templates, thus the use of templates can make code somewhat less portable. Support may also be poor when a C++ compiler is being used with a linker that is not C++-aware, or when attempting to use templates across shared library boundaries. Most modern compilers however now have fairly robust and standard template support, and the new C++ standard, C++11, further addresses these issues.

Almost all compilers produce confusing, long, or sometimes unhelpful error messages when errors are detected in code that uses templates. This can make templates difficult to develop.

Finally, the use of templates requires the compiler to generate a separate *instance* of the templated class or function for every permutation of type parameters used with it. (This is necessary because types in C++ are not all the same size, and the sizes of data fields are important to how classes work.) So the indiscriminate use of templates can lead to code bloat, resulting in excessively large executables. However, judicious use of template specialization and derivation can dramatically reduce such code bloat in some cases:

So, can derivation be used to reduce the problem of code replicated because templates are used? This would involve deriving a template from an ordinary class. This technique proved successful in curbing code bloat in real use. People who do not use a technique like this have found that replicated code can cost megabytes of code space even in moderate size programs.

— Bjarne Stroustrup, The Design and Evolution of C++, 1994

In simple cases templates can be transformed into generics (not causing code bloat) by creating a class getting a parameter derived from a type in compile time and wrapping a template around this class. It is a nice approach for creating generic heap-based containers.

The extra instantiations generated by templates can also cause debuggers to have difficulty working gracefully with templates. For example, setting a debug breakpoint within a template from a source file may either miss setting the breakpoint in the actual instantiation desired or may set a breakpoint in every place the template is instantiated.

Also, because the compiler needs to perform macro-like expansions of templates and generate different instances of them at compile time, the implementation source code for the templated class or function must be available (e.g. included in a header) to the code using it. Templated classes or functions, including much of the Standard Template Library (STL), if not included in header files, cannot be compiled. (This is in contrast to non-templated code, which may be compiled to binary, providing only a declarations header file for code using it.) This may be a disadvantage by exposing the implementing code, which removes some abstractions, and could restrict its use in closed-source projects.

Templates in D

The D programming language supports templates based in design on C++. Most C++ template idioms will carry over to D without alteration, but D adds some additional functionality:

- Template parameters in D are not restricted to just types and primitive values, but also allow arbitrary compile-time values (such as strings and struct literals), and aliases to arbitrary identifiers, including other templates or template instantiations.

- Template constraints and the static if statement provide an alternative to C++'s substitution failure is not an error (SFINAE) mechanism, similar to C++ concepts.

- The is(...) expression allows speculative instantiation to verify an object's traits at compile time.

- The auto keyword and the typeof expression allow type inference for variable declarations and function return values, which in turn allows "Voldemort types" (types which do not have a global name).

Templates in D use a different syntax as in C++: whereas in C++ template parameters are wrapped in angular brackets (Template<param1, param2>), D uses an exclamation sign and parentheses: Template!(param1, param2). This avoids the C++ parsing difficulties due to ambiguity with comparison operators. If there is only one parameter, the parentheses can be omitted.

Conventionally, D combines the above features to provide compile-time polymorphism using trait-based generic programming. For example, an input range is defined as any type that satisfies the checks performed by isInputRange, which is defined as follows:

```
template isInputRange(R)

{

    enum bool isInputRange = is(typeof(

    (inout int = 0)

    {

        R r = R.init;       // can define a range object

        if (r.empty) {}     // can test for empty

        r.popFront();       // can invoke popFront()

        auto h = r.front;   // can get the front of the range

    }));

}
```

A function that accepts only input ranges can then use the above template in a template constraint:

```
auto fun(Range)(Range range)

    if (isInputRange!Range)

{

    // ...

}
```

Code Generation

In addition to template metaprogramming, D also provides several features to enable compile-time code generation:

- The import expression allows reading a file from disk and using its contents as a string expression.

- Compile-time reflection allows enumerating and inspecting declarations and their members during compilation.

- User-defined attributes allow users to attach arbitrary identifiers to declarations, which can then be enumerated using compile-time reflection.

- Compile-Time Function Execution (CTFE) allows a subset of D (restricted to safe operations) to be interpreted during compilation.

- String mixins allow evaluating and compiling the contents of a string expression as D code that becomes part of the program.

Combining the above allows generating code based on existing declarations. For example, D serialization frameworks can enumerate a type's members and generate specialized functions for each serialized type to perform serialization and deserialization. User-defined attributes could further indicate serialization rules.

The import expression and compile-time function execution also allow efficiently implementing domain-specific languages. For example, given a function that takes a string containing an HTML template and returns equivalent D source code, it is possible to use it in the following way:

```
// Import the contents of example.htt as a string manifest constant.

enum htmlTemplate = import("example.htt");



// Transpile the HTML template to D code.

enum htmlDCode = htmlTemplateToD(htmlTemplate);



// Paste the contents of htmlDCode as D code.

mixin(htmlDCode);
```

Genericity in Eiffel

Generic classes have been a part of Eiffel since the original method and language design. The foundation publications of Eiffel, use the term *genericity* to describe the creation and use of generic classes.

Basic/Unconstrained Genericity

Generic classes are declared with their class name and a list of one or more *formal generic parameters*. In the following code, class LIST has one formal generic parameter G

```
class

    LIST [G]

        . . .
```

```
feature    -- Access

    item: G

            -- The item currently pointed to by cursor

            ...

feature    -- Element change

    put (new_item: G)

            -- Add `new_item' at the end of the list

            ...
```

The formal generic parameters are placeholders for arbitrary class names that will be supplied when a declaration of the generic class is made, as shown in the two *generic derivations* below, where ACCOUNT and DEPOSIT are other class names. ACCOUNT and DEPOSIT are considered *actual generic parameters* as they provide real class names to substitute for G in actual use.

```
list_of_accounts: LIST [ACCOUNT]

        -- Account list

list_of_deposits: LIST [DEPOSIT]

        -- Deposit list
```

Within the Eiffel type system, although class LIST [G] is considered a class, it is not considered a type. However, a generic derivation of LIST [G] such as LIST [ACCOUNT] is considered a type.

Constrained Genericity

For the list class shown above, an actual generic parameter substituting for G can be any other available class. To constrain the set of classes from which valid actual generic parameters can be chosen, a *generic constraint* can be specified. In the declaration of class SORTED_LIST below, the generic constraint dictates that any valid actual generic parameter will be a class that inherits from class COMPARABLE. The generic constraint ensures that elements of a SORTED_LIST can in fact be sorted.

```
class

    SORTED_LIST [G -> COMPARABLE]
```

Generics in Java

Support for the *generics*, or "containers-of-type-T" was added to the Java programming language in 2004 as part of J2SE 5.0. In Java, generics are only checked at compile time for type correctness. The generic type information is then removed via a process called type erasure, to maintain compatibility with old JVM implementations, making it unavailable at runtime. For example, a

List<String> is converted to the raw type List. The compiler inserts type casts to convert the elements to the String type when they are retrieved from the list, reducing performance compared to other implementations such as C++ templates.

Genericity in .NET [C#, VB.NET]

Generics were added as part of .NET Framework 2.0 in November 2005, based on a research prototype from Microsoft Research started in 1999. Although similar to generics in Java, .NET generics do not apply type erasure, but implement generics as a first class mechanism in the runtime using reification. This design choice provides additional functionality, such as allowing reflection with preservation of generic types, as well as alleviating some of the limitations of erasure (such as being unable to create generic arrays). This also means that there is no performance hit from runtime casts and normally expensive boxing conversions. When primitive and value types are used as generic arguments, they get specialized implementations, allowing for efficient generic collections and methods. As in C++ and Java, nested generic types such as Dictionary<string, List<int>> are valid types, however are advised against for member signatures in code analysis design rules.

.NET allows six varieties of generic type constraints using the where keyword including restricting generic types to be value types, to be classes, to have constructors, and to implement interfaces. Below is an example with an interface constraint:

```
using System;

class Sample
{

    static void Main()

    {

        int[] array = { 0, 1, 2, 3 };

        MakeAtLeast<int>(array, 2); // Change array to { 2, 2, 2, 3 }

        foreach (int i in array)

            Console.WriteLine(i); // Print results.

        Console.ReadKey(true);

    }


    static void MakeAtLeast<T>(T[] list, T lowest) where T : IComparable<T>

    {

        for (int i = 0; i < list.Length; i++)
```

```
        if (list[i].CompareTo(lowest) < 0)

            list[i] = lowest;

    }

}
```

The MakeAtLeast() method allows operation on arrays, with elements of generic type T. The method's type constraint indicates that the method is applicable to any type T that implements the generic IComparable<T> interface. This ensures a compile time error, if the method is called if the type does not support comparison. The interface provides the generic method CompareTo(T).

The above method could also be written without generic types, simply using the non-generic Array type. However, since arrays are contravariant, the casting would not be type safe, and compiler may miss errors that would otherwise be caught while making use of the generic types. In addition, the method would need to access the array items as objects instead, and would require casting to compare two elements. (For value types like types such as int this requires a boxing conversion, although this can be worked around using the Comparer<T> class, as is done in the standard collection classes.)

A notable behavior of static members in a generic .NET class is static member instantiation per run-time type.

```
    //A generic class

    public class GenTest<T>

    {

        //A static variable - will be created for each type on refraction

        static CountedInstances OnePerType = new CountedInstances();


        //a data member

        private T mT;

        //simple constructor

        public GenTest(T pT)

        {

            mT = pT;

        }

    }


    //a class
```

```
public class CountedInstances
{
    //Static variable - this will be incremented once per instance
    public static int Counter;

    //simple constructor
    public CountedInstances()
    {
        //increase counter by one during object instantiation
        CountedInstances.Counter++;
    }
}

//main code entry point
//at the end of execution, CountedInstances.Counter = 2
GenTest<int> g1 = new GenTest<int>(1);

GenTest<int> g11 = new GenTest<int>(11);

GenTest<int> g111 = new GenTest<int>(111);

GenTest<double> g2 = new GenTest<double>(1.0);
```

Genericity in Delphi

Delphi's Object Pascal dialect acquired generics in the Delphi 2007 release, initially only with the (now discontinued) .NET compiler before being added to the native code one in the Delphi 2009 release. The semantics and capabilities of Delphi generics are largely modelled on those had by generics in .NET 2.0, though the implementation is by necessity quite different. Here's a more or less direct translation of the first C# example shown above:

```
program Sample;


{$APPTYPE CONSOLE}


uses
```

```
  Generics.Defaults; //for IComparer<>


type

  TUtils = class

    class procedure MakeAtLeast<T>(Arr: TArray<T>; const Lowest: T;

      Comparer: IComparer<T>); overload;

      class procedure MakeAtLeast<T>(Arr: TArray<T>; const Lowest: T);
overload;

  end;


class procedure TUtils.MakeAtLeast<T>(Arr: TArray<T>; const Lowest: T;

  Comparer: IComparer<T>);

var

  I: Integer;

begin

  if Comparer = nil then Comparer := TComparer<T>.Default;

  for I := Low(Arr) to High(Arr) do

    if Comparer.Compare(Arr[I], Lowest) < 0 then

      Arr[I] := Lowest;

end;


class procedure TUtils.MakeAtLeast<T>(Arr: TArray<T>; const Lowest: T);

begin

  MakeAtLeast<T>(Arr, Lowest, nil);

end;


var

  Ints: TArray<Integer>;
```

```
  Value: Integer;

begin

  Ints := TArray<Integer>.Create(0, 1, 2, 3);

  TUtils.MakeAtLeast<Integer>(Ints, 2);

  for Value in Ints do

    WriteLn(Value);

  ReadLn;

end.
```

As with C#, methods as well as whole types can have one or more type parameters. In the example, TArray is a generic type (defined by the language) and MakeAtLeast a generic method. The available constraints are very similar to the available constraints in C#: any value type, any class, a specific class or interface, and a class with a parameterless constructor. Multiple constraints act as an additive union.

Genericity in Free Pascal

Free Pascal implemented generics before Delphi, and with different syntax and semantics. However, work is now underway to implement Delphi generics alongside native FPC ones. This allows Free Pascal programmers to use generics in whatever style they prefer.

Delphi and Free Pascal example:

```
// Delphi style

unit A;


{$ifdef fpc}

  {$mode delphi}

{$endif}


interface


type

  TGenericClass<T> = class

    function Foo(const AValue: T): T;
```

```
  end;


implementation


function TGenericClass<T>.Foo(const AValue: T): T;
begin
  Result := AValue + AValue;
end;


end.
// Free Pascal's ObjFPC style
unit B;
{$ifdef fpc}
  {$mode objfpc}
{$endif}


interface


type
  generic TGenericClass<T> = class
    function Foo(const AValue: T): T;
  end;


implementation
function TGenericClass.Foo(const AValue: T): T;
begin
  Result := AValue + AValue;
end;


end.
```

```
// example usage, Delphi style
program TestGenDelphi;

{$ifdef fpc}
  {$mode delphi}
{$endif}

uses
  A,B;

var
  GC1: A.TGenericClass<Integer>;
  GC2: B.TGenericClass<String>;
begin
  GC1 := A.TGenericClass<Integer>.Create;
  GC2 := B.TGenericClass<String>.Create;
  WriteLn(GC1.Foo(100)); // 200
  WriteLn(GC2.Foo('hello')); // hellohello
  GC1.Free;
  GC2.Free;
end.

// example usage, ObjFPC style
program TestGenDelphi;

{$ifdef fpc}
  {$mode objfpc}
{$endif}

uses
```

```
  A,B;


// required in ObjFPC

type

  TAGenericClassInt = specialize A.TGenericClass<Integer>;

  TBGenericClassString = specialize B.TGenericClass<String>;

var

  GC1: TAGenericClassInt;

  GC2: TBGenericClassString;

begin

  GC1 := TAGenericClassInt.Create;

  GC2 := TBGenericClassString.Create;

  WriteLn(GC1.Foo(100)); // 200

  WriteLn(GC2.Foo('hello')); // hellohello

  GC1.Free;

  GC2.Free;

end.
```

Functional Languages

Genericity in Haskell

The type class mechanism of Haskell supports generic programming. Six of the predefined type classes in Haskell (including Eq, the types that can be compared for equality, and Show, the types whose values can be rendered as strings) have the special property of supporting *derived instances*. This means that a programmer defining a new type can state that this type is to be an instance of one of these special type classes, without providing implementations of the class methods as is usually necessary when declaring class instances. All the necessary methods will be "derived" – that is, constructed automatically – based on the structure of the type. For instance, the following declaration of a type of binary trees states that it is to be an instance of the classes Eq and Show:

```
data BinTree a = Leaf a | Node (BinTree a) a (BinTree a)

      deriving (Eq, Show)
```

This results in an equality function (==) and a string representation function (show) being automatically defined for any type of the form BinTree T provided that T itself supports those operations.

The support for derived instances of Eq and Show makes their methods == and show generic in a qualitatively different way from parametrically polymorphic functions: these "functions" (more accurately, type-indexed families of functions) can be applied to values of various types, and although they behave differently for every argument type, little work is needed to add support for a new type. Ralf Hinze (2004) has shown that a similar effect can be achieved for user-defined type classes by certain programming techniques. Other researchers have proposed approaches to this and other kinds of genericity in the context of Haskell and extensions to Haskell (discussed below).

PolyP

PolyP was the first generic programming language extension to Haskell. In PolyP, generic functions are called *polytypic*. The language introduces a special construct in which such polytypic functions can be defined via structural induction over the structure of the pattern functor of a regular datatype. Regular datatypes in PolyP are a subset of Haskell datatypes. A regular datatype t must be of kind $* \to *$, and if a is the formal type argument in the definition, then all recursive calls to t must have the form $t\ a$. These restrictions rule out higher-kinded datatypes as well as nested datatypes, where the recursive calls are of a different form. The flatten function in PolyP is here provided as an example:

```
flatten :: Regular d => d a -> [a]

flatten = cata fl


polytypic fl :: f a [a] -> [a]

  case f of

    g+h -> either fl fl

    g*h -> \(x,y) -> fl x ++ fl y

    ()  -> \x -> []

    Par -> \x -> [x]

    Rec -> \x -> x

    d@g -> concat . flatten . pmap fl

    Con t -> \x -> []


cata :: Regular d => (FunctorOf d a b -> b) -> d a -> b
```

Generic Haskell

Generic Haskell is another extension to Haskell, developed at Utrecht University in the Netherlands. The extensions it provides are:

Duke, the Java mascot

Sun Microsystems released the first public implementation as Java 1.0 in 1995. It promised "Write Once, Run Anywhere" (WORA), providing no-cost run-times on popular platforms. Fairly secure and featuring configurable security, it allowed network- and file-access restrictions. Major web browsers soon incorporated the ability to run *Java applets* within web pages, and Java quickly became popular. The Java 1.0 compiler was re-written in Java by Arthur van Hoff to comply strictly with the Java 1.0 language specification. With the advent of *Java 2* (released initially as J2SE 1.2 in December 1998 – 1999), new versions had multiple configurations built for different types of platforms. *J2EE* included technologies and APIs for enterprise applications typically run in server environments, while *J2ME* featured APIs optimized for mobile applications. The desktop version was renamed *J2SE*. In 2006, for marketing purposes, Sun renamed new *J2* versions as *Java EE*, *Java ME*, and *Java SE*, respectively.

James Gosling, the creator of Java (2008)

In 1997, Sun Microsystems approached the ISO/IEC JTC 1 standards body and later the Ecma International to formalize Java, but it soon withdrew from the process. Java remains a *de facto* standard, controlled through the Java Community Process. At one time, Sun made most of its Java implementations available without charge, despite their proprietary software status. Sun generated revenue from Java through the selling of licenses for specialized products such as the Java Enterprise System.

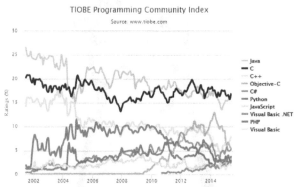

The TIOBE programming language popularity index graph from 2002 to 2015.
Over the course of a decade Java (blue) and C (black) competing for the top position.

On November 13, 2006, Sun released much of its Java virtual machine (JVM) as free and open-source software, (FOSS), under the terms of the GNU General Public License (GPL). On May 8, 2007, Sun finished the process, making all of its JVM's core code available under free software/open-source distribution terms, aside from a small portion of code to which Sun did not hold the copyright.

Sun's vice-president Rich Green said that Sun's ideal role with regard to Java was as an "evangelist". Following Oracle Corporation's acquisition of Sun Microsystems in 2009–10, Oracle has described itself as the "steward of Java technology with a relentless commitment to fostering a community of participation and transparency". This did not prevent Oracle from filing a lawsuit against Google shortly after that for using Java inside the Android SDK. Java software runs on everything from laptops to data centers, game consoles to scientific supercomputers. On April 2, 2010, James Gosling resigned from Oracle.

In January 2016, Oracle announced that Java runtime environments based on JDK 9 will discontinue the browser plugin.

Principles

There were five primary goals in the creation of the Java language:

1. It must be "simple, object-oriented, and familiar".

2. It must be "robust and secure".

3. It must be "architecture-neutral and portable".

4. It must execute with "high performance".

5. It must be "interpreted, threaded, and dynamic".

Versions

As of 2015, only Java 8 is officially supported. Major release versions of Java, along with their release dates:

- JDK 1.0 (January 23, 1996)

- JDK 1.1 (February 19, 1997)

- J2SE 1.2 (December 8, 1998)

- J2SE 1.3 (May 8, 2000)

- J2SE 1.4 (February 6, 2002)

- J2SE 5.0 (September 30, 2004)

- Java SE 6 (December 11, 2006)

- Java SE 7 (July 28, 2011)

- Java SE 8 (March 18, 2014)

Practices

Java Platform

One design goal of Java is portability, which means that programs written for the Java platform must run similarly on any combination of hardware and operating system with adequate runtime support. This is achieved by compiling the Java language code to an intermediate representation called Java bytecode, instead of directly to architecture-specific machine code. Java bytecode instructions are analogous to machine code, but they are intended to be executed by a virtual machine (VM) written specifically for the host hardware. End users commonly use a Java Runtime Environment (JRE) installed on their own machine for standalone Java applications, or in a web browser for Java applets.

Standard libraries provide a generic way to access host-specific features such as graphics, threading, and networking.

The use of universal bytecode makes porting simple. However, the overhead of interpreting bytecode into machine instructions made interpreted programs almost always run more slowly than native executables. Just-in-time (JIT) compilers that compile bytecodes to machine code during runtime were introduced from an early stage. Java itself is platform-independent and is adapted to the particular platform it is to run on by a Java virtual machine for it, which translates the Java bytecode into the platform's machine language.

Implementations

Oracle Corporation is the current owner of the official implementation of the Java SE platform, following their acquisition of Sun Microsystems on January 27, 2010. This implementation is based on the original implementation of Java by Sun. The Oracle implementation is available for Microsoft Windows (still works for XP, while only later versions currently officially supported), macOS, Linux, and Solaris. Because Java lacks any formal standardization recognized by Ecma International, ISO/IEC, ANSI, or other third-party standards organization, the Oracle implementation is the de facto standard.

The Oracle implementation is packaged into two different distributions: The Java Runtime Environment (JRE) which contains the parts of the Java SE platform required to run Java programs and is intended for end users, and the Java Development Kit (JDK), which is intended for software developers and includes development tools such as the Java compiler, Javadoc, Jar, and a debugger.

OpenJDK is another notable Java SE implementation that is licensed under the GNU GPL. The implementation started when Sun began releasing the Java source code under the GPL. As of Java SE 7, OpenJDK is the official Java reference implementation.

The goal of Java is to make all implementations of Java compatible. Historically, Sun's trademark license for usage of the Java brand insists that all implementations be "compatible". This resulted in a legal dispute with Microsoft after Sun claimed that the Microsoft implementation did not support RMI or JNI and had added platform-specific features of their own. Sun sued in 1997, and, in 2001, won a settlement of US$20 million, as well as a court order enforcing the terms of the license from Sun. As a result, Microsoft no longer ships Java with Windows.

Platform-independent Java is essential to Java EE, and an even more rigorous validation is required to certify an implementation. This environment enables portable server-side applications.

Performance

Programs written in Java have a reputation for being slower and requiring more memory than those written in C++. However, Java programs' execution speed improved significantly with the introduction of just-in-time compilation in 1997/1998 for Java 1.1, the addition of language features supporting better code analysis (such as inner classes, the StringBuilder class, optional assertions, etc.), and optimizations in the Java virtual machine, such as HotSpot becoming the default for Sun's JVM in 2000. With Java 1.5, the performance was improved with the addition of the java.util.concurrent package, including Lock free implementations of the ConcurrentMaps and other multi-core collections, and it was improved further Java 1.6.

Some platforms offer direct hardware support for Java; there are microcontrollers that can run Java in hardware instead of a software Java virtual machine, and some ARM based processors could have hardware support for executing Java bytecode through their Jazelle option, though support has mostly been dropped in current implementations of ARM.

Automatic Memory Management

Java uses an automatic garbage collector to manage memory in the object lifecycle. The programmer determines when objects are created, and the Java runtime is responsible for recovering the memory once objects are no longer in use. Once no references to an object remain, the unreachable memory becomes eligible to be freed automatically by the garbage collector. Something similar to a memory leak may still occur if a programmer's code holds a reference to an object that is no longer needed, typically when objects that are no longer needed are stored in containers that are still in use. If methods for a nonexistent object are called, a "null pointer exception" is thrown.

One of the ideas behind Java's automatic memory management model is that programmers can be spared the burden of having to perform manual memory management. In some languages, memory for the creation of objects is implicitly allocated on the stack or explicitly allocated and deallocated from the heap. In the latter case, the responsibility of managing memory resides with the programmer. If the program does not deallocate an object, a memory leak occurs. If the program attempts to access or deallocate memory that has already been deallocated, the result is undefined and difficult to predict, and the program is likely to become unstable and/or crash. This can be partially remedied by the use of smart pointers, but these add overhead and complexity. Note that garbage collection does not prevent "logical" memory leaks, *i.e.*, those where the memory is still referenced but never used.

Garbage collection may happen at any time. Ideally, it will occur when a program is idle. It is guaranteed to be triggered if there is insufficient free memory on the heap to allocate a new object; this can cause a program to stall momentarily. Explicit memory management is not possible in Java.

Java does not support C/C++ style pointer arithmetic, where object addresses and unsigned integers (usually long integers) can be used interchangeably. This allows the garbage collector to relocate referenced objects and ensures type safety and security.

As in C++ and some other object-oriented languages, variables of Java's primitive data types are either stored directly in fields (for objects) or on the stack (for methods) rather than on the heap, as is commonly true for non-primitive data types. This was a conscious decision by Java's designers for performance reasons.

Java contains multiple types of garbage collectors. By default, HotSpot uses the parallel scavenge garbage collector. However, there are also several other garbage collectors that can be used to manage the heap. For 90% of applications in Java, the Concurrent Mark-Sweep (CMS) garbage collector is sufficient. Oracle aims to replace CMS with the Garbage-First collector (G1).

Syntax

The syntax of Java is largely influenced by C++. Unlike C++, which combines the syntax for structured, generic, and object-oriented programming, Java was built almost exclusively as an object-oriented language. All code is written inside classes, and every data item is an object, with the exception of the primitive data types, (*i.e.* integers, floating-point numbers, boolean values, and characters), which are not objects for performance reasons. Java reuses some popular aspects of C++ (such as printf() method).

Unlike C++, Java does not support operator overloading or multiple inheritance for *classes*, though multiple inheritance is supported for interfaces. This simplifies the language and aids in preventing potential errors and anti-pattern design.

Java uses comments similar to those of C++. There are three different styles of comments: a single line style marked with two slashes (//), a multiple line style opened with /* and closed with */, and the Javadoc commenting style opened with /** and closed with */. The Javadoc style of commenting allows the user to run the Javadoc executable to create documentation for the program and can be read by some integrated development environments (IDEs) such as Eclipse to allow developers to access documentation within the IDE.

Example

```
// This is an example of a single line comment using two slashes

/* This is an example of a multiple line comment using the slash and as-
terisk.

 This type of comment can be used to hold a lot of information or deac-
tivate

 code, but it is very important to remember to close the comment. */

package fibsandlies;

import java.util.HashMap;

/**

 * This is an example of a Javadoc comment; Javadoc can compile documen-
tation

 * from this text. Javadoc comments must immediately precede the class,
method, or field being documented.

 */

public class FibCalculator extends Fibonacci implements Calculator {

    private static Map<Integer, Integer> memoized = new HashMap<Integer,
Integer>();

    /*

     * The main method written as follows is used by the JVM as a start-
ing point for the program.

     */

    public static void main(String[] args) {

        memoized.put(1, 1);

        memoized.put(2, 1);

        System.out.println(fibonacci(12)); //Get the 12th Fibonacci number
and print to console

    }

    /**

     * An example of a method written in Java, wrapped in a class.

     * Given a non-negative number FIBINDEX, returns
```

```
 *  the Nth Fibonacci number, where N equals FIBINDEX.
 *  @param fibIndex The index of the Fibonacci number
 *  @return The Fibonacci number
 */
public static int fibonacci(int fibIndex) {
    if (memoized.containsKey(fibIndex)) {
        return memoized.get(fibIndex);
    } else {
        int answer = fibonacci(fibIndex - 1) + fibonacci(fibIndex - 2);
        memoized.put(fibIndex, answer);
        return answer;
    }
}
}
```

"Hello World" Example

The traditional "Hello, world!" program can be written in Java as:

```
class HelloWorldApp {
    public static void main(String[] args) {
        System.out.println("Hello World!"); // Prints the string to the
console.
    }
}
```

Source files must be named after the public class they contain, appending the suffix .java, for example, HelloWorldApp.java. It must first be compiled into bytecode, using a Java compiler, producing a file named HelloWorldApp.class. Only then can it be executed, or "launched". The Java source file may only contain one public class, but it can contain multiple classes with other than public access and any number of public inner classes. When the source file contains multiple classes, make one class "public" and name the source file with that public class name.

A class that is not declared public may be stored in any .java file. The compiler will generate a class file for each class defined in the source file. The name of the class file is the name of the class, with

.class appended. For class file generation, anonymous classes are treated as if their name were the concatenation of the name of their enclosing class, a $, and an integer.

The keyword public denotes that a method can be called from code in other classes, or that a class may be used by classes outside the class hierarchy. The class hierarchy is related to the name of the directory in which the .java file is located. This is called an access level modifier. Other access level modifiers include the keywords private and protected.

The keyword static in front of a method indicates a static method, which is associated only with the class and not with any specific instance of that class. Only static methods can be invoked without a reference to an object. Static methods cannot access any class members that are not also static. Methods that are not designated static are instance methods and require a specific instance of a class to operate.

The keyword void indicates that the main method does not return any value to the caller. If a Java program is to exit with an error code, it must call System.exit() explicitly.

The method name "main" is not a keyword in the Java language. It is simply the name of the method the Java launcher calls to pass control to the program. Java classes that run in managed environments such as applets and Enterprise JavaBeans do not use or need a main() method. A Java program may contain multiple classes that have main methods, which means that the VM needs to be explicitly told which class to launch from.

The main method must accept an array of String objects. By convention, it is referenced as args although any other legal identifier name can be used. Since Java 5, the main method can also use variable arguments, in the form of public static void main(String... args), allowing the main method to be invoked with an arbitrary number of String arguments. The effect of this alternate declaration is semantically identical (the args parameter is still an array of String objects), but it allows an alternative syntax for creating and passing the array.

The Java launcher launches Java by loading a given class (specified on the command line or as an attribute in a JAR) and starting its public static void main(String[]) method. Stand-alone programs must declare this method explicitly. The String[] args parameter is an array of String objects containing any arguments passed to the class. The parameters to main are often passed by means of a command line.

Printing is part of a Java standard library: The System class defines a public static field called out. The out object is an instance of the PrintStream class and provides many methods for printing data to standard out, including println(String) which also appends a new line to the passed string.

The string "Hello World!" is automatically converted to a String object by the compiler.

Special Classes

Applet

Java applets are programs that are embedded in other applications, typically in a Web page displayed in a web browser.

```
// Hello.java

import javax.swing.JApplet;

import java.awt.Graphics;

public class Hello extends JApplet {

    public void paintComponent(final Graphics g) {

        g.drawString("Hello, world!", 65, 95);

    }

}
```

The import statements direct the Java compiler to include the javax.swing.JApplet and java.awt. Graphics classes in the compilation. The import statement allows these classes to be referenced in the source code using the *simple class name* (i.e. JApplet) instead of the *fully qualified class name* (*FQCN*, i.e. javax.swing.JApplet).

The Hello class extends (subclasses) the JApplet (Java Applet) class; the JApplet class provides the framework for the host application to display and control the lifecycle of the applet. The JApplet class is a JComponent (Java Graphical Component) which provides the applet with the capability to display a graphical user interface (GUI) and respond to user events.

The Hello class overrides the paintComponent(Graphics) method (additionally indicated with the annotation, supported as of JDK 1.5, Override) inherited from the Container superclass to provide the code to display the applet. The paintComponent() method is passed a Graphics object that contains the graphic context used to display the applet. The paintComponent() method calls the graphic context drawString(String, int, int) method to display the "Hello, world!" string at a pixel offset of (65, 95) from the upper-left corner in the applet's display.

```
<!DOCTYPE HTML PUBLIC "-//W3C//DTD HTML 4.01//EN"

"http://www.w3.org/TR/html4/strict.dtd">

<!-- Hello.html -->

<html>

    <head>

        <title>Hello World Applet</title>

    </head>

    <body>

        <applet code="Hello.class" width="200" height="200">

        </applet>
```

```
    </body>
```

```
</html>
```

An applet is placed in an HTML document using the <applet> HTML element. The applet tag has three attributes set: code="Hello" specifies the name of the JApplet class and width="200" height="200" sets the pixel width and height of the applet. Applets may also be embedded in HTML using either the object or embed element, although support for these elements by web browsers is inconsistent. However, the applet tag is deprecated, so the object tag is preferred where supported.

The host application, typically a Web browser, instantiates the Hello applet and creates an Applet-Context for the applet. Once the applet has initialized itself, it is added to the AWT display hierarchy. The paintComponent() method is called by the AWT event dispatching thread whenever the display needs the applet to draw itself.

Servlet

Java Servlet technology provides Web developers with a simple, consistent mechanism for extending the functionality of a Web server and for accessing existing business systems. Servlets are server-side Java EE components that generate responses (typically HTML pages) to requests (typically HTTP requests) from clients. A servlet can almost be thought of as an applet that runs on the server side—without a face.

```java
// Hello.java

import java.io.*;

import javax.servlet.*;

public class Hello extends GenericServlet {

    public void service(final ServletRequest request, final ServletResponse response)

    throws ServletException, IOException {

        response.setContentType("text/html");

        final PrintWriter pw = response.getWriter();

        try {

            pw.println("Hello, world!");

        } finally {

            pw.close();

        }

    }

}
```

The import statements direct the Java compiler to include all the public classes and interfaces from the java.io and javax.servlet packages in the compilation. Packages make Java well suited for large scale applications.

The Hello class extends the GenericServlet class; the GenericServlet class provides the interface for the server to forward requests to the servlet and control the servlet's lifecycle.

The Hello class overrides the service(ServletRequest, ServletResponse) method defined by the Servlet interface to provide the code for the service request handler. The service() method is passed: a ServletRequest object that contains the request from the client and a ServletResponse object used to create the response returned to the client. The service() method declares that it throws the exceptions ServletException and IOException if a problem prevents it from responding to the request.

The setContentType(String) method in the response object is called to set the MIME content type of the returned data to "text/html". The getWriter() method in the response returns a Print-Writer object that is used to write the data that is sent to the client. The println(String) method is called to write the "Hello, world!" string to the response and then the close() method is called to close the print writer, which causes the data that has been written to the stream to be returned to the client.

JavaServer Pages

JavaServer Pages (JSP) are server-side Java EE components that generate responses, typically HTML pages, to HTTP requests from clients. JSPs embed Java code in an HTML page by using the special delimiters <% and %>. A JSP is compiled to a Java *servlet*, a Java application in its own right, the first time it is accessed. After that, the generated servlet creates the response.

Swing Application

Swing is a graphical user interface library for the Java SE platform. It is possible to specify a different look and feel through the pluggable look and feel system of Swing. Clones of Windows, GTK+, and Motif are supplied by Sun. Apple also provides an Aqua look and feel for macOS. Where prior implementations of these looks and feels may have been considered lacking, Swing in Java SE 6 addresses this problem by using more native GUI widget drawing routines of the underlying platforms.

This example Swing application creates a single window with "Hello, world!" inside:

```java
// Hello.java (Java SE 5)

import javax.swing.*;

public class Hello extends JFrame {

    public Hello() {

        super("hello");

        super.setDefaultCloseOperation(WindowConstants.EXIT_ON_CLOSE);
```

```
        super.add(new JLabel("Hello, world!"));

        super.pack();

        super.setVisible(true);

    }

    public static void main(final String[] args) {

        new Hello();

    }

}
```

The first import includes all the public classes and interfaces from the javax.swing package.

The Hello class extends the JFrame class; the JFrame class implements a window with a title bar and a close control.

The Hello() constructor initializes the frame by first calling the superclass constructor, passing the parameter "hello", which is used as the window's title. It then calls the setDefaultCloseOperation(int) method inherited from JFrame to set the default operation when the close control on the title bar is selected to WindowConstants.EXIT_ON_CLOSE – this causes the JFrame to be disposed of when the frame is closed (as opposed to merely hidden), which allows the Java virtual machine to exit and the program to terminate. Next, a JLabel is created for the string "Hello, world!" and the add(Component) method inherited from the Container superclass is called to add the label to the frame. The pack() method inherited from the Window superclass is called to size the window and lay out its contents.

The main() method is called by the Java virtual machine when the program starts. It instantiates a new Hello frame and causes it to be displayed by calling the setVisible(boolean) method inherited from the Component superclass with the boolean parameter true. Once the frame is displayed, exiting the main method does not cause the program to terminate because the AWT event dispatching thread remains active until all of the Swing top-level windows have been disposed.

Generics

In 2004, generics were added to the Java language, as part of J2SE 5.0. Prior to the introduction of generics, each variable declaration had to be of a specific type. For container classes, for example, this is a problem because there is no easy way to create a container that accepts only specific types of objects. Either the container operates on all subtypes of a class or interface, usually Object, or a different container class has to be created for each contained class. Generics allow compile-time type checking without having to create many container classes, each containing almost identical code. In addition to enabling more efficient code, certain runtime exceptions are prevented from occurring, by issuing compile-time errors. If Java prevented all runtime type errors (ClassCastException's) from occurring, it would be type safe.

In 2016, the type system was shown not to be safe at all, it was proven unsound.

Criticism

Criticisms directed at Java include the implementation of generics, speed, the handling of unsigned numbers, the implementation of floating-point arithmetic, and a history of security vulnerabilities in the primary Java VM implementation HotSpot.

Use Outside of the Java Platform

The Java programming language requires the presence of a software platform in order for compiled programs to be executed. Oracle supplies the Java platform for use with Java. The Android SDK is an alternative software platform, used primarily for developing Android applications.

Android

The Android operating system makes extensive use of Java-related technology.

The Java language is a key pillar in Android, an open source mobile operating system. Although Android, built on the Linux kernel, is written largely in C, the Android SDK uses the Java language as the basis for Android applications. The bytecode language supported by the Android SDK is incompatible with Java bytecode and runs on its own virtual machine, optimized for low-memory devices such as smartphones and tablet computers. Depending on the Android version, the bytecode is either interpreted by the Dalvik virtual machine or compiled into native code by the Android Runtime.

Android does not provide the full Java SE standard library, although the Android SDK does include an independent implementation of a large subset of it. It supports Java 6 and some Java 7 features, offering an implementation compatible with the standard library (Apache Harmony).

Controversy

The use of Java-related technology in Android led to a legal dispute between Oracle and Google. On May 7, 2012, a San Francisco jury found that if APIs could be copyrighted, then Google had infringed Oracle's copyrights by the use of Java in Android devices. District Judge William Haskell Alsup ruled on May 31, 2012, that APIs cannot be copyrighted, but this was reversed by the United States Court of Appeals for the Federal Circuit in May 2014. On May 26, 2016, the district court decided in favor of Google, ruling the copyright infringement of the Java API in Android constitutes fair use.

Class Libraries

The Java Class Library is the standard library, developed to support application development in Java. It is controlled by Sun Microsystems in cooperation with others through the Java Community Process program. Companies or individuals participating in this process can influence the design and development of the APIs. This process has been a subject of controversy. The class library contains features such as:

- The core libraries, which include:

    o   IO/NIO

    o   Networking

    o   Reflection

    o   Concurrency

    o   Generics

    o   Scripting/Compiler

    o   Functional Programming (Lambda, Streaming)

    o   Collection libraries that implement data structures such as lists, dictionaries, trees, sets, queues and double-ended queue, or stacks

    o   XML Processing (Parsing, Transforming, Validating) libraries

    o   Security

    o   Internationalization and localization libraries

- The integration libraries, which allow the application writer to communicate with external systems. These libraries include:

    o   The Java Database Connectivity (JDBC) API for database access

    o   Java Naming and Directory Interface (JNDI) for lookup and discovery

    o   RMI and CORBA for distributed application development

    o   JMX for managing and monitoring applications

- User interface libraries, which include:

    o   The (heavyweight, or native) Abstract Window Toolkit (AWT), which provides GUI components, the means for laying out those components and the means for handling events from those components

- o   The (lightweight) Swing libraries, which are built on AWT but provide (non-native) implementations of the AWT widgetry

- o   APIs for audio capture, processing, and playback

- o   JavaFX

- A platform dependent implementation of the Java virtual machine that is the means by which the bytecodes of the Java libraries and third party applications are executed

- Plugins, which enable applets to be run in web browsers

- Java Web Start, which allows Java applications to be efficiently distributed to end users across the Internet

- Licensing and documentation

Documentation

Javadoc is a comprehensive documentation system, created by Sun Microsystems, used by many Java developers. It provides developers with an organized system for documenting their code. Javadoc comments have an extra asterisk at the beginning, i.e. the delimiters are /** and */, whereas the normal multi-line comments in Java are set off with the delimiters /* and */.

Editions

Sun has defined and supports four editions of Java targeting different application environments and segmented many of its APIs so that they belong to one of the platforms. The platforms are:

- Java Card for smartcards.

- Java Platform, Micro Edition (Java ME) – targeting environments with limited resources.

- Java Platform, Standard Edition (Java SE) – targeting workstation environments.

- Java Platform, Enterprise Edition (Java EE) – targeting large distributed enterprise or Internet environments.

The classes in the Java APIs are organized into separate groups called packages. Each package contains a set of related interfaces, classes, and exceptions. Refer to the separate platforms for a description of the packages available.

Sun also provided an edition called PersonalJava that has been superseded by later, standards-based Java ME configuration-profile pairings.

C++ is a general-purpose programming language. It has imperative, object-oriented and generic programming features, while also providing facilities for low-level memory manipulation.

It was designed with a bias toward system programming and embedded, resource-constrained and large systems, with performance, efficiency and flexibility of use as its design highlights. C++ has also been found useful in many other contexts, with key strengths being software infrastructure and resource-constrained applications, including desktop applications, servers (e.g. e-commerce, web search or SQL servers), and performance-critical applications (e.g. telephone switches or space probes). C++ is a compiled language, with implementations of it available on many platforms. Many vendors provide C++ compilers, including the Free Software Foundation, Microsoft, Intel, and IBM.

C++ is standardized by the International Organization for Standardization (ISO), with the latest standard version ratified and published by ISO in December 2014 as *ISO/IEC 14882:2014* (informally known as C++14). The C++ programming language was initially standardized in 1998 as *ISO/IEC 14882:1998*, which was then amended by the C++03, *ISO/IEC 14882:2003*, standard. The current C++14 standard supersedes these and C++11, with new features and an enlarged standard library. Before the initial standardization in 1998, C++ was developed by Bjarne Stroustrup at Bell Labs since 1979, as an extension of the C language as he wanted an efficient and flexible language similar to C, which also provided high-level features for program organization. The C++17 standard is due in July 2017, with the draft largely implemented by some compilers already, and C++20 is the next planned standard thereafter.

Many other programming languages have been influenced by C++, including C#, D, Java, and newer versions of C.

History

Bjarne Stroustrup, the creator of C++

In 1979, Bjarne Stroustrup, a Danish computer scientist, began work on "C with Classes", the predecessor to C++. The motivation for creating a new language originated from Stroustrup's experience in programming for his Ph.D. thesis. Stroustrup found that Simula had features that were very helpful for large software development, but the language was too slow for practical use, while BCPL was fast but too low-level to be suitable for large software development. When Stroustrup started working in AT&T Bell Labs, he had the problem of analyzing the UNIX kernel with respect to distributed computing. Remembering his Ph.D. experience, Stroustrup set out to enhance the C language with Simula-like features. C was chosen because it was general-purpose, fast, portable and widely used. As well as C and Simula's influences, other languages also influenced C++, including ALGOL 68, Ada, CLU and ML.

Initially, Stroustrup's "C with Classes" added features to the C compiler, Cpre, including classes, derived classes, strong typing, inlining and default arguments.

In 1983, "C with Classes" was renamed to "C++" (++ being the increment operator in C), adding new features that included virtual functions, function name and operator overloading, references, constants, type-safe free-store memory allocation (new/delete), improved type checking, and BCPL style single-line comments with two forward slashes (//). Furthermore, it included the development of a standalone compiler for C++, Cfront.

In 1985, the first edition of *The C++ Programming Language* was released, which became the definitive reference for the language, as there was not yet an official standard. The first commercial implementation of C++ was released in October of the same year.

In 1989, C++ 2.0 was released, followed by the updated second edition of *The C++ Programming Language* in 1991. New features in 2.0 included multiple inheritance, abstract classes, static member functions, const member functions, and protected members. In 1990, *The Annotated C++ Reference Manual* was published. This work became the basis for the future standard. Later feature additions included templates, exceptions, namespaces, new casts, and a boolean type.

After the 2.0 update, C++ evolved relatively slowly until, in 2011, the C++11 standard was released, adding numerous new features, enlarging the standard library further, and providing more facilities to C++ programmers. After a minor C++14 update released in December 2014, various new additions are planned for July 2017 and 2020.

Etymology

According to Stroustrup: "the name signifies the evolutionary nature of the changes from C". This name is credited to Rick Mascitti (mid-1983) and was first used in December 1983. When Mascitti was questioned informally in 1992 about the naming, he indicated that it was given in a tongue-in-cheek spirit. The name comes from C's ++ operator (which increments the value of a variable) and a common naming convention of using "+" to indicate an enhanced computer program.

During C++'s development period, the language had been referred to as "new C" and "C with Classes" before acquiring its final name.

Philosophy

Throughout C++'s life, its development and evolution has been informally governed by a set of rules that its evolution should follow:

- It must be driven by actual problems and its features should be useful immediately in real world programs.

- Every feature should be implementable (with a reasonably obvious way to do so).

- Programmers should be free to pick their own programming style, and that style should be fully supported by C++.

- Allowing a useful feature is more important than preventing every possible misuse of C++.

- It should provide facilities for organising programs into well-defined separate parts, and provide facilities for combining separately developed parts.

- No implicit violations of the type system (but allow explicit violations; that is, those explicitly requested by the programmer).

- User-created types need to have the same support and performance as built-in types.

- Unused features should not negatively impact created executables (e.g. in lower performance).

- There should be no language beneath C++ (except assembly language).

- C++ should work alongside other existing programming languages, rather than fostering its own separate and incompatible programming environment.

- If the programmer's intent is unknown, allow the programmer to specify it by providing manual control.

Standardization

Year	C++ Standard	Informal name
1998	ISO/IEC 14882:1998	C++98
2003	ISO/IEC 14882:2003	C++03
2011	ISO/IEC 14882:2011	C++11
2014	ISO/IEC 14882:2014	C++14
2017	to be determined	C++17
2020	to be determined	C++20

C++ is standardized by an ISO working group known as JTC1/SC22/WG21. So far, it has published four revisions of the C++ standard and is currently working on the next revision, C++17.

In 1998, the ISO working group standardized C++ for the first time as *ISO/IEC 14882:1998*, which is informally known as *C++98*. In 2003, it published a new version of the C++ standard called *ISO/IEC 14882:2003*, which fixed problems identified in C++98.

The next major revision of the standard was informally referred to as "C++0x", but it was not released until 2011. C++11 (14882:2011) included many additions to both the core language and the standard library.

In 2014, C++14 (also known as C++1y) was released as a small extension to C++11, featuring mainly bug fixes and small improvements. The Draft International Standard ballot procedures completed in mid-August 2014.

After C++14, a major revision, informally known as C++17 or C++1z, is expected in July 2017, which is feature-complete.

As part of the standardization process, ISO also publishes technical reports and specifications:

- ISO/IEC TR 18015:2006 on the use of C++ in embedded systems and on performance implications of C++ language and library features,

- ISO/IEC TR 19768:2007 (also known as the C++ Technical Report 1) on library extensions mostly integrated into C++11,

- ISO/IEC TR 29124:2010 on special mathematical functions,

- ISO/IEC TR 24733:2011 on decimal floating point arithmetic,

- ISO/IEC TS 18822:2015 on the standard filesystem library,

- ISO/IEC TS 19570:2015 on parallel versions of the standard library algorithms,

- ISO/IEC TS 19841:2015 on software transactional memory,

- ISO/IEC TS 19568:2015 on a new set of library extensions, some of which are already integrated into C++17,

- ISO/IEC TS 19217:2015 on the C++ Concepts

More technical specifications are in development and pending approval, including concurrency library extensions, a networking standard library, ranges, and modules.

Language

The C++ language has two main components: a direct mapping of hardware features provided primarily by the C subset, and zero-overhead abstractions based on those mappings. Stroustrup describes C++ as "a light-weight abstraction programming language [designed] for building and using efficient and elegant abstractions"; and "offering both hardware access and abstraction is the basis of C++. Doing it efficiently is what distinguishes it from other languages".

C++ inherits most of C's syntax. The following is Bjarne Stroustrup's version of the Hello world program that uses the C++ Standard Library stream facility to write a message to standard output:

```
#include <iostream>

int main()

{

        std::cout << "Hello, world!\n";

    return 0;

}
```

Within functions that define a non-void return type, failure to return a value before control reaches the end of the function results in undefined behaviour (compilers typically provide the means to issue a diagnostic in such a case). The sole exception to this rule is the main function, which implicitly returns a value of zero.

Object Storage

As in C, C++ supports four types of memory management: static storage duration objects, thread storage duration objects, automatic storage duration objects, and dynamic storage duration objects.

Static Storage Duration Objects

Static storage duration objects are created before main() is entered and destroyed in reverse order of creation after main() exits. The exact order of creation is not specified by the standard (though there are some rules defined below) to allow implementations some freedom in how to organize their implementation. More formally, objects of this type have a lifespan that "shall last for the duration of the program".

Static storage duration objects are initialized in two phases. First, "static initialization" is performed, and only *after* all static initialization is performed, "dynamic initialization" is performed. In static initialization, all objects are first initialized with zeros; after that, all objects that have a constant initialization phase are initialized with the constant expression (i.e. variables initialized with a literal or constexpr). Though it is not specified in the standard, the static initialization phase can be completed at compile time and saved in the data partition of the executable. Dynamic initialization involves all object initialization done via a constructor or function call (unless the function is marked with constexpr, in C++11). The dynamic initialization order is defined as the order of declaration within the compilation unit (i.e. the same file). No guarantees are provided about the order of initialization between compilation units.

Thread Storage Duration Objects

Variables of this type are very similar to static storage duration objects. The main difference is the creation time is just prior to thread creation and destruction is done after the thread has been joined.

Automatic Storage Duration Objects

The most common variable types in C++ are local variables inside a function or block, and temporary variables. The common feature about automatic variables is that they have a lifetime that is limited to the scope of the variable. They are created and potentially initialized at the point of declaration and destroyed in the *reverse* order of creation when the scope is left.

Local variables are created as the point of execution passes the declaration point. If the variable has a constructor or initializer this is used to define the initial state of the object. Local variables are destroyed when the local block or function that they are declared in is closed. C++ destructors for local variables are called at the end of the object lifetime, allowing a discipline for automatic resource management termed RAII, which is widely used in C++.

Member variables are created when the parent object is created. Array members are initialized from 0 to the last member of the array in order. Member variables are destroyed when the parent object is destroyed in the reverse order of creation. i.e. If the parent is an "automatic object" then it will be destroyed when it goes out of scope which triggers the destruction of all its members.

Temporary variables are created as the result of expression evaluation and are destroyed when the statement containing the expression has been fully evaluated (usually at the ; at the end of a statement).

Dynamic Storage Duration Objects

These objects have a dynamic lifespan and are created with a call to new and destroyed explicitly with a call to delete.

Templates

C++ templates enable generic programming. C++ supports function, class, alias and variable templates. Templates may be parameterized by types, compile-time constants, and other templates. Templates are implemented by *instantiation* at compile-time. To instantiate a template, compilers substitute specific arguments for a template's parameters to generate a concrete function or class instance. Some substitutions are not possible; these are eliminated by an overload resolution policy described by the phrase "Substitution failure is not an error" (SFINAE). Templates are a powerful tool that can be used for generic programming, template metaprogramming, and code optimization, but this power implies a cost. Template use may increase code size, because each template instantiation produces a copy of the template code: one for each set of template arguments, however, this is the same or smaller amount of code that would be generated if the code was written by hand. This is in contrast to run-time generics seen in other languages (e.g., Java) where at compile-time the type is erased and a single template body is preserved.

Templates are different from macros: while both of these compile-time language features enable conditional compilation, templates are not restricted to lexical substitution. Templates are aware of the semantics and type system of their companion language, as well as all compile-time type definitions, and can perform high-level operations including programmatic flow control based on evaluation of strictly type-checked parameters. Macros are capable of conditional control over compilation based on predetermined criteria, but cannot instantiate new types, recurse, or perform type evaluation and in effect are limited to pre-compilation text-substitution and text-inclusion/exclusion. In other words, macros can control compilation flow based on pre-defined symbols but cannot, unlike templates, independently instantiate new symbols. Templates are a tool for static polymorphism and generic programming.

In addition, templates are a compile time mechanism in C++ that is Turing-complete, meaning that any computation expressible by a computer program can be computed, in some form, by a template metaprogram prior to runtime.

In summary, a template is a compile-time parameterized function or class written without knowledge of the specific arguments used to instantiate it. After instantiation, the resulting code is equivalent to code written specifically for the passed arguments. In this manner, templates provide a way to decouple generic, broadly applicable aspects of functions and classes (encoded in templates) from specific aspects (encoded in template parameters) without sacrificing performance due to abstraction.

Objects

C++ introduces object-oriented programming (OOP) features to C. It offers classes, which provide the four features commonly present in OOP (and some non-OOP) languages: abstraction, encapsulation, inheritance, and polymorphism. One distinguishing feature of C++ classes compared to classes in other programming languages is support for deterministic destructors, which in turn provide support for the Resource Acquisition is Initialization (RAII) concept.

Encapsulation

Encapsulation is the hiding of information to ensure that data structures and operators are used as intended and to make the usage model more obvious to the developer. C++ provides the ability to define classes and functions as its primary encapsulation mechanisms. Within a class, members can be declared as either public, protected, or private to explicitly enforce encapsulation. A public member of the class is accessible to any function. A private member is accessible only to functions that are members of that class and to functions and classes explicitly granted access permission by the class ("friends"). A protected member is accessible to members of classes that inherit from the class in addition to the class itself and any friends.

The OO principle is that all of the functions (and only the functions) that access the internal representation of a type should be encapsulated within the type definition. C++ supports this (via member functions and friend functions), but does not enforce it: the programmer can declare parts or all of the representation of a type to be public, and is allowed to make public entities that are not part of the representation of the type. Therefore, C++ supports not just OO programming, but other decomposition paradigms, like modular programming.

It is generally considered good practice to make all data private or protected, and to make public only those functions that are part of a minimal interface for users of the class. This can hide the details of data implementation, allowing the designer to later fundamentally change the implementation without changing the interface in any way.

Inheritance

Inheritance allows one data type to acquire properties of other data types. Inheritance from a base class may be declared as public, protected, or private. This access specifier determines whether unrelated and derived classes can access the inherited public and protected members of the base class. Only public inheritance corresponds to what is usually meant by "inheritance". The other two forms are much less frequently used. If the access specifier is omitted, a "class" inherits privately, while a "struct" inherits publicly. Base classes may be declared as virtual; this is called virtual inheritance. Virtual inheritance ensures that only one instance of a base class exists in the inheritance graph, avoiding some of the ambiguity problems of multiple inheritance.

Multiple inheritance is a C++ feature not found in most other languages, allowing a class to be derived from more than one base class; this allows for more elaborate inheritance relationships. For example, a "Flying Cat" class can inherit from both "Cat" and "Flying Mammal". Some other languages, such as C# or Java, accomplish something similar (although more limited) by allowing inheritance of multiple interfaces while restricting the number of base classes to one (interfaces, unlike classes, provide only declarations of member functions, no implementation or member data). An interface as in C# and Java can be defined in C++ as a class containing only pure virtual functions, often known as an abstract base class or "ABC". The member functions of such an abstract base class are normally explicitly defined in the derived class, not inherited implicitly. C++ virtual inheritance exhibits an ambiguity resolution feature called dominance.

Operators and Operator Overloading

Operators that cannot be overloaded	
Operator	**Symbol**
Scope resolution operator	`::`
Conditional operator	`?:`
dot operator	`.`
Member selection operator	`.*`
"sizeof" operator	`sizeof`
"typeid" operator	`typeid`

C++ provides more than 35 operators, covering basic arithmetic, bit manipulation, indirection, comparisons, logical operations and others. Almost all operators can be overloaded for user-defined types, with a few notable exceptions such as member access (. and .*) as well as the conditional operator. The rich set of overloadable operators is central to making user-defined types in C++ seem like built-in types.

Overloadable operators are also an essential part of many advanced C++ programming techniques, such as smart pointers. Overloading an operator does not change the precedence of calculations involving the operator, nor does it change the number of operands that the operator uses (any operand may however be ignored by the operator, though it will be evaluated prior to execution). Overloaded "&&" and "||" operators lose their short-circuit evaluation property.

Polymorphism

Polymorphism enables one common interface for many implementations, and for objects to act differently under different circumstances.

C++ supports several kinds of *static* (resolved at compile-time) and *dynamic* (resolved at run-time) polymorphisms, supported by the language features described above. Compile-time polymorphism does not allow for certain run-time decisions, while runtime polymorphism typically incurs a performance penalty.

Static Polymorphism

Function overloading allows programs to declare multiple functions having the same name but with different arguments (i.e. *ad hoc* polymorphism). The functions are distinguished by the number or types of their formal parameters. Thus, the same function name can refer to different functions depending on the context in which it is used. The type returned by the function is not used to distinguish overloaded functions and would result in a compile-time error message.

When declaring a function, a programmer can specify for one or more parameters a default value. Doing so allows the parameters with defaults to optionally be omitted when the function is called, in which case the default arguments will be used. When a function is called with fewer arguments than there are declared parameters, explicit arguments are matched to parameters in left-to-right order, with any unmatched parameters at the end of the parameter list being assigned their default arguments. In many cases, specifying default arguments in a single function declaration is preferable to providing overloaded function definitions with different numbers of parameters.

Templates in C++ provide a sophisticated mechanism for writing generic, polymorphic code (i.e. parametric polymorphism). In particular, through the Curiously Recurring Template Pattern, it's possible to implement a form of static polymorphism that closely mimics the syntax for overriding virtual functions. Because C++ templates are type-aware and Turing-complete, they can also be used to let the compiler resolve recursive conditionals and generate substantial programs through template metaprogramming. Contrary to some opinion, template code will not generate a bulk code after compilation with the proper compiler settings.

Dynamic Polymorphism

Inheritance

Variable pointers and references to a base class type in C++ can also refer to objects of any derived classes of that type. This allows arrays and other kinds of containers to hold pointers to objects of differing types (references cannot be directly held in containers). This enables dynamic (run-time) polymorphism, where the referred objects can behave differently depending on their (actual, derived) types.

C++ also provides the dynamic_cast operator, which allows code to safely attempt conversion of an object, via a base reference/pointer, to a more derived type: *downcasting*. The *attempt* is necessary as often one does not know which derived type is referenced. (*Upcasting*, conversion to a more general type, can always be checked/performed at compile-time via static_cast, as ancestral classes are specified in the derived class's interface, visible to all callers.) dynamic_cast relies on run-time type information (RTTI), metadata in the program that enables differentiating types and their relationships. If a dynamic_cast to a pointer fails, the result is the nullptr constant, whereas if the destination is a reference (which cannot be null), the cast throws an exception. Objects *known* to be of a certain derived type can be cast to that with static_cast, bypassing RTTI and the safe runtime type-checking of dynamic_cast, so this should be used only if the programmer is very confident the cast is, and will always be, valid.

Virtual Member Functions

Ordinarily, when a function in a derived class overrides a function in a base class, the function to call is determined by the type of the object. A given function is overridden when there exists no difference in the number or type of parameters between two or more definitions of that function. Hence, at compile time, it may not be possible to determine the type of the object and therefore the correct function to call, given only a base class pointer; the decision is therefore put off until runtime. This is called dynamic dispatch. Virtual member functions or *methods* allow the most specific implementation of the function to be called, according to the actual run-time type of the object. In C++ implementations, this is commonly done using virtual function tables. If the object type is known, this may be bypassed by prepending a fully qualified class name before the function call, but in general calls to virtual functions are resolved at run time.

In addition to standard member functions, operator overloads and destructors can be virtual. As a rule of thumb, if any function in the class is virtual, the destructor should be as well. As the type of an object at its creation is known at compile time, constructors, and by extension copy constructors, cannot be virtual. Nonetheless a situation may arise where a copy of an object needs to be created when a pointer to a derived object is passed as a pointer to a base object. In such a case, a common solution is to create a clone() (or similar) virtual function that creates and returns a copy of the derived class when called.

A member function can also be made "pure virtual" by appending it with = o after the closing parenthesis and before the semicolon. A class containing a pure virtual function is called an *abstract class*. Objects cannot be created from an abstract class; they can only be derived from. Any derived class inherits the virtual function as pure and must provide a non-pure definition of it (and all other pure virtual functions) before objects of the derived class can be created. A program that attempts to create an object of a class with a pure virtual member function or inherited pure virtual member function is ill-formed.

Lambda Expressions

C++ provides support for anonymous functions, which are also known as lambda expressions and have the following form:

```
[capture](parameters) -> return_type { function_body }
```

The [capture] list supports the definition of closures. Such lambda expressions are defined in the standard as syntactic sugar for an unnamed function object. An example lambda function may be defined as follows:

```
[](int x, int y) -> int { return x + y; }
```

Exception Handling

Exception handling is used to communicate the existence of a runtime problem or error from where it was detected to where the issue can be handled. It permits this to be done in a uniform manner and separately from the main code, while detecting all errors. Should an error occur, an exception is thrown (raised), which is then caught by the nearest suitable exception handler. The exception causes the current scope to be exited, and also each outer scope (propagation) until a suitable handler is found, calling in turn the destructors of any objects in these exited scopes. At the same time, an exception is presented as an object carrying the data about the detected problem.

The exception-causing code is placed inside a try block. The exceptions are handled in separate catch blocks (the handlers); each try block can have multiple exception handlers, as it is visible in the example below:

```
#include <iostream>

#include <vector>

#include <stdexcept>


int main() {

    try {
```

```
        std::vector<int> vec{3,4,3,1};

        int i{vec.at(4)}; // Throws an exception, std::out_of_range (in-
dexing for vec is from 0-3 not 1-4)

    }\


    // An exception handler, catches std::out_of_range, which is thrown
by vec.at(4)

    catch (std::out_of_range& e) {

        std::cerr << "Accessing a non-existent element: " << e.what() <<
'\n';

    }


    // To catch any other standard library exceptions (they derive from
std::exception)

    catch (std::exception& e) {

        std::cerr << "Exception thrown: " << e.what() << '\n';

    }


    // Catch any unrecognised exceptions (i.e. those which don't derive
from std::exception)

    catch (...) {

        std::cerr << "Some fatal error\n";

    }

}
```

It is also possible to raise exceptions purposefully, using the throw keyword; these exceptions are handled in the usual way. In some cases, exceptions cannot be used due to technical reasons. One such example is a critical component of an embedded system, where every operation must be guaranteed to complete within a specified amount of time. This cannot be determined with exceptions as no tools exist to determine the minimum time required for an exception to be handled.

Standard Library

The C++ standard consists of two parts: the core language and the standard library. C++ programmers expect the latter on every major implementation of C++; it includes vectors, lists, maps, algorithms (find, for_each, binary_search, random_shuffle, etc.), sets, queues, stacks, arrays, tuples, input/output facilities (iostream, for reading from and writing to the console and files), smart pointers for automatic memory management, regular expression support, multi-threading library, atomics support (allowing a variable to be read or written to by at most one thread at a time without any external synchronisation), time utilities (measurement, getting current time, etc.), a system for converting error reporting that doesn't use C++ exceptions into C++ exceptions, a random number generator and a slightly modified version of the C standard library (to make it comply with the C++ type system).

A large part of the C++ library is based on the Standard Template Library (STL). Useful tools provided by the STL include containers as the collections of objects (such as vectors and lists), iterators that provide array-like access to containers, and algorithms that perform operations such as searching and sorting.

Furthermore, (multi)maps (associative arrays) and (multi)sets are provided, all of which export compatible interfaces. Therefore, using templates it is possible to write generic algorithms that work with any container or on any sequence defined by iterators. As in C, the features of the library are accessed by using the #include directive to include a standard header. C++ provides 105 standard headers, of which 27 are deprecated.

The standard incorporates the STL that was originally designed by Alexander Stepanov, who experimented with generic algorithms and containers for many years. When he started with C++, he finally found a language where it was possible to create generic algorithms (e.g., STL sort) that perform even better than, for example, the C standard library qsort, thanks to C++ features like using inlining and compile-time binding instead of function pointers. The standard does not refer to it as "STL", as it is merely a part of the standard library, but the term is still widely used to distinguish it from the rest of the standard library (input/output streams, internationalization, diagnostics, the C library subset, etc.).

Most C++ compilers, and all major ones, provide a standards conforming implementation of the C++ standard library.

Compatibility

To give compiler vendors greater freedom, the C++ standards committee decided not to dictate the implementation of name mangling, exception handling, and other implementation-specific features. The downside of this decision is that object code produced by different compilers is expected to be incompatible. There were, however, attempts to standardize compilers for particular machines or operating systems (for example C++ ABI), though they seem to be largely abandoned now.

With C

C++ is often considered to be a superset of C, but this is not strictly true. Most C code can easily be made to compile correctly in C++, but there are a few differences that cause some valid C code to be invalid or behave differently in C++. For example, C allows implicit conversion from void* to other pointer types, but C++ does not (for type safety reasons). Also, C++ defines many new keywords, such as new and class, which may be used as identifiers (for example, variable names) in a C program.

Some incompatibilities have been removed by the 1999 revision of the C standard (C99), which now supports C++ features such as line comments (//), and declarations mixed with code. On the other hand, C99 introduced a number of new features that C++ did not support, were incompatible or redundant in C++, such as variable-length arrays, native complex-number types (however, the std::complex class in the C++ standard library provides similar functionality, although not code-compatible), designated initializers, compound literals, and the restrict keyword. Some of the C99-introduced features were included in the subsequent version of the C++ standard, C++11 (out of those which were not redundant). However, the C++11 standard introduces new incompatibilities, such as disallowing assignment of a string literal to a character pointer, which remains valid C.

To intermix C and C++ code, any function declaration or definition that is to be called from/used both in C and C++ must be declared with C linkage by placing it within an extern "C" {/*...*/} block. Such a function may not rely on features depending on name mangling (i.e., function overloading).

Criticism

Despite its widespread adoption, many programmers have criticized the C++ language, including Linus Torvalds, Richard Stallman, and Ken Thompson. Issues include a lack of reflection or garbage collection, slow compilation times, perceived feature creep, and verbose error messages, particularly from template metaprogramming.

To avoid the problems that exist in C++, and to increase productivity, some people suggest alternative languages newer than C++, such as D, Go, Rust and Vala.

References

- Mooers, Calvin. "TRAC, A Procedure-Describing Language for the Reactive Typewriter". Archived from the original on 2001-04-25. Retrieved March 9, 2012

- Fowler, Charles B. (October 1967). "The Museum of Music: A History of Mechanical Instruments". Music Educators Journal. Music Educators Journal, Vol. 54, No. 2. 54 (2): 45–49. doi:10.2307/3391092. JSTOR 3391092

- Lerdorf, Rasmus (2007-04-26). "PHP on Hormones – history of PHP presentation by Rasmus Lerdorf given at the MySQL Conference in Santa Clara, California". The Conversations Network. Retrieved 2009-12-11

- Lee, Kent D. (15 December 2008). Programming Languages: An Active Learning Approach. Springer Science & Business Media. pp. 9–10. ISBN 978-0-387-79422-8

- Lämmel, Ralf; Peyton Jones, Simon. "Scrap Your Boilerplate: A Practical Design Pattern for Generic Programming" (PDF). Microsoft. Retrieved 16 October 2016

- Gamma, Erich; Helm, Richard; Johnson, Ralph; Vlissides, John (1994). Design Patterns. Addison-Wesley. ISBN 0-201-63361-2

- Harry. H. Chaudhary (28 July 2014). "Cracking The Java Programming Interview :: 2000+ Java Interview Que/Ans". Retrieved 29 May 2016

- Fuegi, J.; Francis, J. (2003). "Lovelace & babbage and the creation of the 1843 'notes'". IEEE Annals of the History of Computing. 25 (4): 16. doi:10.1109/MAHC.2003.1253887

- Alexander Stepanov; Paul McJones (June 19, 2009). Elements of Programming. Addison-Wesley Professional. ISBN 978-0-321-63537-2

- B. Stroustrup (interviewed by Sergio De Simone) (30 April 2015). "Stroustrup: Thoughts on C++17 - An Interview". Retrieved 8 July 2015

- Stroustrup, Bjarne (1994). "15.5 Avoiding Code Replication". The Design and Evolution of C++. Reading, Massachusetts: Addison-Wesley. pp. 346–348. ISBN 978-81-317-1608-3

- Mycroft, Alan (2013). "C and C++ Exceptions | Templates" (PDF). Cambridge Computer Laboratory - Course Materials 2013-14. Retrieved 30 August 2016

- Alex Homer; Dave Sussman; Rob Howard; Brian Francis; Karli Watson; Richard Anderson (2004). Professional ASP.NET 1.1. Wiley. p. 71. ISBN 0-7645-5890-0. Retrieved 2008-10-08

- Platt, David (2012-06-01). "Don't Get Me Started – The Silent Majority: Why Visual Basic 6 Still Thrives". MSDN Magazine. Retrieved 2012-06-09

3

Significant Aspects of Programming Languages

The set of rules that structures the symbols correctly to produce a programing language is called syntax. Computer language syntax can be divided into three levels, which are words, phrases and context. Data type, structured programming, control flow and programming style are significant and important topics related to programming languages. The following chapter unfolds its crucial aspects in a critical yet systematic manner.

Syntax (Programming Languages)

```python
def add5(x):
    return x+5

def dotwrite(ast):
    nodename = getNodename()
    label=symbol.sym_name.get(int(ast[0]),ast[0])
    print ' %s [label="%s' % (nodename, label),
    if isinstance(ast[1], str):
        if ast[1].strip():
            print '= %s"];' % ast[1]
        else:
            print '"]'
    else:
        print '"];'
        children = []
        for n, child in enumerate(ast[1:]):
            children.append(dotwrite(child))
        print ' %s -> {' % nodename,
        for name in children:
            print '%s' % name,
```

Syntax highlighting and indent style are often used to aid programmers in recognizing elements of source code. Color coded highlighting is used in this piece of code written in Python.

In computer science, the syntax of a computer language is the set of rules that defines the combinations of symbols that are considered to be a correctly structured document or fragment in that language. This applies both to programming languages, where the document represents source code, and markup languages, where the document represents data. The syntax of a language defines its surface form. Text-based computer languages are based on sequences of characters, while visual programming languages are based on the spatial layout and connections between symbols (which may be textual or graphical). Documents that are syntactically invalid are said to have a syntax error.

Syntax – the form – is contrasted with semantics – the meaning. In processing computer languages, semantic processing generally comes after syntactic processing, but in some cases semantic processing is necessary for complete syntactic analysis, and these are done together or concurrently. In a compiler, the syntactic analysis comprises the frontend, while semantic analysis comprises the backend (and middle end, if this phase is distinguished).

Levels of Syntax

Computer language syntax is generally distinguished into three levels:

- Words – the lexical level, determining how characters form tokens;

- Phrases – the grammar level, narrowly speaking, determining how tokens form phrases;

- Context – determining what objects or variables names refer to, if types are valid, etc.

Distinguishing in this way yields modularity, allowing each level to be described and processed separately, and often independently. First a lexer turns the linear sequence of characters into a linear sequence of tokens; this is known as "lexical analysis" or "lexing". Second the parser turns the linear sequence of tokens into a hierarchical syntax tree; this is known as "parsing" narrowly speaking. Thirdly the contextual analysis resolves names and checks types. This modularity is sometimes possible, but in many real-world languages an earlier step depends on a later step – for example, the lexer hack in C is because tokenization depends on context. Even in these cases, syntactical analysis is often seen as approximating this ideal model.

The parsing stage itself can be divided into two parts: the parse tree or "concrete syntax tree" which is determined by the grammar, but is generally far too detailed for practical use, and the abstract syntax tree (AST), which simplifies this into a usable form. The AST and contextual analysis steps can be considered a form of semantic analysis, as they are adding meaning and interpretation to the syntax, or alternatively as informal, manual implementations of syntactical rules that would be difficult or awkward to describe or implement formally.

The levels generally correspond to levels in the Chomsky hierarchy. Words are in a regular language, specified in the lexical grammar, which is a Type-3 grammar, generally given as regular expressions. Phrases are in a context-free language (CFL), generally a deterministic context-free language (DCFL), specified in a phrase structure grammar, which is a Type-2 grammar, generally given as production rules in Backus–Naur form (BNF). Phrase grammars are often specified in much more constrained grammars than full context-free grammars, in order to make them easier to parse; while the LR parser can parse any DCFL in linear time, the simple LALR parser and even simpler LL parser are more efficient, but can only parse grammars whose production rules are constrained. Contextual structure can in principle be described by a context-sensitive grammar, and automatically analyzed by means such as attribute grammars, though in general this step is done manually, via name resolution rules and type checking, and implemented via a symbol table which stores names and types for each scope.

Tools have been written that automatically generate a lexer from a lexical specification written in regular expressions and a parser from the phrase grammar written in BNF: this allows one to use declarative programming, rather than need to have procedural or functional programming. A notable example is the lex-yacc pair. These automatically produce a *concrete* syntax tree; the parser writer must then manually write code describing how this is converted to an *abstract* syntax tree. Contextual analysis is also generally implemented manually. Despite the existence of these automatic tools, parsing is often implemented manually, for various reasons – perhaps the phrase structure is not context-free, or an alternative implementation improves performance or error-reporting, or allows the grammar to be changed more easily. Parsers are often written in functional languages, such as Haskell, in scripting languages, such as Python or Perl, or in C or C++.

Examples of Errors

As an example, (add 1 1) is a syntactically valid Lisp program (assuming the 'add' function exists, else name resolution fails), adding 1 and 1. However, the following are invalid:

```
(_ 1 1)    lexical error: '_' is not valid

(add 1 1   parsing error: missing closing ')'
```

Note that the lexer is unable to identify the first error – all it knows is that, after producing the token LEFT_PAREN, '(' the remainder of the program is invalid, since no word rule begins with '_'. The second error is detected at the parsing stage: The parser has identified the "list" production rule due to the '(' token (as the only match), and thus can give an error message; in general it may be ambiguous.

Type errors and undeclared variable errors are sometimes considered to be syntax errors when they are detected at compile-time (which is usually the case when compiling strongly-typed languages), though it is common to classify these kinds of error as semantic errors instead.

As an example, the Python code

```
'a' + 1
```

contains a type error because it adds a string literal to an integer literal. Type errors of this kind can be detected at compile-time: They can be detected during parsing (phrase analysis) if the compiler uses separate rules that allow "integerLiteral + integerLiteral" but not "stringLiteral + integerLiteral", though it is more likely that the compiler will use a parsing rule that allows all expressions of the form "LiteralOrIdentifier + LiteralOrIdentifier" and then the error will be detected during contextual analysis (when type checking occurs). In some cases this validation is not done by the compiler, and these errors are only detected at runtime.

In a dynamically typed language, where type can only be determined at runtime, many type errors can only be detected at runtime. For example, the Python code

```
a + b
```

is syntactically valid at the phrase level, but the correctness of the types of a and b can only be determined at runtime, as variables do not have types in Python, only values do. Whereas there is disagreement about whether a type error detected by the compiler should be called a syntax error (rather than a static semantic error), type errors which can only be detected at program execution time are always regarded as semantic rather than syntax errors.

Syntax Definition

The syntax of textual programming languages is usually defined using a combination of regular expressions (for lexical structure) and Backus–Naur form (for grammatical structure) to inductively specify syntactic categories (nonterminals) and *terminal* symbols. Syntactic categories are defined by rules called *productions*, which specify the values that belong to a particular syntactic category. Terminal symbols are the concrete characters or strings of characters (for example keywords such as *define*, *if*, *let*, or *void*) from which syntactically valid programs are constructed.

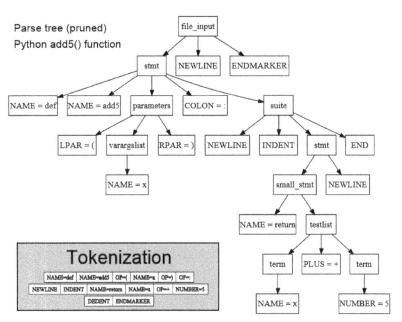

Parse tree of Python code with inset tokenization

A language can have different equivalent grammars, such as equivalent regular expressions (at the lexical levels), or different phrase rules which generate the same language. Using a broader category of grammars, such as LR grammars, can allow shorter or simpler grammars compared with more restricted categories, such as LL grammar, which may require longer grammars with more rules. Different but equivalent phrase grammars yield different parse trees, though the underlying language (set of valid documents) is the same.

Example: Lisp

Below is a simple grammar, defined using the notation of regular expressions and Extended Back-us–Naur form. It describes the syntax of Lisp, which defines productions for the syntactic categories *expression*, *atom*, *number*, *symbol*, and *list*:

```
expression = atom    | list

atom       = number | symbol

number     = [+-]?['0'-'9']+

symbol     = ['A'-'Z''a'-'z'].*

list       = '(', expression*, ')'
```

This grammar specifies the following:

- an *expression* is either an *atom* or a *list*;

- an *atom* is either a *number* or a *symbol*;

- a *number* is an unbroken sequence of one or more decimal digits, optionally preceded by a plus or minus sign;

- a *symbol* is a letter followed by zero or more of any characters (excluding whitespace); and

- a *list* is a matched pair of parentheses, with zero or more *expressions* inside it.

Here the decimal digits, upper- and lower-case characters, and parentheses are terminal symbols.

The following are examples of well-formed token sequences in this grammar: '12345', '()', '(a b c232 (1))'

Complex Grammars

The grammar needed to specify a programming language can be classified by its position in the Chomsky hierarchy. The phrase grammar of most programming languages can be specified using a Type-2 grammar, i.e., they are context-free grammars, though the overall syntax is context-sensitive (due to variable declarations and nested scopes), hence Type-1. However, there are exceptions, and for some languages the phrase grammar is Type-0 (Turing-complete).

In some languages like Perl and Lisp the specification (or implementation) of the language allows constructs that execute during the parsing phase. Furthermore, these languages have constructs that allow the programmer to alter the behavior of the parser. This combination effectively blurs the distinction between parsing and execution, and makes syntax analysis an undecidable problem in these languages, meaning that the parsing phase may not finish. For example, in Perl it is possible to execute code during parsing using a BEGIN statement, and Perl function prototypes may alter the syntactic interpretation, and possibly even the syntactic validity of the remaining code. Colloquially this is referred to as "only Perl can parse Perl" (because code must be executed during parsing, and can modify the grammar), or more strongly "even Perl cannot parse Perl" (because it is undecidable). Similarly, Lisp macros introduced by the defmacro syntax also execute during parsing, meaning that a Lisp compiler must have an entire Lisp run-time system present. In contrast C macros are merely string replacements, and do not require code execution.

Syntax Versus Semantics

The syntax of a language describes the form of a valid program, but does not provide any information about the meaning of the program or the results of executing that program. The meaning given to a combination of symbols is handled by semantics (either formal or hard-coded in a reference implementation). Not all syntactically correct programs are semantically correct. Many syntactically correct programs are nonetheless ill-formed, per the language's rules; and may (depending on the language specification and the soundness of the implementation) result in an error on translation or execution. In some cases, such programs may exhibit undefined behavior. Even when a program is well-defined within a language, it may still have a meaning that is not intended by the person who wrote it.

Using natural language as an example, it may not be possible to assign a meaning to a grammatically correct sentence or the sentence may be false:

- "Colorless green ideas sleep furiously." is grammatically well formed but has no generally accepted meaning.

- "John is a married bachelor." is grammatically well formed but expresses a meaning that cannot be true.

The following C language fragment is syntactically correct, but performs an operation that is not semantically defined (because p is a null pointer, the operations p->real and p->im have no meaning):

```
complex *p = NULL;

complex abs_p = sqrt (p->real * p->real + p->im * p->im);
```

As a simpler example,

```
int x;

printf("%d", x);
```

is syntactically valid, but not semantically defined, as it uses an uninitialized variable. Even though compilers for some programming languages (e.g., Java and C#) would detect uninitialized variable errors of this kind, they should be regarded as semantic errors rather than syntax errors.

Data Type

In computer science and computer programming, a data type or simply type is a classification of data which tells the compiler or interpreter how the programmer intends to use the data. Most programming languages support various types of data, for example: real, integer or Boolean. A Data type provides a set of values from which an expression (i.e. variable, function ...) may take its values. The type defines the operations that can be done on the data, the meaning of the data, and the way values of that type can be stored.

Overview

Data types are used within type systems, which offer various ways of defining, implementing and using them. Different type systems ensure varying degrees of type safety.

Almost all programming languages explicitly include the notion of data type, though different languages may use different terminology. Common data types include:

- integers
- booleans
- characters
- floating-point numbers
- alphanumeric strings

For example, in the Java programming language, the "int" type represents the set of 32-bit integers ranging in value from -2,147,483,648 to 2,147,483,647, as well as the operations that can be performed on integers, such as addition, subtraction, and multiplication. Colors, on the other hand, are represented by three bytes denoting the amounts each of red, green, and blue, and one string representing that color's name; allowable operations include addition and subtraction, but not multiplication.

Most programming languages also allow the programmer to define additional data types, usually by combining multiple elements of other types and defining the valid operations of the new data type. For example, a programmer might create a new data type named "complex number" that would include real and imaginary parts. A data type also represents a constraint placed upon the interpretation of data in a type system, describing representation, interpretation and structure of values or objects stored in computer memory. The type system uses data type information to check correctness of computer programs that access or manipulate the data.

Most data types in statistics have comparable types in computer programming, and vice versa.

Definition of a "Type"

(Parnas, Shore & Weiss 1976) identified five definitions of a "type" that were used—sometimes implicitly—in the literature. Types including behavior align more closely with object-oriented models, whereas a structured programming model would tend to not include code, and are called plain old data structures.

The five types are:

Syntactic

> A type is a purely syntactic label associated with a variable when it is declared. Such definitions of "type" do not give any semantic meaning to types.

Representation

> A type is defined in terms of its composition of more primitive types—often machine types.

Representation and behaviour

> A type is defined as its representation and a set of operators manipulating these representations.

Value space

> A type is a set of possible values which a variable can possess. Such definitions make it possible to speak about (disjoint) unions or Cartesian products of types.

Value space and behaviour

> A type is a set of values which a variable can possess and a set of functions that one can apply to these values.

The definition in terms of a representation was often done in imperative languages such as ALGOL and Pascal, while the definition in terms of a value space and behaviour was used in higher-level languages such as Simula and CLU.

Classes of Data Types

Machine Data Types

All data in computers based on digital electronics is represented as bits (alternatives 0 and 1) on the lowest level. The smallest addressable unit of data is usually a group of bits called a byte (usually an octet, which is 8 bits). The unit processed by machine code instructions is called a word (as of 2011, typically 32 or 64 bits). Most instructions interpret the word as a binary number, such that a 32-bit word can represent unsigned integer values from 0 to or signed integer values from 0 to $2^{32}-1$. Because of two's complement, the machine language and machine doesn't need to distinguish between these unsigned and signed data types for the most part.

There is a specific set of arithmetic instructions that use a different interpretation of the bits in word as a floating-point number.

Machine data types need to be *exposed* or made available in systems or low-level programming languages, allowing fine-grained control over hardware. The C programming language, for instance, supplies integer types of various widths, such as short and long. If a corresponding native type does not exist on the target platform, the compiler will break them down into code using types that do exist. For instance, if a 32-bit integer is requested on a 16 bit platform, the compiler will tacitly treat it as an array of two 16 bit integers.

Several languages allow binary and hexadecimal literals, for convenient manipulation of machine data.

In higher level programming, machine data types are often hidden or *abstracted* as an implementation detail that would render code less portable if exposed. For instance, a generic numeric type might be supplied instead of integers of some specific bit-width.

Boolean Type

The Boolean type represents the values true and false. Although only two values are possible, they are rarely implemented as a single binary digit for efficiency reasons. Many programming languages do not have an explicit Boolean type, instead interpreting (for instance) 0 as false and other values as true. Boolean data simply refers to the logical structure of how the language is interpreted to the machine language. In this case a Boolean 0 refers to the logic False. True is always a non zero, especially a one which is known as Boolean 1.

Numeric Types

Such as:

- The integer data types, or "whole numbers". May be sub-typed according to their ability to contain negative values (e.g. unsigned in C and C++). May also have a small number of predefined subtypes (such as short and long in C/C++); or allow users to freely define subranges such as 1..12 (e.g. Pascal/Ada).

- Floating point data types, usually represent values as high-precision fractional values (rational numbers, mathematically), but are sometimes misleadingly called reals (evocative of mathematical real numbers). They usually have predefined limits on both their maximum values and their precision. Output of these values are often represented in a decimal number format.

- Fixed point data types are convenient for representing monetary values. They are often implemented internally as integers, leading to predefined limits.

- Bignum or arbitrary precision numeric types lack predefined limits. They are not primitive types, and are used sparingly for efficiency reasons.

Composite Types

Composite types are derived from more than one primitive type. This can be done in a number of ways. The ways they are combined are called data structures. Composing a primitive type into a compound type generally results in a new type, e.g. *array-of-integer* is a different type to *integer*.

- An array stores a number of elements of the same type in a specific order. They are accessed randomly using an integer to specify which element is required (although the elements may be of almost any type). Arrays may be fixed-length or expandable.

  o A list is similar to an array, but its contents are strung together by a series of references to the next element.

- Record (also called tuple or struct) Records are among the simplest data structures. A record is a value that contains other values, typically in fixed number and sequence and typically indexed by names. The elements of records are usually called *fields* or *members*.

- Union. A union type definition will specify which of a number of permitted primitive types may be stored in its instances, e.g. "float or long integer". Contrast with a record, which could be defined to contain a float *and* an integer; whereas, in a union, there is only one type allowed at a time.

  o A tagged union (also called a variant, variant record, discriminated union, or disjoint union) contains an additional field indicating its current type, for enhanced type safety.

- A set is an abstract data structure that can store certain values, without any particular order, and no repeated values. Values themselves are not retrieved from sets, rather one tests a value for membership to obtain a boolean "in" or "not in".

- An object contains a number of data fields, like a record, and also a number of subroutines for accessing or modifying them, called methods.

Many others are possible, but they tend to be further variations and compounds of the above.

Enumerations

The enumerated type has distinct values, which can be compared and assigned, but which do not necessarily have any particular concrete representation in the computer's memory; compilers and interpreters can represent them arbitrarily. For example, the four suits in a deck of playing cards may be four enumerators named *CLUB*, *DIAMOND*, *HEART*, *SPADE*, belonging to an enumerated type named *suit*. If a variable *V* is declared having *suit* as its data type, one can assign any of those four values to it. Some implementations allow programmers to assign integer values to the enumeration values, or even treat them as type-equivalent to integers.

String and Text Types

Such as:

- Alphanumeric character. A letter of the alphabet, digit, blank space, punctuation mark, etc.

- Alphanumeric strings, a sequence of characters. They are typically used to represent words and text.

Character and string types can store sequences of characters from a character set such as ASCII. Since most character sets include the digits, it is possible to have a numeric string, such as "1234". However, many languages treat these as belonging to a different type to the numeric value 1234.

Character and string types can have different subtypes according to the required character "width". The original 7-bit wide ASCII was found to be limited, and superseded by 8 and 16-bit sets, which can encode a wide variety of non-Latin alphabets (Hebrew, Chinese) and other symbols. Strings may be either stretch-to-fit or of fixed size, even in the same programming language. They may also be subtyped by their maximum size.

Note: strings are not primitive in all languages, for instance C: they may be composed from arrays of characters.

Other Types

Types can be based on, or derived from, the basic types explained above. In some languages, such as C, functions have a type derived from the type of their return value.

Pointers and References

The main non-composite, derived type is the pointer, a data type whose value refers directly to (or "points to") another value stored elsewhere in the computer memory using its address. It is a primitive kind of reference. (In everyday terms, a page number in a book could be considered a piece of data that refers to another one). Pointers are often stored in a format similar to an integer; however, attempting to dereference or "look up" a pointer whose value was never a valid memory address would cause a program to crash. To ameliorate this potential problem, pointers are considered a separate type to the type of data they point to, even if the underlying representation is the same.

Function Types

Abstract Data Types

Any type that does not specify an implementation is an abstract data type. For instance, a stack (which is an abstract type) can be implemented as an array (a contiguous block of memory containing multiple values), or as a linked list (a set of non-contiguous memory blocks linked by pointers).

Abstract types can be handled by code that does not know or "care" what underlying types are contained in them. Programming that is agnostic about concrete data types is called generic programming. Arrays and records can also contain underlying types, but are considered concrete because they specify how their contents or elements are laid out in memory.

Examples include:

- A queue is a first-in first-out list. Variations are Deque and Priority queue.

- A set can store certain values, without any particular order, and with no repeated values.

- A stack is a last-in, first out data structure.

- A tree is a hierarchical structure.

- A graph.

- A hash, dictionary, map or associative array is a more flexible variation on a record, in which name-value pairs can be added and deleted freely.

- A smart pointer is the abstract counterpart to a pointer. Both are kinds of references.

Utility Types

For convenience, high-level languages may supply ready-made "real world" data types, for instance *times*, *dates* and *monetary values* and *memory*, even where the language allows them to be built from primitive types.

Type Systems

A type system associates types with each computed value. By examining the flow of these values, a type system attempts to prove that no *type errors* can occur. The type system in question determines what constitutes a type error, but a type system generally seeks to guarantee that operations expecting a certain kind of value are not used with values for which that operation does not make sense.

A compiler may use the static type of a value to optimize the storage it needs and the choice of algorithms for operations on the value. In many C compilers the float data type, for example, is represented in 32 bits, in accord with the IEEE specification for single-precision floating point numbers. They will thus use floating-point-specific microprocessor operations on those values (floating-point addition, multiplication, etc.).

The depth of type constraints and the manner of their evaluation affect the *typing* of the language. A programming language may further associate an operation with varying concrete algorithms on each type in the case of type polymorphism. Type theory is the study of type systems, although the concrete type systems of programming languages originate from practical issues of computer architecture, compiler implementation, and language design.

Type systems may be variously static or dynamic, strong or weak typing, and so forth.

Structured Programming

Structured programming is a programming paradigm aimed at improving the clarity, quality, and development time of a computer program by making extensive use of subroutines, block structures, for and while loops—in contrast to using simple tests and jumps such as the *go to* statement which could lead to "spaghetti code" causing difficulty to both follow and maintain.

It emerged in the late 1950s with the appearance of the ALGOL 58 and ALGOL 60 programming languages, with the latter including support for block structures. Contributing factors to its popularity and widespread acceptance, at first in academia and later among practitioners, include the discovery of what is now known as the structured program theorem in 1966, and the publication of the influential "Go To Statement Considered Harmful" open letter in 1968 by Dutch computer scientist Edsger W. Dijkstra, who coined the term "structured programming".

Structured programming is most frequently used with deviations that allow for clearer programs in some particular cases, such as when exception handling has to be performed.

Elements

Control Structures

Following the structured program theorem, all programs are seen as composed of control structures:

- "Sequence"; ordered statements or subroutines executed in sequence.

- "Selection"; one or a number of statements is executed depending on the state of the program. This is usually expressed with keywords such as if..then..else..endif.

- "Iteration"; a statement or block is executed until the program reaches a certain state, or operations have been applied to every element of a collection. This is usually expressed with keywords such as while, repeat, for or do..until. Often it is recommended that each loop should only have one entry point (and in the original structural programming, also only one exit point, and a few languages enforce this).

- "Recursion"; a statement is executed by repeatedly calling itself until termination conditions are met. While similar in practice to iterative loops, recursive loops may be more computationally efficient, and are implemented differently as a cascading stack.

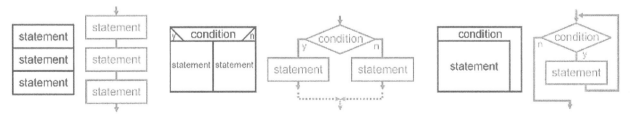

Graphical representations of the three basic patterns using NS diagrams (blue) and flow charts (green).

Subroutines

Subroutines; callable units such as procedures, functions, methods, or subprograms are used to allow a sequence to be referred to by a single statement.

Blocks

Blocks are used to enable groups of statements to be treated as if they were one statement. *Block-structured* languages have a syntax for enclosing structures in some formal way, such as an if-statement bracketed by if..fi as in ALGOL 68, or a code section bracketed by BEGIN..END, as in PL/I, whitespace indentation as in Python - or the curly braces {...} of C and many later languages.

Structured Programming Languages

It is possible to do structured programming in any programming language, though it is preferable to use something like a procedural programming language. Some of the languages initially used for structured programming include: ALGOL, Pascal, PL/I and Ada – but most new procedural programming languages since that time have included features to encourage structured programming, and sometimes deliberately left out features – notably GOTO – in an effort to make unstructured programming more difficult. *Structured programming* (sometimes known as modular programming) enforces a logical structure on the program being written to make it more efficient and easier to understand and modify.

History

Theoretical Foundation

The structured program theorem provides the theoretical basis of structured programming. It states that three ways of combining programs—sequencing, selection, and iteration—are sufficient to express any computable function. This observation did not originate with the structured programming movement; these structures are sufficient to describe the instruction cycle of a central processing unit, as well as the operation of a Turing machine. Therefore, a processor is always executing a "structured program" in this sense, even if the instructions it reads from memory are not part of a structured program. However, authors usually credit the result to a 1966 paper by Böhm and Jacopini, possibly because Dijkstra cited this paper himself. The structured program theorem does not address how to write and analyze a usefully structured program. These issues were addressed during the late 1960s and early 1970s, with major contributions by Dijkstra, Robert W. Floyd, Tony Hoare, Ole-Johan Dahl, and David Gries.

Debate

P. J. Plauger, an early adopter of structured programming, described his reaction to the structured program theorem:

> Us converts waved this interesting bit of news under the noses of the unreconstructed assembly-language programmers who kept trotting forth twisty bits of logic and saying, 'I betcha can't structure this.' Neither the proof by Böhm and Jacopini nor our repeated suc-

cesses at writing structured code brought them around one day sooner than they were ready to convince themselves.

Donald Knuth accepted the principle that programs must be written with provability in mind, but he disagreed (and still disagrees) with abolishing the GOTO statement. In his 1974 paper, "Structured Programming with Goto Statements", he gave examples where he believed that a direct jump leads to clearer and more efficient code without sacrificing provability. Knuth proposed a looser structural constraint: It should be possible to draw a program's flow chart with all forward branches on the left, all backward branches on the right, and no branches crossing each other. Many of those knowledgeable in compilers and graph theory have advocated allowing only reducible flow graphs

Structured programming theorists gained a major ally in the 1970s after IBM researcher Harlan Mills applied his interpretation of structured programming theory to the development of an indexing system for the *New York Times* research file. The project was a great engineering success, and managers at other companies cited it in support of adopting structured programming, although Dijkstra criticized the ways that Mills's interpretation differed from the published work.

As late as 1987 it was still possible to raise the question of structured programming in a computer science journal. Frank Rubin did so in that year with an open letter titled ""GOTO considered harmful" considered harmful". Numerous objections followed, including a response from Dijkstra that sharply criticized both Rubin and the concessions other writers made when responding to him.

Outcome

By the end of the 20th century nearly all computer scientists were convinced that it is useful to learn and apply the concepts of structured programming. High-level programming languages that originally lacked programming structures, such as FORTRAN, COBOL, and BASIC, now have them.

Common Deviations

While goto has now largely been replaced by the structured constructs of selection (if/then/else) and repetition (while and for), few languages are purely structured. The most common deviation, found in many languages, is the use of a return statement for early exit from a subroutine. This results in multiple exit points, instead of the single exit point required by structured programming. There are other constructions to handle cases that are awkward in purely structured programming.

Early Exit

The most common deviation from structured programming is early exit from a function or loop. At the level of functions, this is a return statement. At the level of loops, this is a break statement (terminate the loop) or continue statement (terminate the current iteration, proceed with next iteration). In structured programming, these can be replicated by adding additional branches or tests, but for returns from nested code this can add significant complexity. C is an early and prominent example of these constructs. Some newer languages also have "labeled breaks", which allow breaking out of more than just the innermost loop. Exceptions also allow early exit, but have further consequences, and thus are treated below.

Multiple exits can arise for a variety of reasons, most often either that the subroutine has no more work to do (if returning a value, it has completed the calculation), or has encountered "exceptional" circumstances that prevent it from continuing, hence needing exception handling.

The most common problem in early exit is that cleanup or final statements are not executed – for example, allocated memory is not deallocated, or open files are not closed, causing memory leaks or resource leaks. These must be done at each return site, which is brittle and can easily result in bugs. For instance, in later development, a return statement could be overlooked by a developer, and an action which should be performed at the end of a subroutine (e.g., a trace statement) might not be performed in all cases. Languages without a return statement, such as standard Pascal don't have this problem.

Most modern languages provide language-level support to prevent such leaks. Most commonly this is done via unwind protection, which ensures that certain code is guaranteed to be run when execution exits a block; this is a structured alternative to having a cleanup block and a goto. This is most often known as try...finally, and considered a part of exception handling. Various techniques exist to encapsulate resource management. An alternative approach, found primarily in C++, is Resource Acquisition Is Initialization, which uses normal stack unwinding (variable deallocation) at function exit to call destructors on local variables to deallocate resources.

Kent Beck, Martin Fowler and co-authors have argued in their refactoring books that nested conditionals may be harder to understand than a certain type of flatter structure using multiple exits predicated by guard clauses. Their 2009 book flatly states that "one exit point is really not a useful rule. Clarity is the key principle: If the method is clearer with one exit point, use one exit point; otherwise don't". They offer a cookbook solution for transforming a function consisting only of nested conditionals into a sequence of guarded return (or throw) statements, followed by a single unguarded block, which is intended to contain the code for the common case, while the guarded statements are supposed to deal with the less common ones (or with errors). Herb Sutter and Andrei Alexandrescu also argue in their 2004 C++ tips book that the single-exit point is an obsolete requirement.

In his 2004 textbook, David Watt writes that "single-entry multi-exit control flows are often desirable". Using Tennent's framework notion of sequencer, Watt uniformly describes the control flow constructs found in contemporary programming languages and attempts to explain why certain types of sequencers are preferable to others in the context of multi-exit control flows. Watt writes that unrestricted gotos (jump sequencers) are bad because the destination of the jump is not self-explanatory to the reader of a program until the reader finds and examines the actual label or address that is the target of the jump. In contrast, Watt argues that the conceptual intent of a return sequencer is clear from its own context, without having to examine its destination. Watt writes that a class of sequencers known as *escape sequencers*, defined as a "sequencer that terminates execution of a textually enclosing command or procedure", encompasses both breaks from loops (including multi-level breaks) and return statements. Watt also notes that while jump sequencers (gotos) have been somewhat restricted in languages like C, where the target must be an inside the local block or an encompassing outer block, that restriction alone is not sufficient to make the intent of gotos in C self-describing and so they can still produce "spaghetti code". Watt also examines how exception sequencers differ from escape and jump sequencers.

In contrast to the above, Bertrand Meyer wrote in his 2009 textbook that instructions like break and continue "are just the old goto in sheep's clothing" and strongly advised against their use.

Exception Handling

Based on the coding error from the Ariane 501 disaster, software developer Jim Bonang argues that any exceptions thrown from a function violate the single-exit paradigm, and proposes that all inter-procedural exceptions should be forbidden. In C++ syntax, this is done by declaring all function signatures as throw() Bonang proposes that all single-exit conforming C++ should be written along the lines of:

```
bool myCheck1() throw()

{

  bool success = false;

  try {

    // do something that may throw exceptions

    if(myCheck2() == false) {

      throw SomeInternalException();

    }

    // other code similar to the above

    success = true;

  }

  catch(...) { // all exceptions caught and logged

  }

  return success;

}
```

Peter Ritchie also notes that, in principle, even a single throw right before the return in a function constitutes a violation of the single-exit principle, but argues that Dijkstra's rules were written in a time before exception handling became a paradigm in programming languages, so he proposes to allow any number of throw points in addition to a single return point. He notes that solutions which wrap exceptions for the sake of creating a single-exit have higher nesting depth and thus are more difficult to comprehend, and even accuses those who propose to apply such solutions to programming languages which support exceptions of engaging in cargo cult thinking.

David Watt also analyzes exception handling in the framework of sequencers. Watt notes that an abnormal situation (generally exemplified with arithmetic overflows or input/output failures like file not found) is a kind of error that "is detected in some low-level program unit, but [for which] a handler is more naturally located in a high-level program unit". For example, a program might contain several calls to read files, but the action to perform when a file is not found depends on the meaning (purpose) of the file in question to the program and thus a handling routine for this abnormal situation cannot be located in low-level system code. Watts further notes that introducing status flags testing in the caller, as single-exit structured programming or even (multi-exit) return sequencers would entail, results in a situation where "the application code tends to get cluttered by tests of status flags" and that "the programmer might forgetfully or lazily omit to test a status flag. In fact, abnormal situations represented by status flags are by default ignored!" He notes that in contrast to status flags testing, exceptions have the opposite default behavior, causing the program to terminate unless the programmer explicitly deals with the exception in some way, possibly by adding code to willfully ignore it. Based on these arguments, Watt concludes that jump sequencers or escape sequencers aren't as suitable as a dedicated exception sequencer with the semantics discussed above.

The textbook by Louden and Lambert emphasizes that exception handling differs from structured programming constructs like while loops because the transfer of control "is set up at a different point in the program than that where the actual transfer takes place. At the point where the transfer actually occurs, there may be no syntactic indication that control will in fact be transferred." Computer science professor Arvind Kumar Bansal also notes that in languages which implement exception handling, even control structures like for, which have the single-exit property in absence of exceptions, no longer have it in presence of exceptions, because an exception can prematurely cause an early exit in any part of the control structure; for instance if init() throws an exception in for (init(); check(); increm()), then the usual exit point after check() is not reached. Citing multiple prior studies by others (1999-2004) and their own results, Westley Weimer and George Necula wrote that a significant problem with exceptions is that they "create hidden control-flow paths that are difficult for programmers to reason about".

The necessity to limit code to single-exit points appears in some contemporary programming environments focused on parallel computing, such as OpenMP. The various parallel constructs from OpenMP, like parallel do, do not allow early exits from inside to the outside of the parallel construct; this restriction includes all manner of exits, from break to C++ exceptions, but all of these are permitted inside the parallel construct if the jump target is also inside it.

Multiple Entry

More rarely, subprograms allow multiple *entry*. This is most commonly only *re*-entry into a coroutine (or generator/semicoroutine), where a subprogram yields control (and possibly a value), but can then be resumed where it left off. There are a number of common uses of such programming, notably for streams (particularly input/output), state machines, and concurrency. From a code execution point of view, yielding from a coroutine is closer to structured programming than returning from a subroutine, as the subprogram has not actually terminated, and will continue when called again – it is not an early exit. However, coroutines mean that multiple subprograms have execution state – rather than a single call stack of subroutines – and thus introduce a different form of complexity.

It is very rare for subprograms to allow entry to an arbitrary position in the subprogram, as in this case the program state (such as variable values) is uninitialized or ambiguous, and this is very similar to a goto.

State Machines

Some programs, particularly parsers and communications protocols, have a number of states that follow each other in a way that is not easily reduced to the basic structures, and some programmers implement the state-changes with a jump to the new state. This type of state-switching is often used in the Linux kernel.

However, it is possible to structure these systems by making each state-change a separate subprogram and using a variable to indicate the active state. Alternatively, these can be implemented via coroutines, which dispense with the trampoline.

Programming Style

Programming style is a set of rules or guidelines used when writing the source code for a computer program. It is often claimed that following a particular programming style will help programmers to read and understand source code conforming to the style, and help to avoid introducing errors.

A classic work on the subject was *The Elements of Programming Style*, written in the 1970s, and illustrated with examples from the Fortran and PL/I languages prevalent at the time.

The programming style used in a particular program may be derived from the coding conventions of a company or other computing organization, as well as the preferences of the author of the code. Programming styles are often designed for a specific programming language (or language family): style considered good in C source code may not be appropriate for BASIC source code, and so on. However, some rules are commonly applied to many languages.

Elements of Good Style

Good style is a subjective matter, and is difficult to define. However, there are several elements common to a large number of programming styles. The issues usually considered as part of programming style include the layout of the source code, including indentation; the use of white space around operators and keywords; the capitalization or otherwise of keywords and variable names; the style and spelling of user-defined identifiers, such as function, procedure and variable names; and the use and style of comments.

Code Appearance

Programming styles commonly deal with the visual appearance of source code, with the goal of readability. Software has long been available that formats source code automatically, leaving coders to concentrate on naming, logic, and higher techniques. As a practical point, using a computer to format source code saves time, and it is possible to then enforce company-wide standards without debates.

Indentation

Indent styles assist in identifying control flow and blocks of code. In some programming languages indentation is used to delimit logical blocks of code; correct indentation in these cases is more than a matter of style. In other languages indentation and white space do not affect function, although logical and consistent indentation makes code more readable. Compare:

```
if (hours < 24 && minutes < 60 && seconds < 60) {

    return true;

} else {

    return false;

}
```

or

```
if (hours < 24 && minutes < 60 && seconds < 60)

{

    return true;

}

else

{

    return false;

}
```

with something like

```
if   ( hours    < 24

    && minutes < 60

    && seconds < 60

)

{return      true

; }            else

{return     false

; }
```

The first two examples are probably much easier to read because they are indented in an established way (a "hanging paragraph" style). This indentation style is especially useful when dealing with multiple nested constructs.

Note however that this example is the same as simply:

```
return hours < 24 && minutes < 60 && seconds < 60;
```

ModuLiq

The ModuLiq Zero Indent Style groups with carriage returns rather than indents. Compare all of the above to:

```
if (hours < 24 && minutes < 60 && seconds < 60)

return true;

else

return false;
```

Lua

Lua does not use the traditional curly braces or parenthesis. if/else statements only require the expression be followed by then, and closing the if/else statement with end.

```
if hours < 24 and minutes < 60 and seconds < 60 then

    return true

else

    return false

end
```

Indentation is optional. and,or,not are used in between true/false statements.

They are true/false statements, as

```
print(not true)
```

would mean false.

Python

Python uses indentation to indicate control structures, so *correct indentation* is required. By doing this, the need for bracketing with curly braces (i.e. { and }) is eliminated. On the other hand, copying and pasting Python code can lead to problems, because the indentation level of the pasted code may not be the same as the indentation level of the current line. Such reformatting can be tedious to do by hand, but some text editors and IDEs have features to do it automatically. There are also problems when Python code being rendered unusable when posted on a forum or web page that removes white space, though this problem can be avoided where it is possible to enclose code in white space-preserving tags such as "<pre> ... </pre>" (for HTML), "[code]" ... "[/code]" (for bbcode), etc.

```
if hours < 24 and minutes < 60 and seconds < 60:

    return True
```

```
else:

    return False
```

Notice that Python does not use curly braces, but a regular colon (e.g. else:).

Many Python programmers tend to follow a commonly agreed style guide known as PEP8. There are tools designed to automate PEP8 compliance.

Haskell

Haskell similarly has the off-side rule, i.e. it has a two dimension syntax where indentation is meaningful to define blocks. Although an alternate syntax uses curly braces and semicolons. Haskell is a declarative language, there are statements, but declarations within a Haskell script. Example:

```
let c_1 = 1

    c_2 = 2

in

    f x y = c_1 * x + c_2 * y
```

may be written in one line as:

```
let {c_1=1;c_2=2} in f x y = c_1 * x + c_2 * y
```

Haskell encourage the use of literate programming, where extended text explain the genesis of the code. In literate Haskell scripts (named with the lhs extension), everything is a comment except blocks marked as code. The program can be written in LATEX, in such case the code environment marks what is code. Also each active code paragraph can be marked by preceding and ending it with an empty line, and starting each line of code with a greater than sign and a space. Here an example using LATEX markup:

```
The function \verb+isValidDate+ test if date is valid

\begin{code}

isValidDate :: Date -> Bool

isValidDate date = hh>=0   && mm>=0 && ss>=0

                && hh<24 && mm<60 && ss<60

 where (hh,mm,ss) = fromDate date

\end{code}

observe that in this case the overloaded function is \verb+fromDate ::
Date -> (Int,Int,Int)+.
```

And an example using plain text:

```
The function isValidDate test if date is valid


> isValidDate :: Date -> Bool

> isValidDate date = hh>=0   && mm>=0 && ss>=0

>                    && hh<24 && mm<60 && ss<60

>  where (hh,mm,ss) = fromDate date
```

observe that in this case the overloaded function is fromDate :: Date ->
(Int,Int,Int).

Vertical Alignment

It is often helpful to align similar elements vertically, to make typo-generated bugs more obvious.
Compare:

```
$search = array('a', 'b', 'c', 'd', 'e');

$replacement = array('foo', 'bar', 'baz', 'quux');


// Another example:


$value = 0;

$anothervalue = 1;

$yetanothervalue = 2;
```

with:

```
$search      = array('a',   'b',   'c',   'd',   'e');

$replacement = array('foo', 'bar', 'baz', 'quux');


// Another example:

$value           = 0;

$anothervalue    = 1;

$yetanothervalue = 2;
```

The latter example makes two things intuitively clear that were not clear in the former:

- the search and replace terms are related and match up: they are not discrete variables;

- there is one more search term than there are replacement terms. If this is a bug, it is now more likely to be spotted.

However, note that there are arguments *against* vertical alignment:

- Inter-line false dependencies; tabular formatting creates dependencies across lines. For example, if an identifier with a long name is added to a tabular layout, the column width may have to be increased to accommodate it. This forces a bigger change to the source code than necessary, and the essential change may be lost in the noise. This is detrimental to Revision control where inspecting differences between versions is essential.

- Brittleness; if a programmer does not neatly format the table when making a change, maybe legitimately with the previous point in mind, the result becomes a mess that deteriorates with further such changes. Simple refactoring operations, such as search-and-replace, may also break the formatting.

- Resistance to modification; tabular formatting requires more effort to maintain. This may put off a programmer from making a beneficial change, such as adding, correcting or improving the name of an identifier, because it will mess up the formatting.

- Reliance on mono-spaced font; tabular formatting assumes that the editor uses a fixed-width font. Many modern code editors support proportional fonts, and the programmer may prefer to use a proportional font for readability.

- Tool dependence; some of the effort of maintaining alignment can be alleviated by tools (e.g. a source code editor that supports elastic tabstops), although that creates a reliance on such tools.

For example, if a simple refactoring operation is performed on the code above, renaming variables "$replacement" to "$r" and "$anothervalue" to "$a", the resulting code will look like this:

```
$search       = array('a',    'b',    'c',    'd',    'e');

$r = array('foo', 'bar', 'baz', 'quux');

// Another example:

$value           = 0;

$a     = 1;

$yetanothervalue = 2;
```

The original sequential formatting will still look fine after such change:

```
$search = array('a', 'b', 'c', 'd', 'e');

$r = array('foo', 'bar', 'baz', 'quux');
```

```
// Another example:


$value = 0;

$a = 1;

$yetanothervalue = 2;
```

Spaces

In those situations where some white space is required, the grammars of most free-format languages are unconcerned with the amount that appears. Style related to white space is commonly used to enhance readability. There are currently no known hard facts (conclusions from studies) about which of the whitespace styles have the best readability.

For instance, compare the following syntactically equivalent examples of C code:

```
int i;

for(i=0;i<10;++i){

    printf("%d",i*i+i);

}
```

versus

```
int i;

for (i=0; i<10; ++i) {

    printf("%d", i*i+i);

}
```

versus

```
int i;

for (i = 0; i < 10; ++i) {

    printf("%d", i * i + i);

}
```

Tabs

The use of tabs to create white space presents particular issues when not enough care is taken because the location of the tabulation point can be different depending on the tools being used and even the preferences of the user.

As an example, one programmer prefers tab stops of four and has his toolset configured this way, and uses these to format his code.

```
int     ix;     // Index to scan array

long    sum;    // Accumulator for sum
```

Another programmer prefers tab stops of eight, and his toolset is configured this way. When he examines his code, he may well find it difficult to read.

```
int                 ix;                 // Index to scan array

long    sum;    // Accumulator for sum
```

One widely used solution to this issue may involve forbidding the use of tabs for alignment or rules on how tab stops must be set. Note that tabs work fine provided they are used consistently, restricted to logical indentation, and not used for alignment:

```
class MyClass {

        int foobar(

                int qux, // first parameter

                int quux); // second parameter

        int foobar2(

                int qux, // first parameter

                int quux, // second parameter

                int quuux); // third parameter

};
```

Control Flow

In computer science, control flow (or flow of control) is the order in which individual statements, instructions or function calls of an imperative program are executed or evaluated. The emphasis on explicit control flow distinguishes an *imperative programming* language from a *declarative programming* language.

Within an imperative programming language, a *control flow statement* is a statement which execution results in a choice being made as to which of two or more paths to follow. For non-strict functional languages, functions and language constructs exist to achieve the same result, but they are usually not termed control flow statements.

A set of statements is in turn generally structured as a block, which in addition to grouping, also defines a lexical scope.

Interrupts and signals are low-level mechanisms that can alter the flow of control in a way similar to a subroutine, but usually occur as a response to some external stimulus or event (that can occur asynchronously), rather than execution of an *in-line* control flow statement.

At the level of machine language or assembly language, control flow instructions usually work by altering the program counter. For some central processing units (CPUs), the only control flow instructions available are conditional or unconditional branch instructions, also termed jumps.

Categories

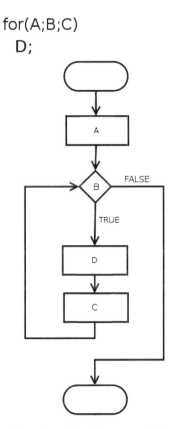

A flow chart showing control flow

The kinds of control flow statements supported by different languages vary, but can be categorized by their effect:

- Continuation at a different statement (unconditional branch or jump)

- Executing a set of statements only if some condition is met (choice - i.e., conditional branch)

- Executing a set of statements zero or more times, until some condition is met (i.e., loop - the same as conditional branch)

- Executing a set of distant statements, after which the flow of control usually returns (subroutines, coroutines, and continuations)

- Stopping the program, preventing any further execution (unconditional halt)

Primitives

Labels

A label is an explicit name or number assigned to a fixed position within the source code, and which may be referenced by control flow statements appearing elsewhere in the source code. A label marks a position within source code, and has no other effect.

Line numbers are an alternative to a named label (and used in some languages such as Fortran and BASIC), that are whole numbers placed at the start of each line of text in the source code. Languages which use these often impose the constraint that the line numbers must increase in value in each following line, but may not require that they be consecutive. For example, in BASIC:

```
10 LET X = 3

20 PRINT X
```

In other languages such as C and Ada, a label is an identifier, usually appearing at the start of a line and immediately followed by a colon. For example, in C:

```
Success: printf("The operation was successful.\n");
```

The language ALGOL 60 allowed both whole numbers and identifiers as labels (both linked by colons to the following statement), but few if any other ALGOL variants allowed whole numbers.

Goto

The *goto* statement (a combination of the English words *go* and *to*, and pronounced accordingly) is the most basic form of unconditional transfer of control.

Although the keyword may either be in upper or lower case depending on the language, it is usually written as:

```
goto label
```

The effect of a goto statement is to cause the next statement to be executed to be the statement appearing at (or immediately after) the indicated label.

Goto statements have been considered harmful by many computer scientists, notably Dijkstra.

Subroutines

The terminology for subroutines varies; they may alternatively be known as routines, procedures, functions (especially if they return results) or methods (especially if they belong to classes or type classes).

In the 1950s, computer memories were very small by current standards so subroutines were used mainly to reduce program size. A piece of code was written once and then used many times from various other places in a program.

Today, subroutines are more often used to help make a program that is more structured, e.g., by isolating some algorithm or hiding some data access method. If many programmers are working on one program, subroutines are one kind of modularity that can help divide the work.

Sequence

In structured programming, the ordered sequencing of successive commands is considered one of the basic control structures, which is used as a building block for programs alongside iteration, recursion and choice.

Minimal Structured Control Flow

In May 1966, Böhm and Jacopini published an article in *Communications of the ACM* which showed that any program with gotos could be transformed into a goto-free form involving only choice (IF THEN ELSE) and loops (WHILE condition DO xxx), possibly with duplicated code and/ or the addition of Boolean variables (true/false flags). Later authors showed that choice can be replaced by loops (and yet more Boolean variables).

That such minimalism is possible does not mean that it is necessarily desirable; after all, computers theoretically need only one machine instruction (subtract one number from another and branch if the result is negative), but practical computers have dozens or even hundreds of machine instructions.

What Böhm and Jacopini's article showed was that all programs could be goto-free. Other research showed that control structures with one entry and one exit were much easier to understand than any other form, mainly because they could be used anywhere as a statement without disrupting the control flow. In other words, they were *composable*. (Later developments, such as non-strict programming languages – and more recently, composable software transactions – have continued this strategy, making components of programs even more freely composable.)

Some academics took a purist approach to the Böhm-Jacopini result and argued that even instructions like break and return from the middle of loops are bad practice as they are not needed in the Böhm-Jacopini proof, and thus they advocated that all loops should have a single exit point. This purist approach is embodied in the language Pascal (designed in 1968–1969), which up to the mid-1990s was the preferred tool for teaching introductory programming in academia. The direct application of the Böhm-Jacopini theorem may result in additional local variables being introduced in the structured chart, and may also result in some code duplication. The latter issue is called the loop and a half problem in this context. Pascal is affected by both of these problems and according to empirical studies cited by Eric S. Roberts, student programmers had difficulty formulating correct solutions in Pascal for several simple problems, including writing a function for searching an element in an array. A 1980 study by Henry Shapiro cited by Roberts found that using only the Pascal-provided control structures, the correct solution was given by only 20% of the subjects, while no subject wrote incorrect code for this problem if allowed to write a return from the middle of a loop.

Control Structures in Practice

Most programming languages with control structures have an initial keyword which indicates the type of control structure involved. Languages then divide as to whether or not control structures have a final keyword.

- No final keyword: ALGOL 60, C, C++, Haskell, Java, Pascal, Perl, PHP, PL/I, Python, PowerShell. Such languages need some way of grouping statements together:

    o   ALGOL 60 and Pascal: begin ... end

    o   C, C++, Java, Perl, PHP, and PowerShell: curly brackets { ... }

    o   PL/I: DO ... END

    o   Python: uses indent level

    o   Haskell: either indent level or curly brackets can be used, and they can be freely mixed

    o   Lua: uses do ... end

- Final keyword: Ada, ALGOL 68, Modula-2, Fortran 77, Mythryl, Visual Basic. The forms of the final keyword vary:

    o   Ada: final keyword is end + *space* + initial keyword e.g., if ... end if, loop ... end loop

    o   ALGOL 68, Mythryl: initial keyword spelled backwards e.g., if ... fi, case ... esac

    o   Fortran 77: final keyword is end + initial keyword e.g., IF ... ENDIF, DO ... ENDDO

    o   Modula-2: same final keyword END for everything

    o   Visual Basic: every control structure has its own keyword. If ... End If; For ... Next; Do ... Loop; While ... Wend

Choice

If-then-(Else) Statements

Conditional expressions and conditional constructs are features of a programming language which perform different computations or actions depending on whether a programmer-specified boolean *condition* evaluates to true or false.

- IF..GOTO. A form found in unstructured languages, mimicking a typical machine code instruction, would jump to (GOTO) a label or line number when the condition was met.

- IF..THEN..(ENDIF). Rather than being restricted to a jump, any simple statement, or nested block, could follow the THEN key keyword. This a structured form.

- IF..THEN..ELSE..(ENDIF). As above, but with a second action to be performed if the condition is false. This is one of the most common forms, with many variations. Some require a terminal ENDIF, others do not. C and related languages do not require a terminal keyword, or a 'then', but do require parentheses around the condition.

- Conditional statements can be and often are nested inside other conditional statements. Some languages allow ELSE and IF to be combined into ELSEIF, avoiding the need to have a series of ENDIF or other final statements at the end of a compound statement.

Less common variations include:

- Some languages, such as Fortran, have a *three-way* or *arithmetic if*, testing whether a numeric value is positive, negative or zero.

- Some languages have a functional form of an if statement, for instance Lisp's cond.

- Some languages have an operator form of an if statement, such as C's ternary operator.

- Perl supplements a C-style if with when and unless.

- Smalltalk uses ifTrue and ifFalse messages to implement conditionals, rather than any fundamental language construct.

Case and Switch Statements

Switch statements (or *case statements*, or *multiway branches*) compare a given value with specified constants and take action according to the first constant to match. There is usually a provision for a default action ("else", "otherwise") to be taken if no match succeeds. Switch statements can allow compiler optimizations, such as lookup tables. In dynamic languages, the cases may not be limited to constant expressions, and might extend to pattern matching, as in the shell script example on the right, where the *) implements the default case as a glob matching any string. Case logic can also be implemented in functional form, as in SQL's decode statement.

Pascal:	Ada:	C:	Shell script:	Lisp:
`case someChar of` `  'a': actionOnA;` `  'x': actionOnX;` `  'y','z':action-` `OnYandZ;` `  else actionOnNo-` `Match;` `end;`	`case someChar is` `  when 'a' =>` `actionOnA;` `  when 'x' =>` `actionOnX;` ` when 'y'	'z'` `=> actionOn-` `YandZ;`  ` when others` `=> actionOnNoM-` `atch;`  `end;`	`switch       (so-` `meChar) {` `  case 'a': ac-` `tionOnA; break;` `  case 'x': ac-` `tionOnX; break;` `  case 'y':` `  case 'z': ac-` `t i o n O n Y a n d Z ;` `break;` `  default: ac-` `tionOnNoMatch;` `}`	`case   $someChar` `in` `  a)    action-` `OnA ;;` `  x)    action-` `OnX ;;` `  [yz])   ac-` `tionOnYandZ ;;` `  *)    action-` `OnNoMatch  ;;` `esac`	`(case someChar` `  ((#\a)      ac-` `tionOnA)` `  ((#\x)      ac-` `tionOnX)` `  ((#\y #\z) ac-` `tionOnYandZ)` `  (else      ac-` `tionOnNoMatch))`

Loops

A loop is a sequence of statements which is specified once but which may be carried out several times in succession. The code "inside" the loop (the *body* of the loop, shown as *xxx*) is obeyed a specified number of times, or once for each of a collection of items, or until some condition is met, or indefinitely.

In functional programming languages, such as Haskell and Scheme, loops can be expressed by using recursion or fixed point iteration rather than explicit looping constructs. Tail recursion is a special case of recursion which can be easily transformed to iteration.

Count-controlled Loops

Most programming languages have constructions for repeating a loop a certain number of times. In most cases counting can go downwards instead of upwards and step sizes other than 1 can be used.

```
FOR I = 1 TO N            | for I := 1 to N do begin

    xxx                   |     xxx

NEXT I                    | end;
--------------------------------------------------------------
DO I = 1,N                | for ( I=1; I<=N; ++I ) {

    xxx                   |     xxx

END DO                    | }
```

In these examples, if N < 1 then the body of loop may execute once (with I having value 1) or not at all, depending on the programming language.

In many programming languages, only integers can be reliably used in a count-controlled loop. Floating-point numbers are represented imprecisely due to hardware constraints, so a loop such as

```
for X := 0.1 step 0.1 to 1.0 do
```

might be repeated 9 or 10 times, depending on rounding errors and/or the hardware and/or the compiler version. Furthermore, if the increment of X occurs by repeated addition, accumulated rounding errors may mean that the value of X in each iteration can differ quite significantly from the expected sequence 0.1, 0.2, 0.3, ..., 1.0.

Condition-controlled Loops

Most programming languages have constructions for repeating a loop until some condition changes. Some variations test the condition at the start of the loop; others test it at the end. If the test is at the start, the body may be skipped completely; if it is at the end, the body is always executed at least once.

```
DO WHILE (test)           | repeat

    xxx                   |     xxx

LOOP                      | until test;
----------------------------------------------------
while (test) {            | do
```

```
        xxx                            |      xxx

    }                                  | while (test);
```

A control break is a value change detection method used within ordinary loops to trigger processing for groups of values. Values are monitored within the loop and a change diverts program flow
to the handling of the group event associated with them.

```
DO UNTIL (End-of-File)

  IF new-zipcode <> current-zipcode

    display_tally(current-zipcode, zipcount)


    current-zipcode = new-zipcode

    zipcount = 0

  ENDIF


  zipcount++

LOOP
```

Collection-controlled Loops

Several programming languages (e.g., Ada, D, C++11, Smalltalk, PHP, Perl, Object Pascal, Java,
C#, MATLAB, Mythryl, Visual Basic, Ruby, Python, JavaScript, Fortran 95 and later) have special
constructs which allow implicit looping through all elements of an array, or all members of a set
or collection.

```
someCollection do: [:eachElement |xxx].

for Item in Collection do begin xxx end;

foreach (item; myCollection) { xxx }

foreach someArray { xxx }

foreach ($someArray as $k => $v) { xxx }

Collection<String> coll; for (String s : coll) {}

foreach (string s in myStringCollection) { xxx }

$someCollection | ForEach-Object { $_ }

forall ( index = first:last:step... )
```

Scala has for-expressions, which generalise collection-controlled loops, and also support other uses, such as asynchronous programming. Haskell has do-expressions and comprehensions, which together provide similar function to for-expressions in Scala.

General Iteration

General iteration constructs such as C's for statement and Common Lisp's do form can be used to express any of the above sorts of loops, and others, such as looping over some number of collections in parallel. Where a more specific looping construct can be used, it is usually preferred over the general iteration construct, since it often makes the purpose of the expression clearer.

Infinite Loops

Infinite loops are used to assure a program segment loops forever or until an exceptional condition arises, such as an error. For instance, an event-driven program (such as a server) should loop forever, handling events as they occur, only stopping when the process is terminated by an operator.

Infinite loops can be implemented using other control flow constructs. Most commonly, in unstructured programming this is jump back up (goto), while in structured programming this is an indefinite loop (while loop) set to never end, either by omitting the condition or explicitly setting it to true, as while (true) .... Some languages have special constructs for infinite loops, typically by omitting the condition from an indefinite loop. Examples include Ada (loop ... end loop), Fortran (DO ... END DO), Go (for { ... }), and Ruby (loop do ... end).

Often, an infinite loop is unintentionally created by a programming error in a condition-controlled loop, wherein the loop condition uses variables that never change within the loop.

Continuation with Next Iteration

Sometimes within the body of a loop there is a desire to skip the remainder of the loop body and continue with the next iteration of the loop. Some languages provide a statement such as continue (most languages), skip, or next (Perl and Ruby), which will do this. The effect is to prematurely terminate the innermost loop body and then resume as normal with the next iteration. If the iteration is the last one in the loop, the effect is to terminate the entire loop early.

Redo Current Iteration

Some languages, like Perl and Ruby, have a redo statement that restarts the current iteration from the start.

Restart Loop

Ruby has a retry statement that restarts the entire loop from the initial iteration.

Early Exit From Loops

When using a count-controlled loop to search through a table, it might be desirable to stop searching as soon as the required item is found. Some programming languages provide a statement such as break (most languages), exit, or last (Perl), which effect is to terminate the current loop immediately, and transfer control to the statement immediately after that loop.

The following example is done in Ada which supports both *early exit from loops* and *loops with test in the middle*. Both features are very similar and comparing both code snippets will show the difference: *early exit* must be combined with an if statement while a *condition in the middle* is a self-contained construct.

```
with Ada.Text IO;

with Ada.Integer Text IO;


procedure Print_Squares is

    X : Integer;

begin

    Read_Data : loop

        Ada.Integer Text IO.Get(X);

    exit Read_Data when X = 0;

        Ada.Text IO.Put (X * X);

        Ada.Text IO.New_Line;

    end loop Read_Data;

end Print_Squares;
```

Python supports conditional execution of code depending on whether a loop was exited early (with a break statement) or not by using an else-clause with the loop. For example,

```
for n in set_of_numbers:

    if isprime(n):

        print "Set contains a prime number"

        break

else:

    print "Set did not contain any prime numbers"
```

The else clause in the above example is linked to the for statement, and not the inner if statement. Both Python's for and while loops support such an else clause, which is executed only if early exit of the loop has not occurred.

Some languages support breaking out of nested loops; in theory circles, these are called multi-level breaks. One common use example is searching a multi-dimensional table. This can be done either via multilevel breaks (break out of N levels), as in bash and PHP, or via labeled breaks (break out and continue at given label), as in Java and Perl. Alternatives to multilevel breaks include single breaks, together with a state variable which is tested to break out another level; exceptions, which are caught at the level being broken out to; placing the nested loops in a function and using return to effect termination of the entire nested loop; or using a label and a goto statement. C does not include a multilevel break, and the usual alternative is to use a goto to implement a labeled break. Python does not have a multilevel break or continue – this was proposed in PEP 3136, and rejected on the basis that the added complexity was not worth the rare legitimate use.

The notion of multi-level breaks is of some interest in theoretical computer science, because it gives rise to what is today called the *Kosaraju hierarchy*. In 1973 S. Rao Kosaraju refined the structured program theorem by proving that it's possible to avoid adding additional variables in structured programming, as long as arbitrary-depth, multi-level breaks from loops are allowed. Furthermore, Kosaraju proved that a strict hierarchy of programs exists: for every integer n, there exists a program containing a multi-level break of depth n that cannot be rewritten as a program with multi-level breaks of depth less than n without introducing added variables.

One can also return out of a subroutine executing the looped statements, breaking out of both the nested loop and the subroutine. There are other proposed control structures for multiple breaks, but these are generally implemented as exceptions instead.

In his 2004 textbook, David Watt uses Tennent's notion of sequencer to explain the similarity between multi-level breaks and return statements. Watt notes that a class of sequencers known as *escape sequencers*, defined as "sequencer that terminates execution of a textually enclosing command or procedure", encompasses both breaks from loops (including multi-level breaks) and return statements. As commonly implemented, however, return sequencers may also carry a (return) value, whereas the break sequencer as implemented in contemporary languages usually cannot.

Loop Variants and Invariants

Loop variants and loop invariants are used to express correctness of loops.

In practical terms, a loop variant is an integer expression which has an initial non-negative value. The variant's value must decrease during each loop iteration but must never become negative during the correct execution of the loop. Loop variants are used to guarantee that loops will terminate.

A loop invariant is an assertion which must be true before the first loop iteration and remain true after each iteration. This implies that when a loop terminates correctly, both the exit condition and the loop invariant are satisfied. Loop invariants are used to monitor specific properties of a loop during successive iterations.

Some programming languages, such as Eiffel contain native support for loop variants and invariants. In other cases, support is an add-on, such as the Java Modeling Language's specification for loop statements in Java.

Loop Sublanguage

Some Lisp dialects provide an extensive sublanguage for describing Loops. An early example can be found in Conversional Lisp of Interlisp. Common Lisp provides a Loop macro which implements such a sublanguage.

Structured Non-local Control Flow

Many programming languages, especially those favoring more dynamic styles of programming, offer constructs for *non-local control flow*. These cause the flow of execution to jump out of a given context and resume at some predeclared point. *Conditions*, *exceptions* and *continuations* are three common sorts of non-local control constructs; more exotic ones also exist, such as generators, coroutines and the async keyword.

Conditions

PL/I has some 22 standard conditions (e.g., ZERODIVIDE SUBSCRIPTRANGE ENDFILE) which can be raised and which can be intercepted by: ON *condition* action; Programmers can also define and use their own named conditions.

Like the *unstructured if*, only one statement can be specified so in many cases a GOTO is needed to decide where flow of control should resume.

Unfortunately, some implementations had a substantial overhead in both space and time (especially SUBSCRIPTRANGE), so many programmers tried to avoid using conditions.

Common Syntax examples:

```
ON condition GOTO label
```

Exceptions

Modern languages have a specialized structured construct for exception handling which does not rely on the use of GOTO or (multi-level) breaks or returns. For example, in C++ one can write:

```
try {
    xxx1                                    // Somewhere in here
    xxx2                                    //     use: '''throw''' some-
Value;
    xxx3
} catch (someClass& someId) {               // catch value of someClass
    actionForSomeClass
} catch (someType& anotherId) {              // catch value of someType
    actionForSomeType
```

```
} catch (...) {                              // catch anything not already
caught

    actionForAnythingElse

}
```

Any number and variety of catch clauses can be used above. If there is no catch matching a particular throw, control percolates back through subroutine calls and/or nested blocks until a matching catch is found or until the end of the main program is reached, at which point the program is forcibly stopped with a suitable error message.

Via C++'s influence, catch is the keyword reserved for declaring a pattern-matching exception handler in other languages popular today, like Java or C#. Some other languages like Ada use the keyword exception to introduce an exception handler and then may even employ a different keyword (when in Ada) for the pattern matching. A few languages like AppleScript incorporate placeholders in the exception handler syntax to automatically extract several pieces of information when the exception occurs. This approach is exemplified below by the on error construct from AppleScript:

```
try

    set myNumber to myNumber / 0

on error e  number n  from f  to t  partial result pr

    if ( e = "Can't divide by zero" ) then display dialog "You must not
do that"

end try
```

David Watt's 2004 textbook also analyzes exception handling in the framework of sequencers. Watt notes that an abnormal situation, generally exemplified with arithmetic overflows or input/output failures like file not found, is a kind of error that "is detected in some low-level program unit, but [for which] a handler is more naturally located in a high-level program unit". For example, a program might contain several calls to read files, but the action to perform when a file is not found depends on the meaning (purpose) of the file in question to the program and thus a handling routine for this abnormal situation cannot be located in low-level system code. Watts further notes that introducing status flags testing in the caller, as single-exit structured programming or even (multi-exit) return sequencers would entail, results in a situation where "the application code tends to get cluttered by tests of status flags" and that "the programmer might forgetfully or lazily omit to test a status flag. In fact, abnormal situations represented by status flags are by default ignored!" Watt notes that in contrast to status flags testing, exceptions have the opposite default behavior, causing the program to terminate unless the programmer explicitly deals with the exception in some way, possibly by adding explicit code to ignore it. Based on these arguments, Watt concludes that jump sequencers or escape sequencers aren't as suitable as a dedicated exception sequencer with the semantics discussed above.

In Object Pascal, D, Java, C#, and Python a finally clause can be added to the try construct. No matter how control leaves the try the code inside the finally clause is guaranteed to execute. This is useful when writing code that must relinquish an expensive resource (such as an opened file or a database connection) when finished processing:

```
FileStream stm = null;                           // C# example

try {

    stm = new FileStream ("logfile.txt", FileMode.Create);

    return ProcessStuff(stm);                    // may throw an exception

} finally {

    if (stm != null)

        stm.Close();

}
```

Since this pattern is fairly common, C# has a special syntax:

```
using (FileStream stm = new FileStream ("logfile.txt", FileMode.Create)) {

    return ProcessStuff(stm);                    // may throw an exception

}
```

Upon leaving the using-block, the compiler guarantees that the stm object is released, effectively binding the variable to the file stream while abstracting from the side effects of initializing and releasing the file. Python's with statement and Ruby's block argument to File.open are used to similar effect.

All the languages mentioned above define standard exceptions and the circumstances under which they are thrown. Users can throw exceptions of their own; in fact C++ allows users to throw and catch almost any type, including basic types like int, whereas other languages like Java aren't as permissive.

Continuations

Async

C# 5.0 introduced the async keyword for supporting asynchronous I/O in a "direct style".

Generators

Generators, also known as semicoroutines, allow control to be yielded to a consumer method temporarily, typically using a yield keyword. Like the async keyword, this supports programming in a "direct style".

Coroutines

Coroutines are functions that can yield control to each other - a form of co-operative multitasking without threads.

Coroutines can be implemented as a library if the programming language provides either continuations or generators - so the distinction between coroutines and generators in practice is a technical detail.

Non-local Control Flow Cross Reference

Proposed Control Structures

In a spoof Datamation article in 1973, R. Lawrence Clark suggested that the GOTO statement could be replaced by the COMEFROM statement, and provides some entertaining examples. COMEFROM was implemented in one esoteric programming language named INTERCAL.

Donald Knuth's 1974 article "Structured Programming with go to Statements", identifies two situations which were not covered by the control structures listed above, and gave examples of control structures which could handle these situations. Despite their utility, these constructs have not yet found their way into mainstream programming languages.

Loop with Test in the Middle

The following was proposed by Dahl in 1972:

```
loop                          loop

    xxx1                          read(char);

while test;                   while not atEndOfFile;

    xxx2                          write(char);

repeat;                       repeat;
```

If *xxx1* is omitted we get a loop with the test at the top. If xxx2 is omitted we get a loop with the test at the bottom. If while is omitted we get an infinite loop. Hence this single construction can replace several constructions in most programming languages. A possible variant is to allow more than one while test; within the loop, but the use of exitwhen appears to cover this case better.

Languages lacking this construct generally emulate it using an equivalent infinite-loop-with-break idiom:

```
while (true) {

    xxx1

    if (not test)

        break

    xxx2

}
```

In Ada, the above loop construct (loop-while-repeat) can be represented using a standard infinite loop (loop - end loop) that has an exit when clause in the middle.

```
with Ada.Text_IO;

with Ada.Integer_Text_IO;

procedure Print_Squares is

    X : Integer;

begin

    Read_Data : loop

        Ada.Integer_Text_IO.Get(X);

    exit Read_Data when X = 0;

        Ada.Text IO.Put (X * X);

        Ada.Text IO.New_Line;

    end loop Read_Data;

end Print_Squares;
```

Naming a loop (like *Read_Data* in this example) is optional but permits leaving the outer loop of several nested loops.

Multiple Early Exit/Exit from Nested Loops

This was proposed by Zahn in 1974. A modified version is presented here.

```
    exitwhen EventA or EventB or EventC;

        xxx

    exits

        EventA: actionA

        EventB: actionB

        EventC: actionC

    endexit;
```

exit when is used to specify the events which may occur within xxx, their occurrence is indicated by using the name of the event as a statement. When some event does occur, the relevant action is carried out, and then control passes just after endexit. This construction provides a very clear separation between determining that some situation applies, and the action to be taken for that situation.

exitwhen is conceptually similar to exception handling, and exceptions or similar constructs are used for this purpose in many languages.

The following simple example involves searching a two-dimensional table for a particular item.

```
exitwhen found or missing;

    for I := 1 to N do

        for J := 1 to M do

            if table[I,J] = target then found;

    missing;

exits

    found:   print ("item is in table");

    missing: print ("item is not in table");

endexit;
```

Security

One way to attack a piece of software is to redirect the flow of execution of a program. A variety of control-flow integrity techniques, including stack canaries, buffer overflow protection, shadow stacks, and vtable pointer verification, are used to defend against these attacks.

References

- David Anthony Watt; William Findlay (2004). Programming language design concepts. John Wiley & Sons. p. 228. ISBN 978-0-470-85320-7

- Payer, Mathias; Kuznetsov, Volodymyr. "On differences between the CFI, CPS, and CPI properties". nebelwelt. net. Retrieved 2016-06-01

- Kenneth C. Louden; Kenneth A. Lambert (2011). Programming Languages: Principles and Practices (3 ed.). Cengage Learning. pp. 422–423. ISBN 1-111-52941-8

- Böhm, C.; Jacopini, G. (May 1966). "Flow diagrams, Turing machines and languages with only two formation rules". Communications of the ACM. 9 (5): 366–371. doi:10.1145/355592.365646

- "The Common Lisp Cookbook - Macros and Backquote". Cl-cookbook.sourceforge.net. 2007-01-16. Retrieved 2013-08-17

- David Anthony Watt; William Findlay (2004). Programming language design concepts. John Wiley & Sons. pp. 215–221. ISBN 978-0-470-85320-7

- Dijkstra, Edsger W. (March 1968). "Letters to the editor: Go to statement considered harmful" (PDF). Communications of the ACM. 11 (3): 147–148. doi:10.1145/362929.362947

- David Anthony Watt; William Findlay (2004). Programming language design concepts. John Wiley & Sons. pp. 221–222. ISBN 978-0-470-85320-7

- Kozen, Dexter (2008). "The Böhm–Jacopini Theorem Is False, Propositionally". Lecture Notes in Computer Science: 177–192. doi:10.1007/978-3-540-70594-9_11

4

An Introduction to Programming Paradigms

Programming paradigms help in the categorization of programming languages based on their specifications. Object-oriented programming, aspect-oriented programming, automata-based programming, flow-based programming, non-structured programming and event-driven programming are some of the types of programming paradigm. The chapter on programming paradigm offers an insightful focus, keeping in mind the complex subject matter.

Programming Paradigm

Programming paradigms are a way to classify programming languages based on their features. Languages can be classified into multiple paradigms.

Some paradigms are concerned mainly with implications for the execution model of the language, such as allowing side effects, or whether the sequence of operations is defined by the execution model. Other paradigms are concerned mainly with the way that code is organized, such as grouping a code into units along with the state that is modified by the code. Yet others are concerned mainly with the style of syntax and grammar.

Common programming paradigms include:

- imperative which allows side effects,

- functional which disallows side effects,

- declarative which does not state the order in which operations execute,

- object-oriented which groups code together with the state the code modifies,

- procedural which groups code into functions,

- logic which has a particular style of execution model coupled to a particular style of syntax and grammar, and

- symbolic programming which has a particular style of syntax and grammar.

For example, languages that fall into the imperative paradigm have two main features: they state the order in which operations occur, with constructs that explicitly control that order, and they allow side effects, in which state can be modified at one point in time, within one unit of code, and then later read at a different point in time inside a different unit of code. The communication between the units of code is not explicit. Meanwhile, in object-oriented programming, code is organized into objects that contain state that is only modified by the code that is part of the object. Most object-oriented languages are also imperative languages. In contrast, languages that fit the declarative paradigm do not state the order in which to execute operations. Instead, they supply a number of operations that are available in the system, along with the conditions under which each is allowed to execute. The implementation of the language's execution model tracks which operations are free to execute and chooses the order on its own. More at Comparison of multi-paradigm programming languages.

Overview

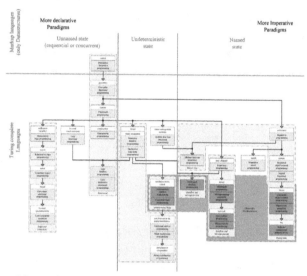

Overview of the various programming paradigms according to Peter Van Roy

Just as software engineering (as a process) is defined by differing *methodologies*, so the programming languages (as models of computation) are defined by differing *paradigms*. Some languages are designed to support one paradigm (Smalltalk supports object-oriented programming, Haskell supports functional programming), while other programming languages support multiple paradigms (such as Object Pascal, C++, Java, C#, Scala, Visual Basic, Common Lisp, Scheme, Perl, PHP, Python, Ruby, Oz, and F#). For example, programs written in C++, Object Pascal or PHP can be purely procedural, purely object-oriented, or can contain elements of both or other paradigms. Software designers and programmers decide how to use those paradigm elements.

In object-oriented programming, programs are treated as a set of interacting objects. In functional programming, programs are treated as a sequence of stateless function evaluations. When programming computers or systems with many processors, in process-oriented programming, programs are treated as sets of concurrent processes acting on logically shared data structures.

Many programming paradigms are as well known for the techniques they *forbid* as for those they *enable*. For instance, pure functional programming disallows use of side-effects, while structured programming disallows use of the goto statement. Partly for this reason, new paradigms are often regarded as doctrinaire or overly rigid by those accustomed to earlier styles. Yet, avoiding certain techniques can make it easier to understand program behavior, and to prove theorems about program correctness.

Programming paradigms can also be compared with *programming models* which allow invoking an execution model by using only an API. Programming models can also be classified into paradigms, based on features of the execution model.

For parallel computing, using a programming model instead of a language is common. The reason is that details of the parallel hardware leak into the abstractions used to program the hardware. This causes the programmer to have to map patterns in the algorithm onto patterns in the execution model (which have been inserted due to leakage of hardware into the abstraction). As a consequence, no one parallel programming language maps well to all computation problems. It is thus more convenient to use a base sequential language and insert API calls to parallel execution models, via a programming model. Such parallel programming models can be classified according to abstractions that reflect the hardware, such as shared memory, distributed memory with message passing, notions of *place* visible in the code, and so forth. These can be considered flavors of programming paradigm that apply to only parallel languages and programming models.

History

Different approaches to programming have developed over time, being identified as such either at the time or retrospectively. An early approach consciously identified as such is structured programming, advocated since the mid 1960s. The concept of a "programming paradigm" as such dates at least to 1978, in the Turing Award lecture of Robert W. Floyd, entitled *The Paradigms of Programming*, which cites the notion of paradigm as used by Thomas Kuhn in his *The Structure of Scientific Revolutions* (1962).

Machine Code

The lowest-level programming paradigms are machine code, which directly represents the instructions (the contents of program memory) as a sequence of numbers, and assembly language where the machine instructions are represented by mnemonics and memory addresses can be given symbolic labels. These are sometimes called first- and second-generation languages.

In the 1960s, assembly languages were developed to support library COPY and quite sophisticated conditional macro generation and preprocessing abilities, CALL to (subroutines), external variables and common sections (globals), enabling significant code re-use and isolation from hardware specifics via use of logical operators such as READ/WRITE/GET/PUT. Assembly was, and still is, used for time critical systems and often in embedded systems as it gives the most direct control of what the machine does.

Procedural Languages

The next advance was the development of procedural languages. These third-generation languages (the first described as high-level languages) use vocabulary related to the problem being solved. For example,

- COmmon Business Oriented Language (COBOL) – uses terms like file, move and copy.

- FORmula TRANslation (FORTRAN) – using mathematical language terminology, it was developed mainly for scientific and engineering problems.

- ALGOrithmic Language (ALGOL) – focused on being an appropriate language to define algorithms, while using mathematical language terminology and targeting scientific and engineering problems just like FORTRAN.

- Programming Language One (PL/I) – a hybrid commercial-scientific general purpose language supporting pointers.

- Beginners All purpose Symbolic Instruction Code (BASIC) – it was developed to enable more people to write programs.

- C – a general-purpose programming language, initially developed by Dennis Ritchie between 1969 and 1973 at AT&T Bell Labs.

All these languages follow the procedural paradigm. That is, they describe, step by step, exactly the procedure that should, according to the particular programmer at least, be followed to solve a specific problem. The efficacy and efficiency of any such solution are both therefore entirely subjective and highly dependent on that programmer's experience, inventiveness, and ability.

Following the widespread use of procedural languages, object-oriented programming (OOP) languages were created, such as Simula, Smalltalk, C++, C#, Eiffel, PHP, and Java. In these languages, data and methods to manipulate it are kept as one unit called an object. The only way that another object or user can access the data is via the object's *methods*. Thus, the inner workings of an object may be changed without affecting any code that uses the object. There is still some controversy raised by Alexander Stepanov, Richard Stallman and other programmers, concerning the efficacy of the OOP paradigm versus the procedural paradigm. The need for every object to have associative methods leads some skeptics to associate OOP with software bloat; an attempt to resolve this dilemma came through polymorphism.

Because object-oriented programming is considered a paradigm, not a language, it is possible to create even an object-oriented assembler language. High Level Assembly (HLA) is an example of this that fully supports advanced data types and object-oriented assembly language programming – despite its early origins. Thus, differing programming paradigms can be seen rather like *motivational memes* of their advocates, rather than necessarily representing progress from one level to the next. Precise comparisons of the efficacy of competing paradigms are frequently made more difficult because of new and differing terminology applied to similar entities and processes together with numerous implementation distinctions across languages.

Further Paradigms

Literate programming, as a form of imperative programming, structures programs as a human-centered web, as in a hypertext essay: documentation is integral to the program, and the program is structured following the logic of prose exposition, rather than compiler convenience.

Independent of the imperative branch, declarative programming paradigms were developed. In these languages, the computer is told what the problem is, not how to solve the problem – the program is structured as a set of properties to find in the expected result, not as a procedure to follow. Given a database or a set of rules, the computer tries to find a solution matching all the desired properties. An archetype of a declarative language is the fourth generation language SQL, and the family of functional languages and logic programming.

Functional programming is a subset of declarative programming. Programs written using this paradigm use functions, blocks of code intended to behave like mathematical functions. Functional languages discourage changes in the value of variables through assignment, making a great deal of use of recursion instead.

The logic programming paradigm views computation as automated reasoning over a body of knowledge. Facts about the problem domain are expressed as logic formulae, and programs are executed by applying inference rules over them until an answer to the problem is found, or the set of formulae is proved inconsistent.

Symbolic programming is a paradigm that describes programs able to manipulate formulas and program components as data. Programs can thus effectively modify themselves, and appear to "learn", making them suited for applications such as artificial intelligence, expert systems, natural language processing and computer games. Languages that support this paradigm include Lisp and Prolog.

Multi-paradigm

A *multi-paradigm programming language* is a programming language that supports more than one programming paradigm. The design goal of such languages is to allow programmers to use the most suitable programming style and associated language constructs for a given job, considering that no single paradigm solves all problems in the easiest or most efficient way.

One example is C#, which includes imperative and object-oriented paradigms, together with a certain level of support for functional programming with features like delegates (allowing functions to be treated as first-order objects), type inference, anonymous functions and Language Integrated Query. Other examples are F#, Python and Scala, which provide similar functionality to C# but also include full support for functional programming (including currying, pattern matching, algebraic data types, lazy evaluation, tail recursion, immutability, etc.). Perhaps the most extreme example is Oz, which has subsets that adhere to logic (Oz descends from logic programming), functional, object-oriented, dataflow concurrent, and other paradigms. Oz was designed over a ten-year period to combine in a harmonious way concepts that are traditionally associated with different programming paradigms. Lisp, while often taught as a functional language, is known for its malleability and thus its ability to engulf many paradigms.

Object-oriented Programming

Object-oriented programming (OOP) is a programming paradigm based on the concept of "objects", which may contain data, in the form of fields, often known as *attributes;* and code, in the form of procedures, often known as *methods*. A feature of objects is that an object's procedures can access and often modify the data fields of the object with which they are associated (objects have a notion of "this" or "self"). In OOP, computer programs are designed by making them out of objects that interact with one another. There is significant diversity of OOP languages, but the most popular ones are class-based, meaning that objects are instances of classes, which typically also determine their type.

Many of the most widely used programming languages (such as C++, Delphi, Java, Python etc.) are multi-paradigm programming languages that support object-oriented programming to a greater or lesser degree, typically in combination with imperative, procedural programming. Significant object-oriented languages include Java, C++, C#, Python, PHP, Ruby, Perl, Object Pascal, Objective-C, Dart, Swift, Scala, Common Lisp, and Smalltalk.

Features

Object-oriented Programming uses objects, but not all of the associated techniques and structures are supported directly in languages that claim to support OOP. The features listed below are, however, common among languages considered strongly class- and object-oriented (or multi-paradigm with OOP support), with notable exceptions mentioned.

Shared with Non-OOP Predecessor Languages

Object-oriented programming languages typically share low-level features with high-level procedural programming languages (which were invented first). The fundamental tools that can be used to construct a program include:

- Variables that can store information formatted in a small number of built-in data types like integers and alphanumeric characters. This may include data structures like strings, lists, and hash tables that are either built-in or result from combining variables using memory pointers

- Procedures – also known as functions, methods, routines, or subroutines – that take input, generate output, and manipulate data. Modern languages include structured programming constructs like loops and conditionals.

Modular programming support provides the ability to group procedures into files and modules for organizational purposes. Modules are namespaced so code in one module will not be accidentally confused with the same procedure or variable name in another file or module.

Objects and Classes

Languages that support object-oriented programming typically use inheritance for code reuse and extensibility in the form of either classes or prototypes. Those that use classes support two main concepts:

- Classes – the definitions for the data format and available procedures for a given type or class of object; may also contain data and procedures (known as class methods) themselves, i.e. classes contains the data members and member functions

- Objects – instances of classes

Objects sometimes correspond to things found in the real world. For example, a graphics program may have objects such as "circle", "square", "menu". An online shopping system might have objects such as "shopping cart", "customer", and "product". Sometimes objects represent more abstract entities, like an object that represents an open file, or an object that provides the service of translating measurements from U.S. customary to metric.

Each object is said to be an instance of a particular class (for example, an object with its name field set to "Mary" might be an instance of class Employee). Procedures in object-oriented programming are known as methods; variables are also known as fields, members, attributes, or properties. This leads to the following terms:

- Class variables – belong to the *class as a whole*; there is only one copy of each one

- Instance variables or attributes – data that belongs to individual *objects*; every object has its own copy of each one

- Member variables – refers to both the class and instance variables that are defined by a particular class

- Class methods – belong to the *class as a whole* and have access only to class variables and inputs from the procedure call

- Instance methods – belong to *individual objects*, and have access to instance variables for the specific object they are called on, inputs, and class variables

Objects are accessed somewhat like variables with complex internal structure, and in many languages are effectively pointers, serving as actual references to a single instance of said object in memory within a heap or stack. They provide a layer of abstraction which can be used to separate internal from external code. External code can use an object by calling a specific instance method with a certain set of input parameters, read an instance variable, or write to an instance variable. Objects are created by calling a special type of method in the class known as a constructor. A program may create many instances of the same class as it runs, which operate independently. This is an easy way for the same procedures to be used on different sets of data.

Object-oriented programming that uses classes is sometimes called class-based programming, while prototype-based programming does not typically use classes. As a result, a significantly different yet analogous terminology is used to define the concepts of *object* and *instance*.

In some languages classes and objects can be composed using other concepts like traits and mixins.

Dynamic Dispatch/message Passing

It is the responsibility of the object, not any external code, to select the procedural code to execute in response to a method call, typically by looking up the method at run time in a table associated with the object. This feature is known as dynamic dispatch, and distinguishes an object from an abstract data type (or module), which has a fixed (static) implementation of the operations for all instances. If there are multiple methods that might be run for a given name, it is known as multiple dispatch.

A method call is also known as *message passing*. It is conceptualized as a message (the name of the method and its input parameters) being passed to the object for dispatch.

Encapsulation

Encapsulation is an Object Oriented Programming concept that binds together the data and functions that manipulate the data, and that keeps both safe from outside interference and misuse. Data encapsulation led to the important OOP concept of data hiding.

If a class does not allow calling code to access internal object data and permits access through methods only, this is a strong form of abstraction or information hiding known as encapsulation. Some languages (Java, for example) let classes enforce access restrictions explicitly, for example denoting internal data with the private keyword and designating methods intended for use by code outside the class with the public keyword. Methods may also be designed public, private, or intermediate levels such as protected (which allows access from the same class and its subclasses, but not objects of a different class). In other languages (like Python) this is enforced only by convention (for example, private methods may have names that start with an underscore). Encapsulation prevents external code from being concerned with the internal workings of an object. This facilitates code refactoring, for example allowing the author of the class to change how objects of that class represent their data internally without changing any external code (as long as "public" method calls work the same way). It also encourages programmers to put all the code that is concerned with a certain set of data in the same class, which organizes it for easy comprehension by other programmers. Encapsulation is a technique that encourages decoupling.

Composition, Inheritance, and Delegation

Objects can contain other objects in their instance variables; this is known as object composition. For example, an object in the Employee class might contain (point to) an object in the Address class, in addition to its own instance variables like "first_name" and "position". Object composition is used to represent "has-a" relationships: every employee has an address, so every Employee object has a place to store an Address object.

Languages that support classes almost always support inheritance. This allows classes to be arranged in a hierarchy that represents "is-a-type-of" relationships. For example, class Employee might inherit from class Person. All the data and methods available to the parent class also appear in the child class with the same names. For example, class Person might define variables "first_name" and "last_name" with method "make_full_name()". These will also be available in class Employee, which might add the variables "position" and "salary". This technique allows easy re-use of the same procedures and data definitions, in addition to potentially mirroring real-world relationships in an intuitive way. Rather than utilizing database tables and programming subroutines, the developer utilizes objects the user may be more familiar with: objects from their application domain.

Subclasses can override the methods defined by superclasses. Multiple inheritance is allowed in some languages, though this can make resolving overrides complicated. Some languages have special support for mixins, though in any language with multiple inheritance, a mixin is simply a class that does not represent an is-a-type-of relationship. Mixins are typically used to add the same methods to multiple classes. For example, class UnicodeConversionMixin might provide a method unicode_to_ascii() when included in class FileReader and class WebPageScraper, which don't share a common parent.

Abstract classes cannot be instantiated into objects; they exist only for the purpose of inheritance into other "concrete" classes which can be instantiated. In Java, the final keyword can be used to prevent a class from being subclassed.

The doctrine of composition over inheritance advocates implementing has-a relationships using composition instead of inheritance. For example, instead of inheriting from class Person, class Employee could give each Employee object an internal Person object, which it then has the opportunity to hide from external code even if class Person has many public attributes or methods. Some languages, like Go do not support inheritance at all.

The "open/closed principle" advocates that classes and functions "should be open for extension, but closed for modification".

Delegation is another language feature that can be used as an alternative to inheritance.

Polymorphism

Subtyping, a form of polymorphism, is when calling code can be agnostic as to whether an object belongs to a parent class or one of its descendants. For example, a function might call "make_full_name()" on an object, which will work whether the object is of class Person or class Employee. This is another type of abstraction which simplifies code external to the class hierarchy and enables strong separation of concerns.

Open Recursion

In languages that support open recursion, object methods can call other methods on the same object (including themselves), typically using a special variable or keyword called this or self. This variable is *late-bound*; it allows a method defined in one class to invoke another method that is defined later, in some subclass thereof.

History

Terminology invoking "objects" and "oriented" in the modern sense of object-oriented programming made its first appearance at MIT in the late 1950s and early 1960s. In the environment of the artificial intelligence group, as early as 1960, "object" could refer to identified items (LISP atoms) with properties (attributes); Alan Kay was later to cite a detailed understanding of LISP internals as a strong influence on his thinking in 1966. Another early MIT example was Sketchpad created by Ivan Sutherland in 1960–61; in the glossary of the 1963 technical report based on his dissertation about Sketchpad, Sutherland defined notions of "object" and "instance" (with the class concept covered by "master" or "definition"), albeit specialized to graphical interaction. Also, an MIT ALGOL version, AED-0, established a direct link between data structures ("plexes", in that dialect) and procedures, prefiguring what were later termed "messages", "methods", and "member functions".

The formal programming concept of objects was introduced in the mid-1960s with Simula 67, a major revision of Simula I, a programming language designed for discrete event simulation, created by Ole-Johan Dahl and Kristen Nygaard of the Norwegian Computing Center in Oslo.

Simula 67 was influenced by SIMSCRIPT and C.A.R. "Tony" Hoare's proposed "record classes". Simula introduced the notion of classes and instances or objects (as well as subclasses, virtual procedures, coroutines, and discrete event simulation) as part of an explicit programming paradigm. The language also used automatic garbage collection that had been invented earlier for the functional programming language Lisp. Simula was used for physical modeling, such as models to study and improve the movement of ships and their content through cargo ports. The ideas of Simula 67 influenced many later languages, including Smalltalk, derivatives of LISP (CLOS), Object Pascal, and C++.

The Smalltalk language, which was developed at Xerox PARC (by Alan Kay and others) in the 1970s, introduced the term *object-oriented programming* to represent the pervasive use of objects and messages as the basis for computation. Smalltalk creators were influenced by the ideas introduced in Simula 67, but Smalltalk was designed to be a fully dynamic system in which classes could be created and modified dynamically rather than statically as in Simula 67. Smalltalk and with it OOP were introduced to a wider audience by the August 1981 issue of *Byte Magazine*.

In the 1970s, Kay's Smalltalk work had influenced the Lisp community to incorporate object-based techniques that were introduced to developers via the Lisp machine. Experimentation with various extensions to Lisp (such as LOOPS and Flavors introducing multiple inheritance and mixins) eventually led to the Common Lisp Object System, which integrates functional programming and object-oriented programming and allows extension via a Meta-object protocol. In the 1980s, there were a few attempts to design processor architectures that included hardware support for objects in memory but these were not successful. Examples include the Intel iAPX 432 and the Linn Smart Rekursiv.

In 1985, Bertrand Meyer produced the first design of the Eiffel language. Focused on software quality, Eiffel is among the purely object-oriented languages, but differs in the sense that the language itself is not only a programming language, but a notation supporting the entire software lifecycle. Meyer described the Eiffel software development method, based on a small number of key ideas from software engineering and computer science, in Object-Oriented Software Construction. Essential to the quality focus of Eiffel is Meyer's reliability mechanism, Design by Contract, which is an integral part of both the method and language.

Object-oriented programming developed as the dominant programming methodology in the early and mid 1990s when programming languages supporting the techniques became widely available. These included Visual FoxPro 3.0, C++, and Delphi. Its dominance was further enhanced by the rising popularity of graphical user interfaces, which rely heavily upon object-oriented programming techniques. An example of a closely related dynamic GUI library and OOP language can be found in the Cocoa frameworks on Mac OS X, written in Objective-C, an object-oriented, dynamic messaging extension to C based on Smalltalk. OOP toolkits also enhanced the popularity of event-driven programming (although this concept is not limited to OOP).

At ETH Zürich, Niklaus Wirth and his colleagues had also been investigating such topics as data abstraction and modular programming (although this had been in common use in the 1960s or earlier). Modula-2 (1978) included both, and their succeeding design, Oberon, included a distinctive approach to object orientation, classes, and such.

Object-oriented features have been added to many previously existing languages, including Ada, BASIC, Fortran, Pascal, and COBOL. Adding these features to languages that were not initially designed for them often led to problems with compatibility and maintainability of code.

More recently, a number of languages have emerged that are primarily object-oriented, but that are also compatible with procedural methodology. Two such languages are Python and Ruby.

Probably the most commercially important recent object-oriented languages are Java, developed by Sun Microsystems, as well as C# and Visual Basic.NET (VB.NET), both designed for Microsoft's .NET platform. Each of these two frameworks shows, in its own way, the benefit of using OOP by creating an abstraction from implementation. VB.NET and C# support cross-language inheritance, allowing classes defined in one language to subclass classes defined in the other language.

Oop Languages

Simula (1967) is generally accepted as being the first language with the primary features of an object-oriented language. It was created for making simulation programs, in which what came to be called objects were the most important information representation. Smalltalk (1972 to 1980) is another early example, and the one with which much of the theory of OOP was developed. Concerning the degree of object orientation, the following distinctions can be made:

- Languages called "pure" OO languages, because everything in them is treated consistently as an object, from primitives such as characters and punctuation, all the way up to whole classes, prototypes, blocks, modules, etc. They were designed specifically to facilitate, even enforce, OO methods. Examples: Python, Ruby, Scala, Smalltalk, Eiffel, Emerald, JADE, Self.

- Languages designed mainly for OO programming, but with some procedural elements. Examples: Java, C++, C#, Delphi/Object Pascal, VB.NET.

- Languages that are historically procedural languages, but have been extended with some OO features. Examples: PHP, Perl, Visual Basic (derived from BASIC), MATLAB, COBOL 2002, Fortran 2003, ABAP, Ada 95, Pascal.

- Languages with most of the features of objects (classes, methods, inheritance), but in a distinctly original form. Examples: Oberon (Oberon-1 or Oberon-2).

- Languages with abstract data type support which may be used to resemble OO programming, but without all features of object-orientation. This includes object-*based* and prototype-based languages. Examples: JavaScript, Lua, Modula-2, CLU.

- Chameleon languages that support multiple paradigms, including OO. Tcl stands out among these for TclOO, a hybrid object system that supports both prototype-based programming and class-based OO.

OOP in Dynamic Languages

In recent years, object-oriented programming has become especially popular in dynamic programming languages. Python, PowerShell, Ruby and Groovy are dynamic languages built on OOP principles, while Perl and PHP have been adding object-oriented features since Perl 5 and PHP 4, and ColdFusion since version 6.

The Document Object Model of HTML, XHTML, and XML documents on the Internet has bindings to the popular JavaScript/ECMAScript language. JavaScript is perhaps the best known prototype-based programming language, which employs cloning from prototypes rather than inheriting from a class (contrast to class-based programming). Another scripting language that takes this approach is Lua.

OOP in a Network Protocol

The messages that flow between computers to request services in a client-server environment can be designed as the linearizations of objects defined by class objects known to both the client and the server. For example, a simple linearized object would consist of a length field, a code point identifying the class, and a data value. A more complex example would be a command consisting of the length and code point of the command and values consisting of linearized objects representing the command's parameters. Each such command must be directed by the server to an object whose class (or superclass) recognizes the command and is able to provide the requested service. Clients and servers are best modeled as complex object-oriented structures. Distributed Data Management Architecture (DDM) took this approach and used class objects to define objects at four levels of a formal hierarchy:

- Fields defining the data values that form messages, such as their length, codepoint and data values.

- Objects and collections of objects similar to what would be found in a Smalltalk program for messages and parameters.

- Managers similar to AS/400 objects, such as a directory to files and files consisting of metadata and records. Managers conceptually provide memory and processing resources for their contained objects.

- A client or server consisting of all the managers necessary to implement a full processing environment, supporting such aspects as directory services, security and concurrency control.

The initial version of DDM defined distributed file services. It was later extended to be the foundation of Distributed Relational Database Architecture (DRDA).

Design Patterns

Challenges of object-oriented design are addressed by several methodologies. Most common is known as the design patterns codified by Gamma *et al.*. More broadly, the term "design patterns" can be used to refer to any general, repeatable solution to a commonly occurring problem in software design. Some of these commonly occurring problems have implications and solutions particular to object-oriented development.

Inheritance and Behavioral Subtyping

It is intuitive to assume that inheritance creates a semantic "is a" relationship, and thus to infer that objects instantiated from subclasses can always be *safely* used instead of those instantiated from the superclass. This intuition is unfortunately false in most OOP languages, in particular in all those that allow mutable objects. Subtype polymorphism as enforced by the type checker in OOP languages (with mutable objects) cannot guarantee behavioral subtyping in any context. Behavioral subtyping is undecidable in general, so it cannot be implemented by a program (compiler). Class or object hierarchies must be carefully designed, considering possible incorrect uses that cannot be detected syntactically. This issue is known as the Liskov substitution principle.

Gang of Four Design Patterns

Design Patterns: Elements of Reusable Object-Oriented Software is an influential book published in 1995 by Erich Gamma, Richard Helm, Ralph Johnson, and John Vlissides, often referred to humorously as the "Gang of Four". Along with exploring the capabilities and pitfalls of object-oriented programming, it describes 23 common programming problems and patterns for solving them. As of April 2007, the book was in its 36th printing.

The book describes the following patterns:

- *Creational patterns* (5): Factory method pattern, Abstract factory pattern, Singleton pattern, Builder pattern, Prototype pattern

- *Structural patterns* (7): Adapter pattern, Bridge pattern, Composite pattern, Decorator pattern, Facade pattern, Flyweight pattern, Proxy pattern

- *Behavioral patterns* (11): Chain-of-responsibility pattern, Command pattern, Interpreter pattern, Iterator pattern, Mediator pattern, Memento pattern, Observer pattern, State pattern, Strategy pattern, Template method pattern, Visitor pattern

Object-orientation and Databases

Both object-oriented programming and relational database management systems (RDBMSs) are extremely common in software today. Since relational databases don't store objects directly (though some RDBMSs have object-oriented features to approximate this), there is a general need to bridge the two worlds. The problem of bridging object-oriented programming accesses and data patterns with relational databases is known as object-relational impedance mismatch. There are a number of approaches to cope with this problem, but no general solution without downsides. One of the most common approaches is object-relational mapping, as found in IDE languages such as Visual FoxPro and libraries such as Java Data Objects and Ruby on Rails' ActiveRecord.

There are also object databases that can be used to replace RDBMSs, but these have not been as technically and commercially successful as RDBMSs.

Real-world Modeling and Relationships

OOP can be used to associate real-world objects and processes with digital counterparts. However, not everyone agrees that OOP facilitates direct real-world mapping or that real-world mapping is even a worthy goal; Bertrand Meyer argues in *Object-Oriented Software Construction* that a program is not a model of the world but a model of some part of the world; "Reality is a cousin twice removed". At the same time, some principal limitations of OOP have been noted. For example, the circle-ellipse problem is difficult to handle using OOP's concept of inheritance.

However, Niklaus Wirth (who popularized the adage now known as Wirth's law: "Software is getting slower more rapidly than hardware becomes faster") said of OOP in his paper, "Good Ideas through the Looking Glass", "This paradigm closely reflects the structure of systems 'in the real world', and it is therefore well suited to model complex systems with complex behaviours" (contrast KISS principle).

Steve Yegge and others noted that natural languages lack the OOP approach of strictly prioritizing *things* (objects/nouns) before *actions* (methods/verbs). This problem may cause OOP to suffer more convoluted solutions than procedural programming.

OOP and Control Flow

OOP was developed to increase the reusability and maintainability of source code. Transparent representation of the control flow had no priority and was meant to be handled by a compiler. With the increasing relevance of parallel hardware and multithreaded coding, developing transparent control flow becomes more important, something hard to achieve with OOP.

Responsibility- vs. Data-driven Design

Responsibility-driven design defines classes in terms of a contract, that is, a class should be defined around a responsibility and the information that it shares. This is contrasted by Wirfs-Brock and Wilkerson with data-driven design, where classes are defined around the data-structures that must be held. The authors hold that responsibility-driven design is preferable.

SOLID and GRASP Guidelines

SOLID is a mnemonic invented by Michael Feathers that stands for and advocates five programming practices:

- Single responsibility principle

- Open/closed principle

- Liskov substitution principle

- Interface segregation principle

- Dependency inversion principle

GRASP (General Responsibility Assignment Software Patterns) is another set of guidelines advocated by Craig Larman.

Criticism

The OOP paradigm has been criticised for a number of reasons, including not meeting its stated goals of reusability and modularity, and for overemphasizing one aspect of software design and modeling (data/objects) at the expense of other important aspects (computation/algorithms).

Luca Cardelli has claimed that OOP code is "intrinsically less efficient" than procedural code, that OOP can take longer to compile, and that OOP languages have "extremely poor modularity properties with respect to class extension and modification", and tend to be extremely complex. The latter point is reiterated by Joe Armstrong, the principal inventor of Erlang, who is quoted as saying:

The problem with object-oriented languages is they've got all this implicit environment that they carry around with them. You wanted a banana but what you got was a gorilla holding the banana and the entire jungle.

A study by Potok et al. has shown no significant difference in productivity between OOP and procedural approaches.

Christopher J. Date stated that critical comparison of OOP to other technologies, relational in particular, is difficult because of lack of an agreed-upon and rigorous definition of OOP; however, Date and Darwen have proposed a theoretical foundation on OOP that uses OOP as a kind of customizable type system to support RDBMS.

In an article Lawrence Krubner claimed that compared to other languages (LISP dialects, functional languages, etc.) OOP languages have no unique strengths, and inflict a heavy burden of unneeded complexity.

Alexander Stepanov compares object orientation unfavourably to generic programming:

I find OOP technically unsound. It attempts to decompose the world in terms of interfaces that vary on a single type. To deal with the real problems you need multisorted algebras — families of interfaces that span multiple types. I find OOP philosophically unsound. It claims that everything is an object. Even if it is true it is not very interesting — saying that everything is an object is saying nothing at all.

Paul Graham has suggested that OOP's popularity within large companies is due to "large (and frequently changing) groups of mediocre programmers". According to Graham, the discipline imposed by OOP prevents any one programmer from "doing too much damage".

Steve Yegge noted that, as opposed to functional programming:

Object Oriented Programming puts the Nouns first and foremost. Why would you go to such lengths to put one part of speech on a pedestal? Why should one kind of concept take precedence over another? It's not as if OOP has suddenly made verbs less important in the way we actually think. It's a strangely skewed perspective.

Rich Hickey, creator of Clojure, described object systems as overly simplistic models of the real world. He emphasized the inability of OOP to model time properly, which is getting increasingly problematic as software systems become more concurrent.

Eric S. Raymond, a Unix programmer and open-source software advocate, has been critical of claims that present object-oriented programming as the "One True Solution", and has written that object-oriented programming languages tend to encourage thickly layered programs that destroy transparency. Raymond compares this unfavourably to the approach taken with Unix and the C programming language.

Rob Pike, a programmer involved in the creation of UTF-8 and Go, has called object-oriented programming "the Roman numerals of computing" and has said that OOP languages frequently shift the focus from data structures and algorithms to types. Furthermore, he cites an instance of a Java professor whose "idiomatic" solution to a problem was to create six new classes, rather than to simply use a lookup table.

Formal Semantics

Objects are the run-time entities in an object-oriented system. They may represent a person, a place, a bank account, a table of data, or any item that the program has to handle.

There have been several attempts at formalizing the concepts used in object-oriented programming. The following concepts and constructs have been used as interpretations of OOP concepts:

- co algebraic data types

- abstract data types (which have existential types) allow the definition of modules but these do not support dynamic dispatch

- recursive types

- encapsulated state

- inheritance

- records are basis for understanding objects if function literals can be stored in fields (like in functional programming languages), but the actual calculi need be considerably more complex to incorporate essential features of OOP. Several extensions of System $F_{<:}$ that deal with mutable objects have been studied; these allow both subtype polymorphism and parametric polymorphism (generics)

Attempts to find a consensus definition or theory behind objects have not proven very successful (however, Abadi & Cardelli, *A Theory of Objects* for formal definitions of many OOP concepts and constructs), and often diverge widely. For example, some definitions focus on mental activities, and some on program structuring. One of the simpler definitions is that OOP is the act of using "map" data structures or arrays that can contain functions and pointers to other maps, all with some syntactic and scoping sugar on top. Inheritance can be performed by cloning the maps (sometimes called "prototyping").

Aspect-oriented Programming

In computing, aspect-oriented programming (AOP) is a programming paradigm that aims to increase modularity by allowing the separation of cross-cutting concerns. It does so by adding additional behavior to existing code (an advice) *without* modifying the code itself, instead separately specifying which code is modified via a "pointcut" specification, such as "log all function calls when the function's name begins with 'set'". This allows behaviors that are not central to the business logic (such as logging) to be added to a program without cluttering the code core to the functionality. AOP forms a basis for aspect-oriented software development.

AOP includes programming methods and tools that support the modularization of concerns at the level of the source code, while "aspect-oriented software development" refers to a whole engineering discipline.

Aspect-oriented programming entails breaking down program logic into distinct parts (so-called *concerns*, cohesive areas of functionality). Nearly all programming paradigms support some level of grouping and encapsulation of concerns into separate, independent entities by providing abstractions (e.g., functions, procedures, modules, classes, methods) that can be used for implementing, abstracting and composing these concerns. Some concerns "cut across" multiple abstractions in a program, and defy these forms of implementation. These concerns are called *cross-cutting concerns* or horizontal concerns.

Logging exemplifies a crosscutting concern because a logging strategy necessarily affects every logged part of the system. Logging thereby *crosscuts* all logged classes and methods.

All AOP implementations have some crosscutting expressions that encapsulate each concern in one place. The difference between implementations lies in the power, safety, and usability of the constructs provided. For example, interceptors that specify the methods to intercept express a limited form of crosscutting, without much support for type-safety or debugging. AspectJ has a number of such expressions and encapsulates them in a special class, an aspect. For example, an aspect can alter the behavior of the base code (the non-aspect part of a program) by applying advice (additional behavior) at various join points (points in a program) specified in a quantification or query called a pointcut (that detects whether a given join point matches). An aspect can also make binary-compatible structural changes to other classes, like adding members or parents.

History

AOP has several direct antecedents A1 and A2: reflection and metaobject protocols, subject-oriented programming, Composition Filters and Adaptive Programming.

Gregor Kiczales and colleagues at Xerox PARC developed the explicit concept of AOP, and followed this with the AspectJ AOP extension to Java. IBM's research team pursued a tool approach over a language design approach and in 2001 proposed Hyper/J and the Concern Manipulation Environment, which have not seen wide usage. The examples use AspectJ as it is the most widely known AOP language.

The Microsoft Transaction Server is considered to be the first major application of AOP followed by Enterprise JavaBeans.

Motivation and Basic Concepts

Typically, an aspect is *scattered* or *tangled* as code, making it harder to understand and maintain. It is scattered by virtue of the function (such as logging) being spread over a number of unrelated functions that might use *its* function, possibly in entirely unrelated systems, different source languages, etc. That means to change logging can require modifying all affected modules. Aspects become tangled not only with the mainline function of the systems in which they are expressed but also with each other. That means changing one concern entails understanding all the tangled concerns or having some means by which the effect of changes can be inferred.

For example, consider a banking application with a conceptually very simple method for transferring an amount from one account to another:

```
void transfer(Account fromAcc, Account toAcc, int amount) throws Exception {

  if (fromAcc.getBalance() < amount)

      throw new InsufficientFundsException();
```

```
    fromAcc.withdraw(amount);

    toAcc.deposit(amount);

}
```

However, this transfer method overlooks certain considerations that a deployed application would require: it lacks security checks to verify that the current user has the authorization to perform this operation; a database transaction should encapsulate the operation in order to prevent accidental data loss; for diagnostics, the operation should be logged to the system log, etc.

A version with all those new concerns, for the sake of example, could look somewhat like this:

void transfer(Account fromAcc, Account toAcc, int amount, User user,

```
        Logger logger, Database database) throws Exception {

    logger.info("Transferring money...");

    if (!isUserAuthorised(user, fromAcc)) {

        logger.info("User has no permission.");

        throw new UnauthorisedUserException();

    }

    if (fromAcc.getBalance() < amount) {

        logger.info("Insufficient funds.");

        throw new InsufficientFundsException();

    }


    fromAcc.withdraw(amount);

    toAcc.deposit(amount);

    database.commitChanges();   // Atomic operation.


    logger.info("Transaction successful.");

}
```

In this example other interests have become *tangled* with the basic functionality (sometimes called the *business logic concern*). Transactions, security, and logging all exemplify *cross-cutting concerns*.

Now consider what happens if we suddenly need to change (for example) the security considerations for the application. In the program's current version, security-related operations appear *scattered* across numerous methods, and such a change would require a major effort.

AOP attempts to solve this problem by allowing the programmer to express cross-cutting concerns in stand-alone modules called *aspects*. Aspects can contain *advice* (code joined to specified points in the program) and *inter-type declarations* (structural members added to other classes). For example, a security module can include advice that performs a security check before accessing a bank account. The pointcut defines the times (join points) when one can access a bank account, and the code in the advice body defines how the security check is implemented. That way, both the check and the places can be maintained in one place. Further, a good pointcut can anticipate later program changes, so if another developer creates a new method to access the bank account, the advice will apply to the new method when it executes.

So for the above example implementing logging in an aspect:

```
aspect Logger {

  void Bank.transfer(Account  fromAcc,  Account  toAcc,  int  amount,  User
user, Logger logger)  {

    logger.info("Transferring money...");

  }


  void Bank.getMoneyBack(User user, int transactionId, Logger logger)  {

    logger.info("User requested money back.");

  }

  // Other crosscutting code.

}
```

One can think of AOP as a debugging tool or as a user-level tool. Advice should be reserved for the cases where you cannot get the function changed (user level) or do not want to change the function in production code (debugging).

Join Point Models

The advice-related component of an aspect-oriented language defines a join point model (JPM). A JPM defines three things:

1. When the advice can run. These are called *join points* because they are points in a running program where additional behavior can be usefully joined. A join point needs to be addressable and understandable by an ordinary programmer to be useful. It should also be stable across inconsequential program changes in order for an aspect to be stable across such changes. Many AOP implementations support method executions and field references as join points.

2. A way to specify (or *quantify*) join points, called *pointcuts*. Pointcuts determine whether a given join point matches. Most useful pointcut languages use a syntax like the base language (for example, AspectJ uses Java signatures) and allow reuse through naming and combination.

3. A means of specifying code to run at a join point. AspectJ calls this *advice*, and can run it before, after, and around join points. Some implementations also support things like defining a method in an aspect on another class.

Join-point models can be compared based on the join points exposed, how join points are specified, the operations permitted at the join points, and the structural enhancements that can be expressed.

AspectJ's Join-point Model

- The join points in AspectJ include method or constructor call or execution, the initialization of a class or object, field read and write access, exception handlers, etc. They do not include loops, super calls, throws clauses, multiple statements, etc.

- Pointcuts are specified by combinations of *primitive pointcut designators* (PCDs).

"Kinded" PCDs match a particular kind of join point (e.g., method execution) and tend to take as input a Java-like signature. One such pointcut looks like this:

```
execution(* set*(*))
```

This pointcut matches a method-execution join point, if the method name starts with "set" and there is exactly one argument of any type.

"Dynamic" PCDs check runtime types and bind variables. For example,

```
this(Point)
```

This pointcut matches when the currently executing object is an instance of class Point. Note that the unqualified name of a class can be used via Java's normal type lookup.

"Scope" PCDs limit the lexical scope of the join point. For example:

```
within(com.company.*)
```

This pointcut matches any join point in any type in the com.company package. The * is one form of the wildcards that can be used to match many things with one signature.

Pointcuts can be composed and named for reuse. For example:

```
pointcut set() : execution(* set*(*) ) && this(Point) && within(com.
company.*);
```

This pointcut matches a method-execution join point, if the method name starts with "set" and this is an instance of type Point in the com.company package. It can be referred to using the name "set()".

- Advice specifies to run at (before, after, or around) a join point (specified with a pointcut) certain code (specified like code in a method). The AOP runtime invokes Advice automatically when the pointcut matches the join point. For example:

```
after() : set() {

  Display.update();

}
```

This effectively specifies: "if the *set()* pointcut matches the join point, run the code Display. update() after the join point completes."

Other Potential Join Point Models

There are other kinds of JPMs. All advice languages can be defined in terms of their JPM. For example, a hypothetical aspect language for UML may have the following JPM:

- Join points are all model elements.

- Pointcuts are some boolean expression combining the model elements.

- The means of affect at these points are a visualization of all the matched join points.

Inter-type Declarations

Inter-type declarations provide a way to express crosscutting concerns affecting the structure of modules. Also known as *open classes* and *extension methods*, this enables programmers to declare in one place members or parents of another class, typically in order to combine all the code related to a concern in one aspect. For example, if a programmer implemented the crosscutting display-update concern using visitors instead, an inter-type declaration using the visitor pattern might look like this in AspectJ:

```
aspect DisplayUpdate {

  void Point.acceptVisitor(Visitor v) {

    v.visit(this);

  }

  // other crosscutting code...

}
```

This code snippet adds the acceptVisitor method to the Point class.

It is a requirement that any structural additions be compatible with the original class, so that clients of the existing class continue to operate, unless the AOP implementation can expect to control all clients at all times.

Implementation

AOP programs can affect other programs in two different ways, depending on the underlying languages and environments:

1. a combined program is produced, valid in the original language and indistinguishable from an ordinary program to the ultimate interpreter

2. the ultimate interpreter or environment is updated to understand and implement AOP features.

The difficulty of changing environments means most implementations produce compatible combination programs through a process known as *weaving* - a special case of program transformation. An aspect weaver reads the aspect-oriented code and generates appropriate object-oriented code with the aspects integrated. The same AOP language can be implemented through a variety of weaving methods, so the semantics of a language should never be understood in terms of the weaving implementation. Only the speed of an implementation and its ease of deployment are affected by which method of combination is used.

Systems can implement source-level weaving using preprocessors (as C++ was implemented originally in CFront) that require access to program source files. However, Java's well-defined binary form enables bytecode weavers to work with any Java program in .class-file form. Bytecode weavers can be deployed during the build process or, if the weave model is per-class, during class loading. AspectJ started with source-level weaving in 2001, delivered a per-class bytecode weaver in 2002, and offered advanced load-time support after the integration of AspectWerkz in 2005.

Any solution that combines programs at runtime has to provide views that segregate them properly to maintain the programmer's segregated model. Java's bytecode support for multiple source files enables any debugger to step through a properly woven .class file in a source editor. However, some third-party decompilers cannot process woven code because they expect code produced by Javac rather than all supported bytecode forms.

Deploy-time weaving offers another approach. This basically implies post-processing, but rather than patching the generated code, this weaving approach *subclasses* existing classes so that the modifications are introduced by method-overriding. The existing classes remain untouched, even at runtime, and all existing tools (debuggers, profilers, etc.) can be used during development. A similar approach has already proven itself in the implementation of many Java EE application servers, such as IBM's WebSphere.

Terminology

Standard terminology used in Aspect-oriented programming may include:

Cross-cutting concerns

> Even though most classes in an OO model will perform a single, specific function, they often share common, secondary requirements with other classes. For example, we may want to add logging to classes within the data-access layer and also to classes in the UI layer whenever a thread enters or exits a method. Further concerns can be related to secu-

rity such as access control or information flow control. Even though each class has a very different primary functionality, the code needed to perform the secondary functionality is often identical.

Advice

This is the additional code that you want to apply to your existing model. In our example, this is the logging code that we want to apply whenever the thread enters or exits a method.

Pointcut

This is the term given to the point of execution in the application at which cross-cutting concern needs to be applied. In our example, a pointcut is reached when the thread enters a method, and another pointcut is reached when the thread exits the method.

Aspect

The combination of the pointcut and the advice is termed an aspect. In the example above, we add a logging aspect to our application by defining a pointcut and giving the correct advice.

Comparison to Other Programming Paradigms

Aspects emerged from object-oriented programming and computational reflection. AOP languages have functionality similar to, but more restricted than metaobject protocols. Aspects relate closely to programming concepts like subjects, mixins, and delegation. Other ways to use aspect-oriented programming paradigms include Composition Filters and the hyperslices approach. Since at least the 1970s, developers have been using forms of interception and dispatch-patching that resemble some of the implementation methods for AOP, but these never had the semantics that the cross-cutting specifications provide written in one place.

Designers have considered alternative ways to achieve separation of code, such as C#'s partial types, but such approaches lack a quantification mechanism that allows reaching several join points of the code with one declarative statement.

Though it may seem unrelated, in testing, the use of mocks or stubs requires the use of AOP techniques, like around advice, and so forth. Here the collaborating objects are for the purpose of the test, a cross cutting concern. Thus the various Mock Object frameworks provide these features. For example, a process invokes a service to get a balance amount. In the test of the process, where the amount comes from is unimportant, only that the process uses the balance according to the requirements.

Adoption Issues

Programmers need to be able to read code and understand what is happening in order to prevent errors. Even with proper education, understanding crosscutting concerns can be difficult without proper support for visualizing both static structure and the dynamic flow of a program. Beginning in 2002, AspectJ began to provide IDE plug-ins to support the visualizing of crosscutting concerns. Those features, as well as aspect code assist and refactoring are now common.

Given the power of AOP, if a programmer makes a logical mistake in expressing crosscutting, it can lead to widespread program failure. Conversely, another programmer may change the join points in a program – e.g., by renaming or moving methods – in ways that the aspect writer did not anticipate, with unforeseen consequences. One advantage of modularizing crosscutting concerns is enabling one programmer to affect the entire system easily; as a result, such problems present as a conflict over responsibility between two or more developers for a given failure. However, the solution for these problems can be much easier in the presence of AOP, since only the aspect needs to be changed, whereas the corresponding problems without AOP can be much more spread out.

Criticism

The most basic criticism of the effect of AOP is that control flow is obscured, and is not only worse than the much-maligned GOTO, but is in fact closely analogous to the joke COME FROM statement. The *obliviousness of application*, which is fundamental to many definitions of AOP (the code in question has no indication that an advice will be applied, which is specified instead in the pointcut), means that the advice is not visible, in contrast to an explicit method call. For example, compare the COME FROM program:

```
 5 input x

10 print 'result is :'

15 print x


20 come from 10

25      x = x * x

30 return
```

with an AOP fragment with analogous semantics:

```
main() {

    input x

    print(result(x))

}

input result(int x) { return x }

around(int x): call(result(int)) && args(x) {

    int temp = proceed(x)

//     return temp * temp

}
```

Indeed, the pointcut may depend on runtime condition and thus not be statically deterministic. This can be mitigated but not solved by static analysis and IDE support showing which advices *potentially* match.

General criticisms are that AOP purports to improve "both modularity and the structure of code", but some counter that it instead undermines these goals and impedes "independent development and understandability of programs". Specifically, quantification by pointcuts breaks modularity: "one must, in general, have whole-program knowledge to reason about the dynamic execution of an aspect-oriented program." Further, while its goals (modularizing cross-cutting concerns) are well-understood, its actual definition is unclear and not clearly distinguished from other well-established techniques. Cross-cutting concerns potentially cross-cut each other, requiring some resolution mechanism, such as ordering. Indeed, aspects can apply to themselves, leading to problems such as the liar paradox.

Technical criticisms include that the quantification of pointcuts (defining where advices are executed) is "extremely sensitive to changes in the program", which is known as the *fragile pointcut problem*. The problems with pointcuts are deemed intractable: if one replaces the quantification of pointcuts with explicit annotations, one obtains attribute-oriented programming instead, which is simply an explicit subroutine call and suffers the identical problem of scattering that AOP was designed to solve.

Implementations

The following programming languages have implemented AOP, within the language, or as an external library:

- .NET Framework languages (C# / VB.NET)

    o   PostSharp is a commercial AOP implementation with a free but limited edition.

    o   Unity, It provides an API to facilitate proven practices in core areas of programming including data access, security, logging, exception handling and others.

- ActionScript

- Ada

- AutoHotkey

- C / C++

- COBOL

- The Cocoa Objective-C frameworks

- ColdFusion

- Common Lisp

- Delphi

- Delphi Prism

- e (IEEE 1647)

- Emacs Lisp

- Groovy

- Haskell

- Java

  ○ AspectJ

- JavaScript

- Logtalk

- Lua

- make

- Matlab

- ML

- Perl

- PHP

- Prolog

- Python

- Racket

- Ruby

- Squeak Smalltalk

- UML 2.0

- XML

Automata-based Programming

Automata-based programming is a programming paradigm in which the program or part of it is thought of as a model of a finite state machine (FSM) or any other (often more complicated) formal automaton. Sometimes a potentially infinite set of possible states is introduced, and such a set can have a complicated structure, not just an enumeration.

FSM-based programming is generally the same, but, formally speaking, doesn't cover all possible variants, as FSM stands for finite state machine, and automata-based programming doesn't necessarily employ FSMs in the strict sense.

The following properties are key indicators for automata-based programming:

1. The time period of the program's execution is clearly separated down to the *steps of the automaton*. Each of the *steps* is effectively an execution of a code section (same for all the steps), which has a single entry point. Such a section can be a function or other routine, or just a cycle body. The step section might be divided down to subsections to be executed depending on different states, although this is not necessary.

2. Any communication between the steps is only possible via the explicitly noted set of variables named *the state*. Between any two steps, the program (or its part created using the automata-based technique) can not have implicit components of its state, such as local (stack) variables' values, return addresses, the current instruction pointer, etc. That is, the state of the whole program, taken at any two moments of entering the step of the automaton, can only differ in the values of the variables being considered as the state of the automaton.

The whole execution of the automata-based code is a (possibly explicit) cycle of the automaton's steps.

Another reason for using the notion of automata-based programming is that the programmer's style of thinking about the program in this technique is very similar to the style of thinking used to solve mathematical tasks using Turing machines, Markov algorithms, etc.

Example

Consider a program in C that reads a text from *standard input stream*, line by line, and prints the first word of each line. It is clear we need first to read and skip the leading spaces, if any, then read characters of the first word and print them until the word ends, and then read and skip all the remaining characters until the end-of-line character is encountered. Upon reaching the end of line character (regardless of the stage), we restart the algorithm from the beginning, and upon encountering the *end of file* condition (regardless of the stage), we terminate the program.

Traditional (Imperative) Program in C

The program which solves the example task in traditional (imperative) style can look something like this:

```c
#include <stdio.h>

#include <ctype.h>

int main(void)

{

    int c;

    do {

        do {
```

```
        c = getchar();
    } while(c == ` `);
    while(c != EOF && !isspace(c) && c != '\n') {
        putchar(c);
        c = getchar();
    }
    putchar('\n');
    while(c != EOF && c != '\n')
        c = getchar();
    } while(c != EOF);
    return 0;
}
```

Automata-based Style Program

The same task can be solved by thinking in terms of finite state machines. Note that line parsing has three stages: skipping the leading spaces, printing the word and skipping the trailing characters. Let's call them states before, inside and after. The program may now look like this:

```
#include <stdio.h>
#include <ctype.h>
int main(void)
{
    enum states {
        before, inside, after
    } state;
    int c;
    state = before;
    while((c = getchar()) != EOF) {
        switch(state) {
            case before:
```

```
                    if(c != ' ') {

                        putchar(c);

                        if(c != '\n')

                            state = inside;

                    }

                    break;

                case inside:

                    if(!isspace(c))

                        putchar(c);

                    else {

                        putchar('\n');

                        if(c == '\n')

                            state = before;

                        else

                            state = after;

                    }

                    break;

                case after:

                    if(c == '\n')

                        state = before;

            }

        }

    return 0;

}
```

Although the code now looks longer, it has at least one significant advantage: there's only one *reading* (that is, call to the getchar() function) instruction in the program. Besides that, there's only one loop instead of the four the previous versions had.

In this program, the body of the while loop is the automaton step, and the loop itself is the *cycle of the automaton's work.*

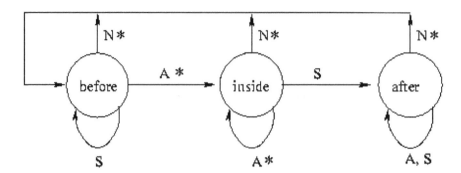

The program implements (models) the work of a *finite state machine* shown on the picture. The N denotes the end of line character, the S denotes spaces, and the **A** stands for all the other characters. The automaton follows exactly one *arrow* on each step depending on the current state and the encountered character. Some state switches are accompanied with printing the character; such arrows are marked with asterisks.

It is not absolutely necessary to divide the code down to separate handlers for each unique state. Furthermore, in some cases the very notion of the *state* can be composed of several variables' values, so that it could be impossible to handle each possible state explicitly. In the discussed program it is possible to reduce the code length by noticing that the actions taken in response to the end of line character are the same for all the possible states. The following program is equal to the previous one but is a bit shorter:

```
#include <stdio.h>

#include <ctype.h>

int main(void)

{

    enum states {

        before, inside, after

    } state;

    int c;

    state = before;

    while((c = getchar()) != EOF) {

        if(c == '\n') {

            putchar('\n');

            state = before;

        } else
```

```
        switch(state) {

            case before:

                if(c != ` `) {

                    putchar(c);

                    state = inside;

                }

                break;

            case inside:

                if(c == ` `) {

                    state = after;

                } else {

                    putchar(c);

                }

                break;

            case after:

                break;

        }

    }

    if(state != before)

        putchar(`\n`);

    return 0;

}
```

A Separate Function for the Automation Step

The most important property of the previous program is that the automaton step code section is clearly localized. With a separate function for it, we can better demonstrate this property:

```
#include <stdio.h>

enum states { before, inside, after };

void step(enum states *state, int c)
```

```
{
    if(c == '\n') {

        putchar('\n');

        *state = before;

    } else
    switch(*state) {

        case before:

            if(c != ' ') {

                putchar(c);

                *state = inside;

            }

            break;

        case inside:

            if(c == ' ') {

                *state = after;

            } else {

                putchar(c);

            }

            break;

        case after:

            break;

    }
}
int main(void)
{
    int c;

    enum states state = before;

    while((c = getchar()) != EOF) {
```

```
        step(&state, c);

   }

   if(state != before)

       putchar('\n');

   return 0;

}
```

This example clearly demonstrates the basic properties of automata-based code:

1. time periods of automaton step executions may not overlap

2. the only information passed from the previous step to the next is the explicitly specified *automaton state*

Explicit State Transition Table

A finite automaton can be defined by an explicit state transition table. Generally speaking, an automata-based program code can naturally reflect this approach. In the program below there's an array named the_table, which defines the table. The rows of the table stand for three *states*, while columns reflect the input characters (first for spaces, second for the end of line character, and the last is for all the other characters).

For every possible combination, the table contains the new state number and the flag, which determines whether the automaton must print the symbol. In a real life task, this could be more complicated; e.g., the table could contain pointers to functions to be called on every possible combination of conditions.

```
#include <stdio.h>

enum states { before = 0, inside = 1, after = 2 };

struct branch {

    unsigned char new_state:2; //BIT [1:0]

    unsigned char should_putchar:1; //BIT

};

struct branch the_table = {

                 /* ' '             '\n'          others */

    /* before */ { {before,0}, {before,1}, {inside,1} },

    /* inside */ { {after, 1}, {before,1}, {inside,1} },

    /* after  */ { {after, 0}, {before,1}, {after, 0} }
```

```
};

void step(enum states *state, int c)

{

    int idx2 = (c == ' ') ? 0 : (c == '\n') ? 1 : 2;

    struct branch *b = & the_table[*state][idx2];

    *state = (enum states)(b->new_state);

    if(b->should_putchar) putchar(c);

}
```

Automation and Automata

Automata-based programming indeed closely matches the programming needs found in the field of automation.

A production cycle is commonly modelled as:

- A sequence of stages stepping according to input data (from captors).
- A set of actions performed depending on the current stage.

Various dedicated programming languages allow expressing such a model in more or less sophisticated ways.

Example Program

The example presented above could be expressed according to this view like in the following program. Here pseudo-code uses such conventions:

- 'set' and 'reset' respectively activate & inactivate a logic variable (here a stage)
- ':' is assignment, '=' is equality test

```
SPC : ' '

EOL : '\n'

states : (before, inside, after, end, endplusnl)

setState(c) {

    if c=EOF then if inside or after then set endplusnl else set end

    if before and (c!=SPC and c!=EOL) then set inside

    if inside and (c=SPC or c=EOL) then set after

    if after and c=EOL then set before
```

```
}

doAction(c) {

    if inside then write(c)

    else if c=EOL or endplusnl then write(EOL)

}


cycle {

    set before

    loop {

        c : readCharacter

        setState(c)

        doAction(c)

    }

    until end or endplusnl

}
```

The separation of routines expressing cycle progression on one side, and actual action on the other (matching input & output) allows clearer and simpler code.

Automation & Events

In the field of automation, stepping from step to step depends on input data coming from the machine itself. This is represented in the program by reading characters from a text. In reality, those data inform about position, speed, temperature, etc. of critical elements of a machine.

Like in GUI programming, changes in the machine state can thus be considered as events causing the passage from a state to another, until the final one is reached. The combination of possible states can generate a wide variety of events, thus defining a more complex production cycle. As a consequence, cycles are usually far to be simple linear sequences. There are commonly parallel branches running together and alternatives selected according to different events, schematically represented below:

```
s:stage    c:condition



s1

|
```

```
    |-c2

    |

    s2

    |

    ----------

    |          |

    |-c31      |-c32

    |          |

    s31        s32

    |          |

    |-c41      |-c42

    |          |

    ----------

    |

    s4
```

Using Object-oriented Capabilities

If the implementation language supports object-oriented programming, a simple refactoring is to encapsulate the automaton into an object, thus hiding its implementation details. For example, an object-oriented version in C++ of the same program is below. A more sophisticated refactoring could employ the State pattern.

```cpp
#include <stdio.h>

class StateMachine {
    enum states { before = 0, inside = 1, after = 2 } state;
    struct branch {
        unsigned char new_state:2;
        unsigned char should_putchar:1;
    };
    static struct branch the_table;
public:
```

```
    StateMachine() : state(before) {}

    void FeedChar(int c) {

        int idx2 = (c == ` `) ? 0 : (c == `\n`) ? 1 : 2;

        struct branch *b = & the_table[state][idx2];

        state = (enum states)(b->new_state);

        if(b->should_putchar) putchar(c);

    }

};

struct StateMachine::branch StateMachine::the_table = {

                    /* ` `             `\n`           others */

    /* before */ { {before,0}, {before,1}, {inside,1} },

    /* inside */ { {after, 0}, {before,1}, {inside,1} },

    /* after  */ { {after, 0}, {before,1}, {after, 0} }

};

int main(void)

{

    int c;

    StateMachine machine;

    while((c = getchar()) != EOF)

        machine.FeedChar(c);

    return 0;

}
```

Note: To minimize changes not directly related to the subject of the article, the input/output functions from the standard library of C are being used. Note the use of the ternary operator, which could also be implemented as if-else.

Applications

Automata-based programming is widely used in lexical and syntactic analyses.

Besides that, thinking in terms of automata (that is, breaking the execution process down to *automaton steps* and passing information from step to step through the explicit *state*) is necessary for event-driven programming as the only alternative to using parallel processes or threads.

The notions of states and state machines are often used in the field of formal specification. For instance, UML-based software architecture development uses state diagrams to specify the behaviour of the program. Also various communication protocols are often specified using the explicit notion of *state*.

Thinking in terms of automata (steps and states) can also be used to describe semantics of some programming languages. For example, the execution of a program written in the Refal language is described as a sequence of *steps* of a so-called abstract Refal machine; the state of the machine is a *view* (an arbitrary Refal expression without variables).

Continuations in the Scheme language require thinking in terms of steps and states, although Scheme itself is in no way automata-related (it is recursive). To make it possible the call/cc feature to work, implementation needs to be able to catch a whole state of the executing program, which is only possible when there's no implicit part in the state. Such a *caught state* is the very thing called *continuation*, and it can be considered as the *state* of a (relatively complicated) automaton. The step of the automaton is deducing the next continuation from the previous one, and the execution process is the cycle of such steps.

Alexander Ollongren in his book explains the so-called *Vienna method* of programming languages semantics description which is fully based on formal automata.

The STAT system is a good example of using the automata-based approach; this system, besides other features, includes an embedded language called *STATL* which is purely automata-oriented.

History

Automata-based techniques were used widely in the domains where there are algorithms based on automata theory, such as formal language analyses.

One of the early papers on this is by Johnson et al., 1968.

One of the earliest mentions of automata-based programming as a general technique is found in the paper by Peter Naur, 1963. The author calls the technique *Turing machine approach*, however no real Turing machine is given in the paper; instead, the technique based on states and steps is described.

Compared Against Imperative and Procedural Programming

The notion of state is not exclusive property of automata-based programming. Generally speaking, *state* (or program state) appears during execution of any computer program, as a combination of all information that can change during the execution. For instance, a *state* of a traditional imperative program consists of

1. values of all variables and the information stored within dynamic memory

2. values stored in registers

3. stack contents (including local variables' values and return addresses)

4. current value of the instruction pointer

These can be divided to the explicit part (such as values stored in variables) and the implicit part (return addresses and the instruction pointer).

Having said this, an automata-based program can be considered as a special case of an imperative program, in which implicit part of the state is minimized. The state of the whole program taken at the two distinct moments of entering the *step* code section can differ in the automaton state only. This simplifies the analysis of the program.

Object-oriented Programming Relationship

In the theory of object-oriented programming an object is said to have an internal *state* and is capable of *receiving messages*, *responding* to them, *sending* messages to other objects and changing the internal state during message handling. In more practical terminology, *to call an object's method* is considered the same as *to send a message to the object*.

Thus, on the one hand, objects from object-oriented programming can be considered as automata (or models of automata) whose *state* is the combination of internal fields, and one or more methods are considered to be the *step*. Such methods must not call each other nor themselves, neither directly nor indirectly, otherwise the object can not be considered to be implemented in an automata-based manner.

On the other hand, it is obvious that *object* is good for implementing a model of an automaton. When the automata-based approach is used within an object-oriented language, an automaton model is usually implemented by a class, the *state* is represented with internal (private) fields of the class, and the *step* is implemented as a method; such a method is usually the only non-constant public method of the class (besides constructors and destructors). Other public methods could query the state but don't change it. All the secondary methods (such as particular state handlers) are usually hidden within the private part of the class.

Flow-based Programming

In computer programming, flow-based programming (FBP) is a programming paradigm that defines applications as networks of "black box" processes, which exchange data across predefined connections by message passing, where the connections are specified *externally* to the processes. These black box processes can be reconnected endlessly to form different applications without having to be changed internally. FBP is thus naturally component-oriented.

FBP is a particular form of dataflow programming based on bounded buffers, information packets with defined lifetimes, named ports, and separate definition of connections.

Introduction

Flow-based programming defines applications using the metaphor of a "data factory". It views an application not as a single, sequential process, which starts at a point in time, and then does one thing at a time until it is finished, but as a network of asynchronous processes communicating by means of streams of structured data chunks, called "information packets" (IPs). In this view, the focus is on the application data and the transformations applied to it to produce the desired outputs. The network is defined externally to the processes, as a list of connections which is interpreted by a piece of software, usually called the "scheduler".

The processes communicate by means of fixed-capacity connections. A connection is attached to a process by means of a port, which has a name agreed upon between the process code and the network definition. More than one process can execute the same piece of code. At any point in time, a given IP can only be "owned" by a single process, or be in transit between two processes. Ports may either be simple, or array-type, as used e.g. for the input port of the Collate component described below. It is the combination of ports with asynchronous processes that allows many long-running primitive functions of data processing, such as Sort, Merge, Summarize, etc., to be supported in the form of software black boxes.

Because FBP processes can continue executing as long they have data to work on and somewhere to put their output, FBP applications generally run in less elapsed time than conventional programs, and make optimal use of all the processors on a machine, with no special programming required to achieve this.

The network definition is usually diagrammatic, and is converted into a connection list in some lower-level language or notation. FBP is often a visual programming language at this level. More complex network definitions have a hierarchical structure, being built up from subnets with "sticky" connections. Many other flow based languages/runtimes are built around more traditional programming languages, the most notable example is RaftLib which uses C++ iostream-like operators to specify the flow graph.

FBP has much in common with the Linda language in that it is, in Gelernter and Carriero's terminology, a "coordination language": it is essentially language-independent. Indeed, given a scheduler written in a sufficiently low-level language, components written in different languages can be linked together in a single network. FBP thus lends itself to the concept of domain-specific languages or "mini-languages".

FBP exhibits "data coupling", on coupling as the loosest type of coupling between components. The concept of loose coupling is in turn related to that of service-oriented architectures, and FBP fits a number of the criteria for such an architecture, albeit at a more fine-grained level than most examples of this architecture.

FBP promotes high-level, functional style of specifications that simplify reasoning about system behavior. An example of this is the distributed data flow model for constructively specifying and analyzing the semantics of distributed multi-party protocols.

History

Flow-Based Programming was invented by J. Paul Morrison in the early 1970s, and initially implemented in software for a Canadian bank. FBP at its inception was strongly influenced by some IBM simulation languages of the period, in particular GPSS, but its roots go all the way back to Conway's seminal paper on what he called coroutines.

FBP has undergone a number of name changes over the years: the original implementation was called AMPS (Advanced Modular Processing System). One large application in Canada went live in 1975, and, as of 2013, has been in continuous production use, running daily, for almost 40 years. Because IBM considered the ideas behind FBP "too much like a law of nature" to be patentable they instead put the basic concepts of FBP into the public domain, by means of a Technical Disclosure Bulletin, "Data Responsive Modular, Interleaved Task Programming System", in 1971. An article describing its concepts and experience using it was published in 1978 in the IBM Research IBM Systems Journal under the name DSLM. A second implementation was done as a joint project of IBM Canada and IBM Japan, under the name "Data Flow Development Manager" (DFDM), and was briefly marketed in Japan in the late '80s under the name "Data Flow Programming Manager".

Generally the concepts were referred to within IBM as "Data Flow", but this term was felt to be too general, and eventually the name flow-based programming was adopted.

From the early '80s to 1993 J. Paul Morrison and IBM architect Wayne Stevens refined and promoted the concepts behind FBP. Stevens wrote several articles describing and supporting the FBP concept, and included material about it in several of his books. In 1994 Morrison published a book describing FBP, and providing empirical evidence that FBP led to reduced development times.

Concepts

The following diagram shows the major entities of an FBP diagram (apart from the Information Packets). Such a diagram can be converted directly into a list of connections, which can then be executed by an appropriate engine (software or hardware).

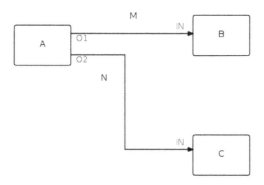

Simple FBP diagram

A, B and C are processes executing code components. O1, O2, and the two INs are ports connecting the connections M and N to their respective processes. It is permitted for processes B and C to be executing the same code, so each process must have its own set of working storage, control blocks, etc. Whether or not they do share code, B and C are free to use the same port names, as port names only have meaning within the components referencing them (and at the network level, of course).

M and N are what are often referred to as "bounded buffers", and have a fixed capacity in terms of the number of IPs that they can hold at any point in time.

The concept of *ports* is what allows the same component to be used at more than one place in the network. In combination with a parametrization ability, called Initial Information Packets (IIPs), ports provide FBP with a component reuse ability, making FBP a component-based architecture. FBP thus exhibits what Raoul de Campo and Nate Edwards of IBM Research have termed configurable modularity.

Information Packets or IPs are allocated in what might be called "IP space" (just as Linda's tuples are allocated in "tuple space"), and have a well-defined lifetime until they are disposed of and their space is reclaimed - in FBP this must be an explicit action on the part of an owning process. IPs traveling across a given connection (actually it is their "handles" that travel) constitute a "stream", which is generated and consumed asynchronously - this concept thus has similarities to the lazy cons concept described in the 1976 article by Friedman and Wise.

IPs are usually structured chunks of data - some IPs, however, may not contain any real data, but are used simply as signals. An example of this is "bracket IPs", which can be used to group data IPs into sequential patterns within a stream, called "substreams". Substreams may in turn be nested. IPs may also be chained together to form "IP trees", which travel through the network as single objects.

The system of connections and processes described above can be "ramified" to any size. During the development of an application, monitoring processes may be added between pairs of processes, processes may be "exploded" to subnets, or simulations of processes may be replaced by the real process logic. FBP therefore lends itself to rapid prototyping.

This is really an assembly line image of data processing: the IPs travelling through a network of processes may be thought of as widgets travelling from station to station in an assembly line. "Machines" may easily be reconnected, taken off line for repair, replaced, and so on. Oddly enough, this image is very similar to that of unit record equipment that was used to process data before the days of computers, except that decks of cards had to be hand-carried from one machine to another.

Implementations of FBP may be non-preemptive or preemptive - the earlier implementations tended to be non-preemptive (mainframe and C language), whereas the latest Java implementation uses Java Thread class and is preemptive.

Examples

"Telegram Problem"

FBP components often form complementary pairs. This example uses two such pairs. The problem described seems very simple as described in words, but in fact is surprisingly difficult to accomplish using conventional procedural logic. The task, called the "Telegram Problem", originally described by Peter Naur, is to write a program which accepts lines of text and generates output lines containing as many words as possible, where the number of characters in each line does not exceed a certain length. The words may not be split and we assume no word is longer than the size of the output lines. This is analogous to the word-wrapping problem in text editors.

In conventional logic, the programmer rapidly discovers that neither the input nor the output structures can be used to drive the call hierarchy of control flow. In FBP, on the other hand, the problem description itself suggests a solution:

- "words" are mentioned explicitly in the description of the problem, so it is reasonable for the designer to treat words as information packets (IPs)

- in FBP there is no single call hierarchy, so the programmer is not tempted to force a sub-pattern of the solution to be the top level.

Here is the most natural solution in FBP (there is no single "correct" solution in FBP, but this seems like a natural fit):

Peter Naur's "Telegram problem"

where DC and RC stand for "DeCompose" and "ReCompose", respectively.

As mentioned above, Initial Information Packets (IIPs) can be used to specify parametric information such as the desired output record length (required by the rightmost two components), or file names. IIPs are data chunks associated with a port in the network definition which become "normal" IPs when a "receive" is issued for the relevant port.

Batch Update

This type of program involves passing a file of "details" (changes, adds and deletes) against a "master file", and producing (at least) an updated master file, and one or more reports. Update programs are generally quite hard to code using synchronous, procedural code, as two (sometimes more) input streams have to be kept synchronized, even though there may be masters without corresponding details, or vice versa.

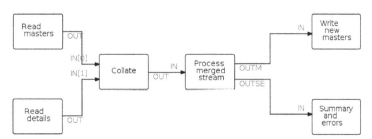

Canonical "batch update" structure

In FBP, a reusable component (Collate), based on the unit record idea of a Collator, makes writing this type of application much easier as Collate merges the two streams and inserts bracket IPs to indicate grouping levels, significantly simplifying the downstream logic. Suppose that one stream ("masters" in this case) consists of IPs with key values of 1, 2 and 3, and the second stream IPs ("details") have key values of 11, 12, 21, 31, 32, 33 and 41, where the first digit corresponds to the master key values. Using bracket characters to represent "bracket" IPs, the collated output stream will be as follows:

```
( m1 d11 d12 )  ( m2 d21 )  ( m3 d31 d32 d33 )  (d41)
```

As there was no master with a value of 4, the last group consists of a single detail (plus brackets).

The structure of the above stream can be described succinctly using a BNF-like notation such as

```
{ ( [m] d* ) }*
```

Collate is a reusable black box which only needs to know where the control fields are in its incoming IPs (even this is not strictly necessary as transformer processes can be inserted upstream to place the control fields in standard locations), and can in fact be generalized to any number of input streams, and any depth of bracket nesting. Collate uses an array-type port for input, allowing a variable number of input streams.

Multiplexing Processes

Flow-based programming supports process multiplexing in a very natural way. Since components are read-only, any number of instances of a given component ("processes") can run asynchronously with each other.

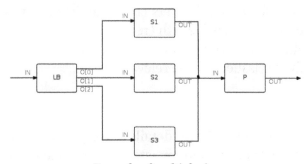

Example of multiplexing

When computers usually had a single processor, this was useful when a lot of I/O was going on; now that machines usually have multiple processors, this is starting to become useful when processes are CPU-intensive as well. The diagram in this section shows a single "Load Balancer" process distributing data between 3 processes, labeled S1, S2 and S3, respectively, which are instances of a single component, which in turn feed into a single process on a "first-come, first served" basis.

Simple Interactive Network

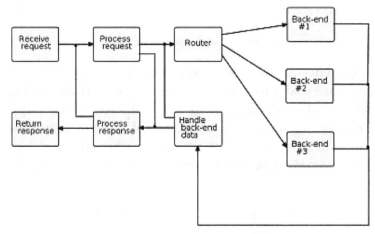

Schematic of general interactive application

In this general schematic, requests (transactions) coming from users enter the diagram at the upper left, and responses are returned at the lower left. The "back ends" (on the right side) communicate with systems at other sites, e.g. using CORBA, MQSeries, etc. The cross-connections represent requests that do not need to go to the back ends, or requests that have to cycle through the network more than once before being returned to the user.

As different requests may use different back-ends, and may require differing amounts of time for the back-ends (if used) to process them, provision must be made to relate returned data to the appropriate requesting transactions, e.g. hash tables or caches.

The above diagram is schematic in the sense that the final application may contain many more processes: processes may be inserted between other processes to manage caches, display connection traffic, monitor throughput, etc. Also the blocks in the diagram may represent "subnets" - small networks with one or more open connections.

Comparison with Other Paradigms and Methodologies

Jackson Structured Programming (JSP) and Jackson System Development (JSD)

This methodology assumes that a program must be structured as a single procedural hierarchy of subroutines. Its starting point is to describe the application as a set of "main lines", based on the input and output data structures. One of these "main lines" is then chosen to drive the whole program, and the others are required to be "inverted" to turn them into subroutines (hence the name "Jackson inversion"). This sometimes results in what is called a "clash", requiring the program to be split into multiple programs or coroutines. When using FBP, this inversion process is not required, as every FBP component can be considered a separate "main line".

FBP and JSP share the concept of treating a program (or some components) as a parser of an input stream.

In Jackson's later work, Jackson System Development (JSD), the ideas were developed further.

In JSD the design is maintained as a network design until the final implementation stage. The model is then transformed into a set of sequential processes to the number of available processors. Jackson discusses the possibility of directly executing the network model that exists prior to this step, in section 1.3 of his book:

> The specification produced at the end of the System Timing step is, in principle, capable of direct execution. The necessary environment would contain a processor for each process, a device equivalent to an unbounded buffer for each data stream, and some input and output devices where the system is connected to the real world. *Such an environment could, of course, be provided by suitable software running on a sufficiently powerful machine. Sometimes, such direct execution of the specification will be possible, and may even be a reasonable choice.*

FBP was recognized by M A Jackson as an approach that follows his method of "Program decomposition into sequential processes communicating by a coroutine-like mechanism"

Applicative Programming

W.B. Ackerman defines an applicative language as one which does all of its processing by means of operators applied to values. The earliest known applicative language was LISP.

An FBP component can be regarded as a function transforming its input stream(s) into its output stream(s). These functions are then combined to make more complex transformations, as shown here:

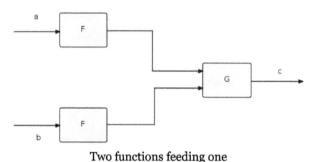

Two functions feeding one

If we label streams, as shown, with lower case letters, then the above diagram can be represented succinctly as follows:

```
c = G(F(a),F(b));
```

Just as in functional notation F can be used twice because it only works with values, and therefore has no side effects, in FBP two instances of a given component may be running concurrently with each other, and therefore FBP components must not have side-effects either. Functional notation could clearly be used to represent at least a part of an FBP network.

The question then arises whether FBP components can themselves be expressed using functional notation. W.H. Burge showed how stream expressions can be developed using a recursive, applicative style of programming, but this work was in terms of (streams of) atomic values. In FBP, it is necessary to be able to describe and process structured data chunks (FBP IPs).

Furthermore, most applicative systems assume that all the data is available in memory at the same time, whereas FBP applications need to be able to process long-running streams of data while still using finite resources. Friedman and Wise suggested a way to do this by adding the concept of "lazy cons" to Burge's work. This removed the requirement that both of the arguments of "cons" be available at the same instant of time. "Lazy cons" does not actually build a stream until both of its arguments are realized - before that it simply records a "promise" to do this. This allows a stream to be dynamically realized from the front, but with an unrealized back end. The end of the stream stays unrealized until the very end of the process, while the beginning is an ever-lengthening sequence of items.

Linda

Many of the concepts in FBP seem to have been discovered independently in different systems over the years. Linda, mentioned above, is one such. The difference between the two techniques is illustrated by the Linda "school of piranhas" load balancing technique - in FBP, this requires an extra "load balancer" component which routes requests to the component in a list which has the smallest number of IPs waiting to be processed. Clearly FBP and Linda are closely related, and one could easily be used to simulate the other.

Object-oriented Programming

An object in OOP can be described as a semi-autonomous unit comprising both information and behaviour. Objects communicate by means of "method calls", which are essentially subroutine calls, done indirectly via the class to which the receiving object belongs. The object's internal data can only be accessed by means of method calls, so this is a form of information hiding or "encapsulation". Encapsulation, however, predates OOP - David Parnas wrote one of the seminal articles on it in the early 70s - and is a basic concept in computing. Encapsulation is the very essence of an FBP component, which may be thought of as a black box, performing some conversion of its input data into its output data. In FBP, part of the specification of a component is the data formats and stream structures that it can accept, and those it will generate. This constitutes a form of design by contract. In addition, the data in an IP can only be accessed directly by the currently owning process. Encapsulation can also be implemented at the network level, by having outer processes protect inner ones.

A paper by C. Ellis and S. Gibbs distinguishes between active objects and passive objects. Passive objects comprise information and behaviour, as stated above, but they cannot determine the *timing* of this behaviour. Active objects on the other hand can do this. In their article Ellis and Gibbs state that active objects have much more potential for the development of maintainable systems than do passive objects. An FBP application can be viewed as a combination of these two types of object, where FBP processes would correspond to active objects, while IPs would correspond to passive objects

Non-structured Programming

Non-structured programming is the historically earliest programming paradigm capable of creating Turing-complete algorithms. It is often contrasted with structured programming paradigms, including procedural, functional, and object-oriented programming.

Unstructured programming has been heavily criticized for producing hardly-readable ("spaghetti") code and is sometimes considered a bad approach for creating major projects, but has been praised for the freedom it offers to programmers and has been compared to how Mozart wrote music.

There are both high- and low-level programming languages that use non-structured programming. Some languages commonly cited as being non-structured include JOSS, FOCAL, TEL-COMP, assembly languages, MS-DOS batch files, and early versions of BASIC, Fortran, COBOL, and MUMPS.

Features and Typical Concepts

Basic Concepts

A program in a non-structured language usually consists of sequentially ordered commands, or statements, usually one in each line. The lines are usually numbered or may have labels: this allows the flow of execution to jump to any line in the program.

Non-structured programming introduces basic control flow concepts such as loops, branches and jumps. Although there is no concept of procedures in the non-structured paradigm, subroutines are allowed. Unlike a procedure, a subroutine may have several entry and exit points, and a direct jump into or out of subroutine is (theoretically) allowed. This flexibility allows realization of coroutines.

There is no concept of locally scoped variables in non-structured programming (although for assembly programs, general purpose registers may serve the same purpose after saving on entry), but labels and variables can have a limited area of effect (for example, a group of lines). This means there is no (automatic) context refresh when calling a subroutine, so all variables might retain their values from the previous call. This makes general recursion difficult, but some cases of recursion—where no subroutine state values are needed after the recursive call—are possible if variables dedicated to the recursive subroutine are explicitly cleared (or re-initialized to their original value) on entry to the subroutine. The depth of nesting also may be limited to one or two levels.

Data Types

Non-structured languages allow only basic data types, such as numbers, strings and arrays (numbered sets of variables of the same type). The introduction of arrays into non-structured languages was a notable step forward, making stream data processing possible despite the lack of structured data types.

Event-driven Programming

In computer programming, event-driven programming is a programming paradigm in which the flow of the program is determined by events such as user actions (mouse clicks, key presses), sensor outputs, or messages from other programs/threads. Event-driven programming is the dominant paradigm used in graphical user interfaces and other applications (e.g. JavaScript web applications) that are centered on performing certain actions in response to user input. This is also true of programming for device drivers (e.g. P in USB device driver stacks)

In an event-driven application, there is generally a main loop that listens for events, and then triggers a callback function when one of those events is detected. In embedded systems the same may be achieved using hardware interrupts instead of a constantly running main loop. Event-driven programs can be written in any programming language, although the task is easier in languages that provide high-level abstractions, such as closures.

Event Handlers

A Trivial Event Handler

Because the code for checking for events and the main loop do not depend on the application, many programming frameworks take care of their implementation and expect the user to provide only the code for the event handlers. In this simple example there may be a call to an event handler called OnKeyEnter() that includes an argument with a string of characters, corresponding to what the user typed before hitting the ENTER key. To add two numbers, storage outside the event handler must be used. The implementation might look like below.

```
globally declare the counter K and the integer T.

OnKeyEnter(character C)

{

    convert C to a number N

    if K is zero store N in T and increment K

    otherwise add N to T, print the result and reset K to zero

}
```

While keeping track of history is straightforward in a batch program, it requires special attention and planning in an event-driven program.

Exception Handlers

In PL/1, even though a program itself may not be predominantly event-driven, certain abnormal events such as a hardware error, overflow or "program checks" may occur that possibly prevent further processing. Exception handlers may be provided by "ON statements" in (unseen) callers to provide housekeeping routines to clean up afterwards before termination.

Creating Event Handlers

The first step in developing an event-driven program is to write a series of subroutines, or methods, called event-handler routines. These routines handle the events to which the main program will respond. For example, a single left-button mouse-click on a command button in a GUI program may trigger a routine that will open another window, save data to a database or exit the application. Many modern-day programming environments provide the programmer with event templates, allowing the programmer to focus on writing the event code.

The second step is to bind event handlers to events so that the correct function is called when the event takes place. Graphical editors combine the first two steps: double-click on a button, and the editor creates an (empty) event handler associated with the user clicking the button and opens a text window so you can edit the event handler.

The third step in developing an event-driven program is to write the main loop. This is a function that checks for the occurrence of events, and then calls the matching event handler to process it. Most event-driven programming environments already provide this main loop, so it need not be specifically provided by the application programmer. RPG, an early programming language from IBM, whose 1960s design concept was similar to event-driven programming discussed above, provided a built-in main I/O loop (known as the "program cycle") where the calculations responded in accordance to 'indicators' (flags) that were set earlier in the cycle.

Common Uses

Most of existing GUI development tools and architectures rely on event-driven programming.

In addition, systems such as Node.js are also event-driven

Criticism

The design of those programs which rely on event-action model has been criticised, and it has been suggested that event-action model leads programmers to create error prone, difficult to extend and excessively complex application code. Table-driven state machines have been advocated as a viable alternative. On the other hand, table-driven state machines themselves suffer from significant weaknesses including "state explosion" phenomenon.

Stackless Threading

An event-driven approach is used in hardware description languages. A thread context only needs a CPU stack while actively processing an event, once done the CPU can move on to process other event-driven threads, which allows an extremely large number of threads to be handled. This is essentially a finite-state machine approach.

Comparison of Multi-paradigm Programming Languages

Programming languages can be grouped by the number and types of paradigms supported.

Criticism

Some programming language researchers criticise the notion of paradigms as a classification of programming languages, e.g. Krishnamurthi. They argue that many programming languages cannot be strictly classified into one paradigm, but rather include features from several paradigms. This is clearly demonstrated in the table below (which is silent on the level of support of different 'paradigms').

Paradigm Summaries

A concise reference for the programming paradigms are listed.

- Concurrent programming – have language constructs for concurrency, these may involve multi-threading, support for distributed computing, message passing, shared resources (including shared memory), or futures

  o Actor programming – concurrent computation with *actors* that make local decisions in response to the environment (capable of selfish or competitive behavior)

- Constraint programming – relations between variables are expressed as constraints (or constraint networks), directing allowable solutions (uses constraint satisfaction or simplex algorithm)

- Dataflow programming – forced recalculation of formulas when data values change (e.g. spreadsheets)

- Declarative programming – describes actions (e.g. HTML describes a page but not how to actually display it)

- Distributed programming – have support for multiple autonomous computers that communicate via computer networks

- Functional programming – uses evaluation of mathematical functions and avoids state and mutable data

- Generic programming – uses algorithms written in terms of to-be-specified-later types that are then instantiated as needed for specific types provided as parameters

- Imperative programming – explicit statements that change a program state

- Logic programming – uses explicit mathematical logic for programming

- Metaprogramming – writing programs that write or manipulate other programs (or themselves) as their data, or that do part of the work at compile time that would otherwise be done at runtime

  o Template metaprogramming – metaprogramming methods in which templates are used by a compiler to generate temporary source code, which is merged by the compiler with the rest of the source code and then compiled

  o Reflective programming – metaprogramming methods in which a program modifies or extends itself

- Object-oriented programming – uses data structures consisting of data fields and methods together with their interactions (objects) to design programs

  o Class-based – object-oriented programming in which inheritance is achieved by defining classes of objects, versus the objects themselves

  o Prototype-based – object-oriented programming that avoids classes and implements inheritance via cloning of instances

- Pipeline programming – a simple syntax change to add syntax to nest function calls to language originally designed with none

- Rule-based programming – a network of rules of thumb that comprise a knowledge base and can be used for expert systems and problem deduction & resolution

- Visual programming – manipulating program elements graphically rather than by specifying them textually (e.g. Simulink); also termed *diagrammatic programming*

References

- Gabe Stein (August 2013). "How an Arcane Coding Method From 1970s Banking Software Could Save the Sanity of Web Developers Everywhere". Retrieved 24 January 2016

- Kindler, E.; Krivy, I. (2011). "Object-Oriented Simulation of systems with sophisticated control". International Journal of General Systems: 313–343

- Lewis, John; Loftus, William (2008). Java Software Solutions Foundations of Programming Design 6th ed. Pearson Education Inc. ISBN 0-321-53205-8. , section 1.6 "Object-Oriented Programming"

- Nørmark, Kurt. Overview of the four main programming paradigms. Aalborg University, 9 May 2011. Retrieved 22 September 2012

- "Automata-based programming" (PDF). Scientific and Technicial Journal of Information Technologies, Mechanics and Optics (53). 2008

- Vivek Gupta, Ethan Jackson, Shaz Qadeer and Sriram Rajamani. "P: Safe Asynchronous Event-Driven Programming". Retrieved 20 February 2017

- John C. Mitchell, Concepts in programming languages, Cambridge University Press, 2003, ISBN 0-521-78098-5, p.278. Lists: Dynamic dispatch, abstraction, subtype polymorphism, and inheritance

- Michael A. Covington (2010-08-23). "CSCI/ARTI 4540/6540: First Lecture on Symbolic Programming and LISP" (PDF). University of Georgia. Retrieved 2013-11-20

- W.P. Stevens, How Data Flow can Improve Application Development Productivity, IBM System Journal, Vol. 21, No. 2, 1982

- Michael Lee Scott, Programming language pragmatics, Edition 2, Morgan Kaufmann, 2006, ISBN 0-12-633951-1, p. 470. Lists encapsulation, inheritance, and dynamic dispatch

- Peter Van Roy (2009-05-12). "Programming Paradigms for Dummies: What Every Programmer Should Know" (PDF). info.ucl.ac.be. Retrieved 2014-01-27

- Jacobsen, Ivar; Magnus Christerson; Patrik Jonsson; Gunnar Overgaard (1992). Object Oriented Software Engineering. Addison-Wesley ACM Press. pp. 43–69. ISBN 0-201-54435-0

- Ross, Doug. "The first software engineering language". LCS/AI Lab Timeline:. MIT Computer Science and Artificial Intelligence Laboratory. Retrieved 13 May 2010

- Dahl, Ole Johan (2004). "The Birth of Object Orientation: the Simula Languages" (PDF). doi:10.1007/978-3-540-39993-3_3. Retrieved 9 June 2016

- Aho, Alfred V.; Ullman, Jeffrey D. (1973). The theory of parsing, translation and compiling. 1. Englewood Cliffs, N. J.: Prentice-Hall. ISBN 0-13-914564-8

- Holmevik, Jan Rune (1994). "Compiling Simula: A historical study of technological genesis" (PDF). IEEE Annals of the History of Computing. 16 (4): 25–37. doi:10.1109/85.329756. Retrieved 12 May 2010

Permissions

We would like to thank the editorial team for lending their expertise to make the book truly unique. They have played a crucial role in the development of this book. Without their invaluable contributions this book wouldn't have been possible. They have made vital efforts to compile up to date information on the varied aspects of this subject to make this book a valuable addition to the collection of many professionals and students.

This book was conceptualized with the vision of imparting up-to-date and integrated information in this field. To ensure the same, a matchless editorial board was set up. Every individual on the board went through rigorous rounds of assessment to prove their worth. After which they invested a large part of their time researching and compiling the most relevant data for our readers.

The editorial board has been involved in producing this book since its inception. They have spent rigorous hours researching and exploring the diverse topics which have resulted in the successful publishing of this book. They have passed on their knowledge of decades through this book. To expedite this challenging task, the publisher supported the team at every step. A small team of assistant editors was also appointed to further simplify the editing procedure and attain best results for the readers.

Apart from the editorial board, the designing team has also invested a significant amount of their time in understanding the subject and creating the most relevant covers. They scrutinized every image to scout for the most suitable representation of the subject and create an appropriate cover for the book.

The publishing team has been an ardent support to the editorial, designing and production team. Their endless efforts to recruit the best for this project, has resulted in the accomplishment of this book. They are a veteran in the field of academics and their pool of knowledge is as vast as their experience in printing. Their expertise and guidance has proved useful at every step. Their uncompromising quality standards have made this book an exceptional effort. Their encouragement from time to time has been an inspiration for everyone.

The publisher and the editorial board hope that this book will prove to be a valuable piece of knowledge for students, practitioners and scholars across the globe.

Index

www.ingramcontent.com/pod-product-compliance
Lightning Source LLC
Jackson TN
JSHW052208130125
77033JS00004B/220